"Marra has produced a first-rate book that t   through the theory and practice of dialectical behavior therapy (DBT). He is a wonderful guide, leading us by the hand, pointing out where we need to attend to theory, empirical research, and clinical observation and intuition. Drawing on the latest acceptance-based and mindfulness approaches, he mixes personal observation with literature review and clinical cases and provides a superb synthesis of the way DBT can be applied to many different psychological problems. Many therapists who have been intrigued by Marsha Linehan's pioneering work will be glad of Thomas Marra's expert guidance in applying it to help a wide variety of their patients."

—J. Mark G. Williams, professor of clinical psychology and Wellcome Principal Research Fellow in the University of Oxford Department of Psychology, Werneford Hospital, in Oxford, UK, and coauthor of *Mindfulness-Based Cognitive Therapy for Depression*

"*Dialectical Behavior Therapy in Private Practice* is a wonderful addition to the busy clinician's resource library for evidence-based clinical practice. Marra summarizes the research to date on DBT and mindfulness applications, and provides the clinical tools for readers to transport this treatment technology into their own clinical practices. Key features of DBT are articulated for a range of clinical problems. Practitioners will likely find the illustrations of subtle distinctions between DBT and other cognitive behavioral interventions extremely useful. Clinical strategies for combining individual therapy and skills training in a private practice setting are also thoroughly considered. The text even comes with PowerPoint presentations and handouts for conducting skills training sessions. *DBT in Private Practice* aptly encompasses both scholarly and practical issues of essential concern to today's providers."

—Denise D. Davis, Ph.D., clinical psychologist and assistant director of clinical training in the Department of Psychology at Vanderbilt University in Nashville, TN

"While many are intrigued by DBT, few practice it. This book will change that as therapists in any practice setting can apply DBT to several diagnoses thanks to the author's guidelines, case transcriptions, and downloadable materials. Written by a masterful clinician, this exciting clinical text represents the cutting edge in cognitive behavior therapy."

—Len Sperry, MD, Ph.D., author of *Cognitive Behavior Therapy of DSM-IV Personality Disorders* and *Handbook of Diagnosis and Treatment of DSM-IV-TR Personality Disorders, Second Edition*

"This book is a valuable compendium of information on how to practice DBT. Marra has succeeded in expanding the focus of DBT to include most forms of psychopathology and provides everything therapists need to begin using DBT in their own practice."

—Susan Bradley MD, FRCP, professor of psychiatry at the University of Toronto and author of *Affect Regulation and the Development of Psychopathology*

"Marra's book, *Dialectal Behavior Therapy in Private Practice*, makes this especially powerful and useful model easily accessible to the practicing clinician. The volume's strength and value come in the clear exposition of the model that is required for the uninitiated, and it is a valuable review for those experienced in DBT. This presentation is essential so that the clinician is not simply mechanically applying techniques without a clear theoretical, philosophical, and conceptual basis for the DBT treatment model. This is a book written by a skilled and knowledgeable clinician for the practicing therapist. The text is clear, the prose easily digested, and the content immediately useful. Worth twice the price of the book are the downloadable forms and worksheets for use with patients and a series of PowerPoint presentations that visually presents the model. This volume has great potential as a teaching text for graduate students in the broad range of clinical education."

—Arthur Freeman, Ed.D., ABPP, professor of psychology and dean of the School of Professional Studies at the University of Saint Francis, Fort Wayne, IN

Dialectical Behavior Therapy

in

Private Practice

THOMAS MARRA, PhD

New Harbinger Publications, Inc.

Publisher's Note

Distributed in Canada by Raincoast Books

Copyright © 2005 by Thomas Marra
New Harbinger Publications, Inc.
5674 Shattuck Avenue
Oakland, CA 94609

Cover design by Amy Shoup
Text design by Michele Waters-Kermes
Acquired by Catharine Sutker

ISBN 978-1-60882-906-4

The Library of Congress has cataloged the hard cover edition as:
ISBN 1-57224-420-8

New Harbinger Publications' website address: www.newharbinger.com

15 14 13

10 9 8 7 6 5 4 3 2 1   First Printing

Contents

Tables and Figures

Acknowledgments

As with the patient workbook format (*Depressed & Anxious: The Dialectical Behavior Therapy Workbook*, New Harbinger Publications, 2004) of this expanded use of DBT to multiple diagnoses, the intellectual contributions of Dr. Marsha Linehan are greatly acknowledged. The neuropsychiatric underpinnings of affect regulation and the development of psychopathology are substantially contributed to by the scholarship of Susan Bradley. Zindel Segal, Mark Williams, and John Teasdale's expansion of mindfulness-based therapy substantially influenced my work, as did those who have expanded the cognitive behavioral tradition to the treatment of personality disorders (such as Aaron Beck, Arthur Freeman, Denise Davis, and Len Sperry). The macro analytic thinking of Daniel Goleman, S. C. Hayes, and Paul Wachtel is also appreciated. To the publisher, Dr. Matt McKay, editor Carole Honeychurch, acquisitions director Catharine Sutker, and the entire production staff of New Harbinger Publications who tolerate my fixations, I owe great debt.

As with the first book, my wife Judy and boys (Steven and Daniel) are due gratitude for their perseverance with me in this continued effort.

INTRODUCTION

How to Use This Book

This book is intended to teach mental-health clinicians a fairly new theoretical orientation to psychotherapy, dialectical behavior therapy (DBT). DBT can effectively treat most (but not all) patients who present for treatment. It is an exciting new development in psychology, since the theory well explains human pain in a language consistent with how patients think and feel. It focuses on the emotions themselves and thus has wide applicability.

Clinicians have many demands placed upon their time. Reading a book from cover to cover is frequently not an option. Therefore, this introduction is intended to help the reader choose chapters to read based upon their interests. Chapter 1 defines DBT and offers a theoretical comparison of DBT to other therapeutic schools of psychology. If you have not read any materials regarding DBT, this chapter is essential. Those well acquainted with DBT may wish to skim or skip both chapters 1 and 2. Those mostly familiar with DBT in the treatment of borderline personality disorder may find chapter 2 interesting, since it reviews research on the applicability of DBT to other disorders.

Chapter 3 is highly theoretical in that it reviews neurological and psychological research demonstrating that emotion regulation is a core therapeutic target for most acute mental disorders. If you're not interested in the psychological and biological substrates that DBT is proposed to treat, you can skip this chapter. However, you should understand the critical role of arousal reduction in DBT psychotherapy, as well as how frequently emotional arousal is beyond the conscious control of the individuals who experience it.

For practitioners mostly interested in practice issues, you can begin with chapter 4, which reviews how patients look and feel and how DBT helps in the change process. Chapter 5 begins a practical explanation of what to do in DBT therapy and how to do it, and is less about why. You should only begin here if you are thoroughly familiar with DBT.

Chapter 6 reviews the applicability of dialectics to many emotional disorders and is recommended in its entirety for most practitioners, even if you tend to treat only certain disorders in your practice. Do not simply skip to the subsections of the chapter that deal with your most frequent patient population treated, because DBT is designed for acute disorders that include comorbidity. The dialectics are frequently found across many different subsections, and in private practice comorbidity is the rule rather than the exception. The research that demonstrates that this is the case is reviewed in chapter 4.

Chapter 7 is essential for professionals with or without previous DBT knowledge, since it reviews how DBT is different from standard cognitive-behavioral treatment approaches, explains how DBT can be conducted in private practice settings, and reviews how DBT is applicable to nonborderline pathologies. Linehan (1993b, 1993c) well reviews the specifics of treatment of borderline personality disorder using DBT, but chapter 7 in this book shows DBT operating in private practice settings, frequently without a treatment team available, and for treatment of disorders other than borderlines.

Finally, this book is written for professionals. Patients can be directed to a number of DBT treatment manuals published elsewhere. While this book provides theory and research to guide the DBT psychotherapy process for professionals, the treatment manuals are essential components for patients, increasing their understanding and application of new psychological coping skills so essential in DBT.

Using self-help manuals in the psychotherapy process can be counterproductive if the therapist doesn't understand the underlying theory and procedures with which the manual is designed to assist. To acquire this necessary understanding, this book is essential reading for therapists who want to successfully integrate DBT-oriented skills training into the therapy process with or without the benefit of patient treatment manuals.

While I've provided some guidelines for skimming the book, I believe that digesting the entire book from cover to cover will provide you with an adequate theoretical foundation to understand DBT, and thus to better understand most of the patients with whom you deal on a daily basis.

The downloadable materials that accompany this book (go to nhpubs.com /29064) serve a number of purposes. First, the PowerPoint slides enable the professional to lead psychosocial skills groups (training in mindfulness, emotion regulation, distress tolerance, meaning-making, and strategic behavior skills). The slides are visual aids for the group leader to use to help focus the group on content to be mastered during each session. Second, the therapist can download forms and worksheets for patients to use. The therapist can print out these forms, photocopy them, and provide them to patients in order to more strategically use DBT in the Hpsychotherapy process. While digesting chapter 7, which deals with the psychoeducational component of treatment, it may be helpful for the reader to run the slide show on the topic (strategic behavior skills, meaning-making skills, mindfulness, emotion regulation, and distress tolerance). The description of the skills in chapter 7 is presented, in outline form for presentation to patients, through the visual aid of PowerPoint.

CHAPTER I

Dialectical Behavior Therapy: A New Theoretical Orientation

This book provides a scholarly expansion of Marsha Linehan's (1993b, 1993c) dialectical behavior therapy (DBT) for the treatment of borderline personality disorder into the broader context of psychotherapy for acute disorders. It teaches therapists to use DBT in private-practice settings and DBT-informed self-help treatment manuals in the psychotherapy process (Marra, 2004).

While DBT was originally conceptualized by Linehan as a method to treat parasuicidal patients (Koerner and Linehan, 2000; Linehan, Armstrong, Suarez, Allmon, and Heard, 1991; Linehan, Heard, and Armstrong, 1993; Linehan, Tutek, Heard, and Armstrong, 1994; Shearin and Linehan, 1994; Westen, 2000), the strategies and techniques she identified have robust applicability beyond borderline personality disorder. In fact, Dr. Linehan has outlined an eclectic treatment approach that is especially powerful with patients who have mood, anxiety, addictive, eating, impulse-control, and personality disorders, thus encompassing most, but not all, diagnostic categories as currently understood.

The approach is effective for patients who experience intense emotional pain or urges that they attempt to avoid or escape, regardless of the diagnosis. This book will thus argue that DBT is an effective, new school of psychotherapy and psychopathology that has wide applicability to many patients.

DBT can be seen as a new school of psychology, rather than a simple set of treatment strategies, since it has an underlying theoretical understanding of pathogenesis (chapter 3), pathotopology (chapter 4), and psychotherapeutic intervention (chapters 5 through 7) to relieve human suffering.

While many therapists consider themselves eclectic since they have not found a theory that explains, predicts, and helps control the kind of problematic behavior they find presented in their patients, theory is nevertheless critically important for therapists, even those who plan no research or writing. Theory defines what should be examined, it proposes causes rather than simply describing problems, and most importantly, it predicts cures. Without an adequate theory of human suffering, the therapist is left with only the patient's own perspective in defining their suffering. If the patient had an adequate and complete understanding of their difficulties, they would not need the therapist's assistance in any substantial way. It is theory, applied to the patient's description and presentation and coupled with the therapeutic relationship itself, that the therapist contributes to the resolution of human difficulties.

While eclecticism offers the advantage that the therapist can pick and choose what seems to fit in a particular patient's problem, it does not provide the prognostic, diagnostic, and intervention prescription that a solid theoretical framework offers. DBT offers psychotherapists the kind of overarching framework that robustly defines psychological pathology frequently seen in both outpatient and inpatient psychological practices.

WHAT IS DBT?

DBT has several core assumptions, regardless of diagnosis. People who suffer intense emotional discomfort frequently engage in emotional escape and avoidance behaviors. The patient attempts to escape from feeling what they feel, in spite of the fact that they may report intense emotional discomfort. In spite of expressed emotional arousal that may be gut-wrenching, they attempt to truncate those feelings to what they perceive are more manageable levels. DBT thus assumes, like psychodynamic approaches, that attempted repression (escape and avoidance) of affect is central to emotional psychopathology.

DBT presumes that the intensity of affect is caused by dialectic conflict between self and environment (see chapter 4), defined as inadequate compromises between competing needs and wants; attachment, trauma, and loss experiences of the patient (see chapter 3); or genetic or kindling effects (chapter 3).

Prolonged intensity of affect results in high baseline arousal even in nonthreatening environments, frantic attempts to reduce such emotional arousal (ineffective operant behavior), and the slow return to the emotional baseline following exposure to threatening situations.

Therapeutic strategies of DBT include both acceptance of the patient's experiences (validation of their emotional pain and suffering) and offering new psychological coping strategies that include a refocus on meaning and substance in their life, exposure to previously intolerated emotions, prevention of emotional escape, and introduction of a behavior focus (a new goal orientation that appreciates and acknowledges emotional pain and suffering but demands new and different solution-focused strategies to deal with them).

DBT assumes that patients accurately report their experiences as perceived and that faulty cognitions do not typically represent the major causative factor in developing or sustaining emotional pain. In fact, thoughts are usually developed to attempt to explain the level of suffering experienced rather than the other way around (Jacobson et al. 1996). Emotions are more likely to spur certain thoughts rather than thoughts growing emotions. People are scientifically trained creatures. They look for explanations for why they feel so desperate and aroused. While cognitive restructuring strategies can result in substantial patient improvement, they do so indirectly by providing validation to the patient that their emotional pain is real and understandable.

DBT thus assumes that emotions themselves (their intensity, duration, and perceived nonspecific manifestation) are the primary causative factor in psychopathology. Neurobiological data suggests that once emotional pain pathways "fire," the frequency of future firing of those same pathways increases. This "kindling" effect is thus a central object of intervention in DBT approaches to suffering. It is only natural and expectable that patients will engage in extreme emotional avoidance and escape given the chronic firing of emotional arousal that such people endure.

DBT also presumes, paradoxically, that while the goal of the patient is to escape and avoid their affect, their very focus on such processes makes them increasingly attentive to (and thus more likely to respond to) affective stimuli. The more they avoid and escape their emotions, the more they experience them. A central principle of DBT, therefore, is that acceptance of emotional pain decreases it.

DBT differs from previous therapeutic approaches in that psychotherapy is oriented around validation (acceptance of the patient's perspectives on their own experience) of the emotional pain the patient suffers and assisting the patient to differentiate acceptance of their pain from approval of it. The patient is thus invited to move back and forth between the dialectic of acceptance and change. (Dialectics involve the polemics, opposites, opposing forces, paradoxes, conflicts, or catch-22s life inevitably brings.) Exposure to emotional pain, together with emotional support and validation, is counterbalanced with distress tolerance strategies that help patients to endure the exposure and increased environmental changes that can prompt new and different feeling states. DBT is thus about balancing therapeutic strategies: some strategies promote change, some strategies promote acceptance of experience as it is, some promote exploration of feelings and history, some promote distraction and arousal reduction, and some strategies are designed to promote the commitment and endurance required to undergo the arduous path of the previous strategies.

Linehan developed her dialectical framework from an understanding that emotional intensity leads to impulse-driven attempts to escape such pain, and that such escape and avoidance behaviors actually increase emotional intensity rather than decrease it (1993b). Addressing our unwillingness to experience our feelings is thus central to the DBT approach to both psychopathology and psychotherapeutic intervention.

Emotional acceptance technologies (both cognitive reorientation and meditative techniques) thus set the stage for decreasing emotional avoidance and escape. Acceptance-based strategies take into account the primordial role of neurological factors in sustaining high arousal. Increasing emotion regulation skills (psycho-education, exposure, and renewed strategic behavior skills) empowers the patient to attend to new cues in problem solving their emotional arousal.

Skills vs. Psychotherapy

Throughout this book reference will be made to psychosocial skills or psychotherapy. The psychological coping skills, those contained in the downloads (nhpubs.com/29064) included with this text, are psychoeducational in nature. The therapist teaches, explains, and reviews concepts important to learning, either in individual coaching sessions or group modalities. The skill sets (meaning making, mindfulness, emotion regulation, distress tolerance, strategic behavior skills) curricula are included in the downloadable material, while the individual psychotherapy process is explored throughout this text. While the most simple treatment configuration is to have one professional teach the skill sets while the other provides DBT psychotherapy, this is frequently impractical in a private practice setting. The therapist should thus be mindful of the notion that a dual approach is necessary: psychological coping skills should be taught to those who are deficient in identified skills, as well as providing general individual psychotherapeutic relief to the patients they treat. When in private solo practice, the therapist will frequently perform both functions (skills training and psychotherapy). Both are critical functions for the therapist, as explored in chapter 7.

Nonspecific Effects of Treatment

DBT assumptions explain why different theoretical orientations, with widely different interventions, still "work." Many research reviews have found that therapeutic interventions derived from widely discrepant theoretical orientations produce equal results (Bradley, 2000; Jacobson et al., 1996; Messer and Warren, 1995; Roth and Fonagy, 1996). The "nonspecific" effects of therapy (those garnered by psychodynamic, existential, interpersonal, and behavioral approaches) have been widely noted. While relationship or therapist effects have been proposed to explain such theoretically incompatible results (Beutler and Howard, 2003; Beutler, Machado, and Neufeldt, 1994; Crits-Christoph et al., 1991; Henry, 1998; Luborsky et al., 1986, 1999; Norcross and Hill, 2003; Wampold, 2001), and DBT acknowledges the therapeutic relationship as a critical factor in patient improvement, DBT would nevertheless posit that the more that different theoretical approaches expose the patient to their own emotions and prevent escape or avoidance from their own emotional process, the greater the patient improves. Emotion regulation, staying close to affect, and assisting the patient to accept rather than reject their experience will result in the greatest therapeutic effects.

DBT AS A THEORETICAL ORIENTATION

Current theoretical orientations in psychology include psychoanalytic (as represented by Freud and his followers), humanistic (as represented by Rogers), gestalt (as represented by Pearls), behaviorism (as represented by Skinner), cognitive behaviorism (as represented by Meichenbaum), social learning approaches (as represented by Bandura), and many eclectic iterations and revisions on these. DBT is a new theoretical school that accepts many of the philosophical assumptions of approaches that preceded it yet combines these assumptions and treatment strategies into a theoretically coherent model of mankind that provides both understanding of emotional pain and strategies to reduce such pain.

Comparisons to Analytic Approaches

DBT shares the rich intellectual tradition of psychoanalytic approaches by embracing the notions of compromise formation, the pleasure principle, cathexis and anticathexis (redefined as attachment and aversion), emotional trauma as requiring extreme psychological defensive mechanisms, and the role of transference in psychological healing. DBT rejects the central notions of a dynamic psychology (one that studies the transformations and exchanges of energy within the personality, such as id, ego, and superego), the central role of the unconscious developmental stages (oral, anal, etc.) in predicting lifelong deficits, and the primitive role of sexuality in explaining pathology.

DBT embraces the central role of compromise formation in defining human suffering, as did Freud (Hall, 1954). Life involves a series of competing, contradictory, and irreconcilable differences in demands, expectations, and desires. Dialectics are the continua that define such competing and contradictory demands upon the person. For example, people in critical emotional pain frequently live out the dialectic that they both want to embrace life and feel that they cannot tolerate what life brings to them. They want both to live and to die. These are incompatible desires, but they are experienced simultaneously in the moment by the person who suffers such a dia-lectic conflict. A compromise must be formed between the two competing demands (see chapter 4), and the adequacy of the formed compromise will define the health and dis-ease of the person.

Note how recognition of the critical importance of dialectics embraces one of the main tenets of psychoanalytic approaches. Freud writes: "It may thus be said that the theory of psychoanalysis is an attempt to account for two striking and unexpected facts of observation . . . the facts of transference and of resistance. Any line of investi-gation which recognizes these two facts and takes them as the starting point of its work may call itself psychoanalysis, though it arrives at results other than my own" (1914, p. 116). While Freud identifies transference and resistance as purely intrapsychic dynamics primarily expressed during the psychotherapy process with the analyst, DBT, like later Adlerian approaches, sees conflict as arising between people and the environment. Extenders of Freud's work historically have given increased rel-evance to social expectations, values, and cognitions (Mosak and Dreikurs, 1973) as well as the importance of interpersonal relationships (ego psychology).

DBT may thus be closer to accepting many of the theoretical foundations of an Adlerian perspective, since Adler proclaims that a person's psychology cannot be understood independent of the field in which they function. Adler found great merit in the study of the person's convictions, including their self-concept, their ideal self, their view of the world, and their personal "right-wrong" code (Mosak and Dreikurs, 1973). Adler defined the goal of therapy, unlike the Freudian notion of rescuing the patient from illness, as liberating the patient's social interest by changing faulty social values such as overgeneralizations, false or impossible goals of "security," misperceptions of life and of life's demands, minimization or denial of one's worth, or faulty ethical values such as "Be first even if you have to climb over others" (Dreikurs, 1957).

DBT also embraces Freud's pleasure principle. Simply put, people try to increase their pleasure and to decrease their pain. People do not consciously and deliberately put themselves in situations and circumstances that are painful. Experienced thera-pists, however, daily see how their patients maintain themselves in violent, emotion-ally abusive, and intolerable environments. Our patients keep themselves in dynamics that cause their pain. So where is Freud's pleasure principle operating? Freud added another powerful notion, that of repression, to explain how painful cir-cumstances can still be the best compromise, at the moment, for the person. He assumes that recognition of the source of their pain would be intolerable, so the per-son represses their wants, urges, or experiences. They may feel pain but not the extent or intensity of emotional pain that would be experienced without the tool of repression. DBT does not assume that repression is the compromise formation. Neither do psychoanalytic approaches—repression is the mechanism used to avoid a compromise. Instead, DBT assumes that the pleasure principle is at work, but the time frame and extant behavioral contingencies explain this.

If life is a series of compromises between multiple competing and contradictory demands, then the pleasure principle predicts that the person will choose to deal with those demands that are most pressing and emotionally meaningful. For example, staying in a physically and emotionally abusive relationship may feel like the most appropriate strategy to avoid abandonment and aloneness (perceived to have an even greater cost to the person than emotional and physical abuse from the person from whom they fear abandonment). So the pleasure principle is clearly at work given the weight or importance of each need and fear of the person at the time.

In the late 1800s, Freud wrote about cathexis and anticathexis. The underlying notion is about urges. "Want" and "need" have a force. Urgency is the sense of desperation that satisfying a need or want is critically important. DBT, along with Eastern meditative traditions, embraces the notion that people become "attached" to either a person, thing, or process and begin to live their lives as if this attachment is more important than other values. Attachment (defined as a deep desire to keep something or someone) causes the person to sustain environments that may have outlived their usefulness. The reverse, aversion (similar to Freud's anticathexis), causes the person to avoid or repel situations that otherwise might continue to be useful to them. The DBT notions of attachment and aversion refer to a clinging to pleasure or pain (the pleasure principle gone amok) when the result does not ultimately bring the desired pleasure or help to avoid the dreaded pain. Moreover, DBT assumes that our behavior is operant. No matter how chaotic and misunderstood our behavior may be, it probably represents frantic attempts to operate on the environment to reduce perceived threat and increase perceived pleasure.

DBT endorses the role of trauma in producing long-lived ineffective strategies to cope with emotional pain. Freud, in his later writings, acknowledged that anxiety was the cause of repression rather than its consequence (Wachtel, 1977). One powerful emotional event (a death, an abandonment, a threat to safety or security from a trusted source, etc.) can override multiple experiences of safety and satisfaction. Emotionally hurtful learning experiences result in kindling effects (see chapter 3) that sustain past behavior in spite of the pleasure principle.

The core of analytic psychotherapy is the transference. Freud assumed that the primitive and repressed psychological processes of the patient would be projected onto the therapist. The more ambiguous and less defined the relationship (if the patient is expected to be emotionally exposed while the therapist is relatively unknown and unknowable), the more projection of the patient's primary issues onto the therapist would likely be. DBT thus turns Freud's strategy of encouraging transference on its head. The therapist takes specific and strategic maneuvers to decrease projection. We don't want the patient to treat us like other valued objects from the past, acting out their past pathology as diagnostic tools for assessment. Instead, the DBT therapist identifies projection and takes active steps to assist the patient to repair the therapeutic relationship through clearly defined, well-expressed definition of the psychotherapy relationship. The humanistic approach of having a real relationship with another person (different from the relationships in the past) who cares is redefined each time projection occurs. Transference is acknowledged as a process that occurs, and one that interferes with therapy. Traditional analytic promotion of the transference is thus discouraged, but the role of transference is acknowledged rather than denied to the patient.

DBT sees the dialectic between competing demands as being between self and society, rather than between consciousness and the unconscious, as in traditional analytical psychotherapy (Whitmont and Kaufmann, 1973). However, the similarity between DBT and psychoanalytic approaches is that helping to define the meaningful connections that conflict brings is at the core of the psychotherapy process. DBT looks for meaning between the person and their perceived wants and demands (typically between person and environment), while analytic approaches look for meaning between consciousness and unconsciousness. Both approaches are looking for meaning.

Comparisons to Humanistic Approaches

The major tenets of humanistic approaches to psychology involve the growth potential of any human being based on relationships defined by realness, caring, and deeply sensitive nonjudgmentalness (Meador and Rogers, 1973). The intended product of the real relationship between the therapist and client is client self-understanding and self-acceptance. The therapeutic relationship is defined by warmth, responsiveness, and a permissive relationship free from coercion or pressure. The therapist is required to get "behind the words" of the client and into their feeling world in order to obtain accurate empathic understanding.

The humanistic hypothesis is that if the therapist is able to obtain genuineness, empathic understanding, and positive regard, then positive personality change will occur in the client (Rogers, 1957). Rogers proposes seven behavior strands within which behavior changes can be described in the client: feelings and personal meanings, manner of experiencing, degree of incongruence, communication of self, manner in which experience is construed, relationship to problems, and manner of relating. Rogers holds that a successful result of humanistic psychotherapy is that the client is more aware of their feelings, owns these feelings as theirs, and is better able to express the feelings as they occur.

Those familiar with DBT will immediately notice the similarities between humanistic approaches and the DBT approach. DBT also assumes that a successful outcome of DBT therapy will be increased exposure to the patient's affect, a result of decreasing the avoidance and escape responses the patient formerly used to reduce dialectical conflict. DBT uses specific strategies (behavioral techniques as well as respectful psychotherapeutic alliance) in order to teach patients to accept their feelings as events that do not necessarily need to be changed (acceptance) and to view their problems as events that need not be interpreted as defining their worth or value as a human being (changing the patient's relationship to their own problems).

While DBT thus has precisely the same goals as humanistic theories of psychotherapy, the difference is that humanistic psychotherapies see the process as directly related to the therapeutic relationship, while DBT sees the benefits as only partially related to the therapeutic relationship and as more substantially related to the technology of behavior change employed by the therapist (strategy and techniques).

Comparison to Gestalt or Existential Theories

Gestalt or existential therapies assume that disturbance is the result of painful polarization between two elements in a psychological process (Kempler, 1973), very similar to the dialectic focus of DBT. According to Gestalt theory, "coming to know" one's own psychological polarizations is the first step toward psychological integration. Direct, interpersonal experience is seen as the key toward the restoration of mental health. This is due to the existential emphasis on experience and perception. The polarizations assumed in Gestalt approaches have to do with attracting and repelling forces, need and fulfillment (need attracts and fulfillment neutralizes or repels), rather than conscious and unconscious conflict. The Gestalt approach is distinguishable from other theories in that the focus is on experience itself and awareness of such experience, again consistent with the DBT approach of reducing avoidance and escape responses to emotional experience.

As with humanistic approaches, Gestalt or existential theory assumes that the relationship is the main therapeutic tool to achieve psychotherapy goals. Thus, it differs from DBT in that DBT relies more heavily on strategic procedures that the therapist introduces to the patient in order to alter their experiences in their day-to-day life outside of the therapy environment. However, the Gestalt perspective that the goal of treatment is to help the patient be who they are, rather than striving for something else, is consistent with the DBT perspective.

Moreover, Gestalt perspectives encourage acknowledgment of affect without necessarily approving of it. The Gestalt personality theory of approbation is relevant here (Kempler, 1973). Gestalt theory states that approval, especially from parents and other authority figures, tends to increase personality disintegration, as the person strives to be who they're supposed to be rather than who they are. Thus, Gestalt approaches are consistent with DBT in that they invite the person to more clearly recognize polarities without prejudging which side of the polarity is right and which side is wrong. Gestalt and existential approaches were also the first to acknowledge the role of validation in treatment, an essential component of DBT approaches as well. The validation is that the patient experiences conflict due to polemic demands, and the role of the therapist is to help the patient "find themselves" by acknowledging their conflict, their experience, and their current awareness.

Comparison to Behavioristic Approaches

One of the first behavioral studies is reported by Watson, who showed that a human infant's fears are learned or conditioned (Watson and Rayner, 1920). However, Joseph Wolpe is generally credited with the beginning of behavior therapy as we know it today (Wolpe, 1958). Wolpe's position was that neurotic behavior was the result of learning in the presence of fear-producing stimuli and reversal could be achieved by relearning emotional responses. In addition to the concurrent behavioral principle that the scientific method should be applied to mental-health discovery, behavioristic presumptions include the notion that knowledge of the history of the individual is not entirely necessary to promote behavioral change. Behaviorists believe that the necessary and sufficient conditions for change exist in the present moment (contingencies of behavior), and that changes in the present contingencies of reinforcement are sufficient to bring lasting therapeutic change to the person.

Behavioral principles of conditioning, extinction, generalization, and counterconditioning are now recognized as incontrovertible elements of learning. Over time, behavioristic perspectives have increasingly included emotional components of human functioning. Anxiety, for example, is now a central aspect of behavioral approaches: ". . . anxiety is a motivating state of arousal and the direction of the behavior thereby motivated is away from the anxiety-stimulating situations. Since any behavior with a history of consistently reducing anxiety tends to be strongly learned, avoidance behaviors may take innumerable forms, some of which may be in the long run highly unadaptive" (Goldstein, 1973, p. 218). So behavioral approaches have long abandoned the Skinnerian model that only observable behavior can be the object of scientific study of human behavior. Many behavior therapists will also agree that interpretive or conversational therapies, such as psychoanalytic approaches, can facilitate extinction of anxiety through nonreinforced exposure to anxiety-provoking cues (Wachtel, 1977).

The Partial Reinforcement Effect

One powerful idea from behavioristic approaches is the notion of intermittent and partial reinforcement. The behavior therapy principle of intermittent reinforcement (similar to the psychoanalytic concept of internalization) is directly relevant to the experience of guilt and shame, central notions of DBT. Helping patients to identify their inadequate dialectic compromises, some of which result from infrequent but powerful intermittent reinforcement, must involve frequent attempts to extinguish shame feelings secondary to their emotional arousal.

What separates behavioristic principles of human behavior from nonbehavioral principles is the notion of determinism and antecedent events (Goldstein, 1973). Behavior therapy specifies that all behavior is contingent upon antecedent events, and DBT embraces this notion of cause and effect. Behavior is a response to stimulation—behavior is elicited—even if the elicitation is to internal events. Nothing is random. Behaviorists believe that the therapeutic relationship is a necessary but not sufficient condition for change, that emotional changes that may occur during the safety of the therapeutic relationship must be generalized to environments outside of the therapy environment in order to be effectively sustained. Perhaps most importantly, behavioristic approaches believe that resistance of the patient to change is meaningless, since it is the therapist and not the patient who must provide the conditions for both emotional and behavioral change. The responsibility for providing a therapeutic environment, under behavior therapy, shifts from the patient to the therapist (Goldstein, 1973).

The Cognitive Revolution in Behaviorism

Techniques of direct reinforcement, aversive therapy, flooding, and counterconditioning have generally been replaced with cognitive behavioral strategies that acknowledge the critical role of the patient's thoughts and expectancies in determining what kind of conditioning occurs in any particular person's environmental history (Beck, Rush, Shaw, and Emery, 1979; Elkin et al., 1989; Jacobson et al., 1996). Rather than being a contradictory perspective, DBT is an outgrowth of behavior therapy in that it fully embraces behavior therapy principles. However, DBT is less cognitive than traditional cognitive behavioral perspectives (Marks and Dar, 2000) since DBT posits that thoughts, per se, are less important than affect regulation (a different kind of exposure—exposure to emotional processes—rather than to thoughts and their attendant emotional arousal).

Most newer psychotherapies following the cognitive behavior model place great emphasis on thoughts per se, as in acceptance and commitment therapy (ACT), where Hayes, Strosahl, and Wilson conclude that "avoidance of aversive private experiences is the natural result of human language" (1999, p. 45). ACT asserts that "language itself enables humans to struggle with their own private experiences in a way that fosters the ubiquity of human misery" (p. 57-58). Thus, even the "third wave" of behaviorism, encompassing acceptance and mindfulness principles, tends to support the primacy of cognitive events as the cause of major emotional dysfunction, although the goals are much the same as DBT. Recent integrative models, even those supported by the National Institute of Mental Health treatment development grants, embrace cognition or thoughts as the center of emotional illness (Vieth et al., 2003). DBT, on the other hand, diminishes the role of cognition as the primary causative factor in major mental disorders.

Fundamentally, DBT differentiates itself from standard cognitive behavioral therapy by placing the major emphasis on emotion regulation (Bohus et al., 2000; Bradley, 2000; Eisenberg et al., 1996; Field, 1994; Kagan, 1994; Lazarus and Folkman, 1984; Shearin and Linehan, 1994; Thompson, 1994; Wagner and Linehan, 1999; Wiser and Telch, 1999) rather than maladaptive thought processes (Beck et al., 1979). DBT proposes that the ability to sustain attention to affect is more important than the ability to change simple behavioral contingencies (Addis and Hatgis, 2000; Bradley, 2000; Carek, 1990; Davidson and Goleman, 1977; Eisenberg et al., 1996; Field, 1994; Goleman, 2003; Gray, 1991; Segal, Williams, and Teasdale, 2002; Teasdale, Segal, and Williams, 1995, 2003; Thompson, 1994). This is due to the pivotal role of affect in sustaining behavioral responses in complex human beings (Bradley, 2000; Carek, 1990; Goleman, 2003; Kagan, 1989; Lazarus and Folkman, 1984; Segal et al., 2002).

DBT thus is different from standard behavioral therapy approaches because it places major responsibility for behavioral change closer to the emotions themselves (Koerner and Linehan, 2000; Linehan, 1987; Linehan et al., 1991, 2002; Rizvi and Linehan, 2001; Segal et al., 2002). Cognition is not a necessary mediating factor. Emotions hurt, and emotional factors, including the behavioral principles of avoidance and escape, are critically important in defining the therapeutic focus of attention (Cassidy and Kobak, 1988; Jacobson et al., 1996; Kagan, 1989; Segal et al., 2002).

So DBT borrows from many intellectual traditions of the past, but is differentiated from those same schools of psychology by assuming that emotional conflict itself creates psychopathological responses. Inadequate compromise formation, the dialectics upon which DBT rests, define its uniqueness. Emotional conflict and fear of one's own emotional arousal result in avoidance and escape behaviors. Yet in complex human beings, the avoidance and escape apply to internal processes rather than external environments, and effectively avoiding or escaping oneself is difficult indeed.

In acute disorders, the intensity of emotional arousal is frequently beyond the conscious control of the person due to neurological kindling effects. Emotional dysregulation results, with secondary guilt and shame responses that increase the very arousal the person attempts to avoid. Increasingly, the person begins to attend more to avoidance and escape of affect and less to the immediate contingencies of reinforcement that sustain the behaviors that cause them pain. DBT is a theory that can effectively assist patients who are in acute phases of mood, anxiety, addictive, eating, impulse-control, and personality disorders.

Chapter Summary

DBT shares an intellectual history with psychoanalytic, humanistic, existential, and behavioristic schools of psychology. It embraces the psychoanalytic notions of conflict and compromise formations, the humanistic emphasis on validation of the patient, the existential focus on experience over thoughts and ideas, and the behavioristic traditions of learning theory and science. DBT is more than eclecticism, however, since it embodies an entire theory of pathogenesis, pathotopology, and treatment applicable to most acute mental disorders.

CHAPTER 2

Evidence for the Effectiveness of DBT

There are three strands of research that support the dialectical approach to psychopathology and psychotherapy. The first and largest is the standard behavior therapy literature covering avoidance, escape, desensitization, and contingencies of reinforcement (learning theory). The second is research on acceptance technologies, such as mindfulness research. The last is the more recent literature on dialectical behavior therapy, per se.

BEHAVIOR THERAPY RESEARCH

While it is beyond the scope of this book to fully explore the research on behavior therapy principles, it should be noted that the literature on avoidance and escape of emotional arousal has been studied for many years (Bandura, Blanchard, and Ritter, 1969; Baum, 1970; Berman and Katzev, 1972; Borkovec and Craighead, 1971; Ferster, 1973; Kazdin, 1973; Rappaport, 1972; Riccio and Silvestri, 1973), and exposure is the preferred method of decreasing avoidance and escape behaviors (Vodde and Gilner, 1971). In fact, there is some evidence that cognitive behavioral strategies, which place emphasis on such things as exploring patient attributions, correcting cognitive distortions, and focusing on patient thoughts, per se, may actually work due to the exposure element of having patients face issues they fear, rather than changing their thoughts as predicted in cognitive behavior theory (Jacobson et al., 1996).

Avoidance is when the patient finds that an experience arouses anxiety and then engages in behavior to decrease such arousal by not coming in contact with the cues that trigger the arousal. Avoidance thus occurs prior to when the emotional arousal begins and, as such, is an anticipatory process. Escape is similar to avoidance, but takes place when the emotional arousal has already begun, causing the person to engage in behavior to terminate the arousal. Avoidance is a powerful negative reinforcer of behavior because it terminates an aversive experience, and escape is a powerful positive reinforcer of behavior because it increases calm. Both positive and negative reinforcement share the same outcome: they increase the frequency of the behavior upon whose occurrence they are contingent. Each time a person avoids or escapes the emotions they do not wish to have, they increase the tendency that they will use that same strategy in the future. The strategy, in the short term, works for them. They feel less anxiety, less depression, or less threat.

Avoidance is anticipatory, and as sentient and creative beings, we humans can take increasingly anticipatory avoidance responses. First, we avoid paniclike responses, but later we learn to avoid high anxiety, moderate arousal, disappointment, interpersonal hurt, or even simple boredom. We can come to fear strong emotions of any sort and to take measures to avoid them rapidly and without conscious effort. Escape is no different. Once an emotion begins, we can develop strategies (distraction, inattentiveness, obsessiveness, or even producing another, less-aversive feeling, such as anger) to avoid the aversive feeling we don't want to feel.

What makes behavior principles appear less useful in clinical private practice is that the contingencies of reinforcement tend to be internal, delayed, and intermittent. But simply because the contingencies of reinforcement are less discernable doesn't make them any less relevant to assisting our patients. The reinforcing value of avoiding or terminating a powerfully aversive emotion (anxiety, depression, addiction, or guilt, for example) frequently is observable only to the person who experiences the emotion. Only through repeated and thorough observation of the person could an outsider begin to notice the contingency of reinforcement. Internal events, by definition, are obscure. Similarly, delayed reinforcement (the behavior or cues that lead to the behavior, which, in clinical private practice, is the emotions themselves) may be far removed from the reinforcing events. For example, a patient may engage in compulsive masturbatory behavior hours prior to the feared performance anxiety of sexual contact with a partner they wish to please. The compulsive behavior (masturbation) thus serves to decrease fear of nonperformance, even though the two events (masturbation and interpersonal sexual contact) are hours apart.

Finally, the intermittent reinforcement principle can be particularly troublesome for the private practitioner who observes the patient's behavior only once or perhaps twice per week. In intermittent reinforcement, the person receives reward for

their behavior only occasionally. However, learning research clearly shows that intermittent reinforcement produces the highest frequency of responding as well as the
highest resistance to extinction (Rimm and Masters, 1979). In other words, when the
reinforcement only sometimes works or even infrequently works, the person is more
likely to engage in the behavior. The frequency of the behavior increases because the
person knows that the desired results only occur occasionally, and thus by engaging
in the behavior rapidly and frequently they are more likely to obtain their desired
result. Of course, behavior therapy theory, like other analytic approaches, does not
propose that this is a conscious or even desired process. It occurs just like gravity,
without intent or planning. Since reinforcement occurs only occasionally, extinction
or termination of the response is slowed. Just because it has not worked in the last
one hundred attempts, the person keeps trying because it worked a few times in the
past with some regularity. We don't give up, because there is memory of when it previously worked.

Exposure technologies (Foa, Rothbaum, and Furr, 2003) are the treatment of
choice to solve avoidance and escape defenses for a variety of specific disorders, as
shown in table 1 . Exposure is a necessary component.

Table 1: Exposure as Treatment of Choice for Avoidant and Escape Defenses	
Problem Area	**Research Studies Demonstrating Exposure Effectiveness**
Anxiety	Berman, Weems, Silverman, and Kurtines, 2000
	Pina, Silverman, Weems, Kurtines, and Goldman, 2003
Fear	Mohlman and Zinbarg, 2000
	Tsao and Craske, 2000
Panic	Huppert and Baker-Morrisette, 2003
	Park et al., 2001
Phobias	Berman et al., 2000
	Coles and Heimberg, 2000
	Craske, DeCola, Sachs, and Pontillo, 2003
	Fava, Grandi, et al., 2001
	Fava, Rafanelli, et al., 2001
	Fernandes, 2003
	Hahlweg, Fiegenbaum, Frank, Schroeder, and von Witzleben, 2001
	Hazlett-Stevens and Borkovec, 2001
	Zoellner, Echiverri, and Craske, 2000

Social phobia	Coles and Heimberg, 2000
	Fava, Grandi, et al., 2001
	Hofmann, 2000
Agoraphobia	Craske et al., 2003
	Fava, Rafanelli, et al., 2001
	Hahlweg et al., 2001
Generalized anxiety disorder	Dugas et al., 2003
	Forsyth and McNeil, 2002
Obsessive-compulsive disorder	Abramowitz, Franklin, and Cahill, 2003
	Abramowitz, Franklin, Street, Kozak, and Foa, 2000
	Franklin, Abramowitz, Kozak, Levitt, and Foa, 2000
Simple obsessive thoughts	Freeston, Leger, and Ladouceur, 2001
Depression	Abramowitz and Foa, 2000
	Abramowitz et al., 2000
Eating disorders	Carter, McIntosh, Joyce, Sullivan, and Bulik, 2003
	Toro et al., 2003
	Tuschen-Caffier, Voegele, Bracht, and Hilbert, 2003
	Wilson and Roberts, 2002
Hypochondriasis	Visser and Bouman, 2001
Comorbid conditions	Abramowitz and Foa, 2000
	Steketee, Chambless, and Tran, 2001

Behavior therapy principles thus offer powerful notions to promote both behavior and emotion change: look for avoidance and escape strategies the patient uses with strong and vulnerable emotions, look for intermittent, delayed, and internal contingencies of reinforcement, and don't expect that the patient understands or intends for any of these processes to be at work.

Behavior therapy has more randomized clinical control studies than any other approach in psychotherapy (Elkin et al., 1989; Lambert, 1992; Roth and Fonagy, 1996; Wampold, 2001), and while it will be argued elsewhere in this book that there is more similarity between treatment approaches than there are theoretically important differences (Hibbs et al., 1991; Jacobson et al., 1996; Messer and Warren, 1995; Roth and Fonagy, 1996), the absolute number, quality, and replication of findings for behavior therapy principles should make mental-health treatment professionals mindful of their power to help change the emotional suffering we find in patients presented in private practice.

So why, in addition to the factors of intermittent, internal, and delayed contingencies that make such effects less readily observable, are there fewer mental-health professionals who adhere to behavior therapy theory than those who describe themselves as theoreticaly eclectic? Perhaps because behavior therapy principles do not describe a language that is consistent with emotionality and arousal. While it well explains maintaining factors and environmental contingencies, behavior therapy as theory fails to fully entertain notions of meaning, the very core of reinforcement or learning theory. Acceptance-based approaches, the second strand of research supporting DBT-based psychotherapy, embrace a language of meaning that is more consistent with how patients feel and think.

MINDFULNESS AND ACCEPTANCE-BASED RESEARCH

Acceptance-based therapy procedures (unlike traditional behavior therapy that attempts to solve problems and engage in behavior and affect change) invite patients to experience their situation without struggle or expectation of change (Kabat-Zinn, 1994). Mindfulness is the most widely accepted technique used to accomplish acceptance-based decreases in agony (Goleman, 2003; Kabat-Zinn, Lipworth, Burney, and Sellers, 1986; Kabat-Zinn et al., 1992; Kabat-Zinn et al., 1998; Miller, Fletcher, and Kabat-Zinn, 1995; Segal et al., 2002; Teasdale et al., 2000; Wegner, 1994). The pioneering research work with mindfulness (to be reviewed below) was originally conducted on chronic pain patients (Kabat-Zinn, Lipworth, and Burney, 1985), but was adopted as a core strategy of DBT used with borderline personality patients (Linehan, 1987, 1993a).

Chronic pain patients offer an unusual challenge to traditional behavior therapy. Behavior therapy offers patients the hope of change of the status quo, while chronic pain patients by definition have little hope of substantially changing their physical pain. These patients typically have had multiple evaluations by physicians, physical therapists, pain specialists, occupational medicine specialists, as well as mental-health specialists. It is unusual for the chronic pain patient to not also be depressed because of the chronicity and intensity of their discomfort. Dr. Kabat-Zinn is the acknowledged leader in using mindfulness-based interventions to treat pain patients.

Dr. Kabat-Zinn taught mindfulness meditation in a ten-week stress-education and relaxation program to train fifty-one chronic pain patients in self-regulation (Kabat-Zinn et al., 1985). The patients were taught detached observation of their pain, specifically attending to their pain rather than avoiding or escaping experience of it. At the time, Kabat-Zinn couched his intervention as increasing the patients' knowledge of their own proprioception. His research showed a reduction of 33 percent in the mean total of a pain rating index at the conclusion of the ten-week program. Large and significant reductions in mood disturbance and psychiatric symptomatology accompanied these changes and were relatively stable up to one and half years later.

The next year, Kabat-Zinn conducted another study on ninety chronic pain patients (Kabat-Zinn et al., 1985). These pain patients were also trained in mindfulness meditation in a ten-week stress-reduction and relaxation program. Self-report indices, including the McGill Pain Questionnaire, the Profile of Mood States, and the Hopkins Symptom Checklist, were administered to the experimental subjects to assess aspects of pain and certain pain-related behaviors. Results show statistically significant reductions in measures of present-moment pain. This is significant in that patients were not taught how to reduce their pain experience per se, but how to attend to their physical pain in a detached and nonjudgmental manner. In addition to the reduction of perceived pain, these experimental subjects showed scores indicative of reductions in negative body image, inhibition of activity by pain, pain symptoms, mood disturbance, and psychological symptomatology, including anxiety and depression. Reduction in perceived pain and increases in psychological health were thus achieved through group mindfulness meditation practice. More objective measures, such as pain-related drug utilization, decreased, and activity levels and feelings of self-esteem increased. Dr. Kabat-Zinn concluded that improvement appeared to be independent of gender, source of referral, and type of pain. A comparison group of twenty-one pain patients did not show significant improvement on these measures after traditional treatment protocols. At follow-up, the improvements observed during the meditation training were maintained up to fifteen months after the meditation training for all measures except present-moment pain. This suggests the importance of continued practice of the meditation techniques with an experienced therapist, in spite of the fact that the majority of subjects reported continued high compliance with the meditation practice as part of their daily lives.

In addition to the robust effectiveness of mindfulness-based treatment effects with chronic pain patients, the experimenters demonstrate that these effects are long lasting and that patients continue to use the mindfulness-based procedures up to four years after the initial ten-week intervention (Kabat-Zinn et al., 1986). Few short-term interventions have shown the staying power and effectiveness that mindfulness-based procedures have shown.

Although mindfulness meditation was originally developed in the Buddhist religious tradition, it has been adopted by Western psychology as a nonreligious strategy to decrease emotional suffering. Hayes and Wilson (2003) provide an elegant description of "experiential avoidance" that mindfulness is designed to treat:

> Experiential avoidance is the phenomenon that occurs when a person is unwilling to remain in contact with particular private experiences (e.g., bodily sensations, emotions, thoughts, memories, behavioral predispositions) and

takes steps to alter the form or frequency of these events and the contexts that occasion them, even when doing so creates life harm. (p. 162)

They note the substantial body of evidence showing that such experiential avoidance is harmful in a variety of psychopathological areas (Hayes, Wilson, Gifford, Follette, and Strosahl, 1996). And they provide a poetic discrimination of acceptance-based psychological treatment strategies from traditional cognitive behavioral approaches:

These new methods . . . seek to increase the range and flexibility of functions that occur in contexts that previously had only literal, avoidant, or evaluative functions. They carry the same message as old-fashioned, functionally oriented behavior therapy, but in a new package that validates and dignifies the importance of human thoughts and feelings and their role in human suffering. . . . Mindfulness, acceptance, and defusion are not just a different way of treating traditionally conceptualized problems of depression or anxiety. They imply a redefinition of the problem, the solution, and how both should be measured. The problem is not the presence of particular thoughts, emotions, sensations, or urges: It is the constriction of a human life. The solution is not removal of difficult private events: It is living a valued life. (pp. 164–165)

The review of mindfulness research here presented is categorized as acceptance-based because mindfulness training is proposed to have several components, only one of which is the actual practice of the meditative process. First, mindfulness is an intentional act. It requires that the meditator be aware of their own attentional and observational process. It thus predicts that there are various kinds of attention and consciousness, and ordinary or automatic consciousness is only one among many ways of experiencing the world. Second, mindfulness encourages nonevaluative contact with events in the moment. Such attention to the functions of evaluative language itself serves to change one's historical and immediate experience. It thus separates analytical thought from experience per se (discriminating observation itself from thoughts about observation). Rather than informing the meditator that their thoughts are distorted (that the patient is wrong), as some cognitive behavioral theories presume, mindfulness invites the meditator to simply notice the evaluations and let them go, when possible. Third, mindfulness invites acceptance of private events that previously may have been ignored or avoided. It increases contact with what is occurring in the meditator's private world. Fourth, mindfulness promotes a principle that experience is valuable. By inviting participation with one's experience (noticing what is going on in the meditator's private world), there is implicit understanding that there is existential meaning to be found by training the mind to observe better and more fully.

Goleman notes that there are two distinct processes involved in meditation: concentration and mindfulness (1978). Davidson and Goleman note in an early review of the literature that meditative attention appears to enhance cortical specificity (increases in brain activity in specific areas), but simple concentration techniques do not (1977). Their early conclusion has been more recently confirmed by Dunn, who used electroencephalographic recordings from ten subjects (including nineteen scalp recording sites) in meditation, concentration, mindfulness, and a normal relaxation control condition (Dunn, Hartigan, and Mikulas, 1999). The subjects were assessed both after initial training and after prolonged training. During each recording session, all subjects performed three tasks: an eyes-closed relaxed baseline, a concentration meditation, and a mindfulness meditation. Analysis of all standard frequency bandwidth data showed strong mean amplitude frequency differences between the two meditation conditions and relaxation over numerous cortical sites. Significant differences were obtained between concentration and mindfulness states at all bandwidths, showing the superiority of mindfulness. Results suggest that concentration and mindfulness meditations may be unique forms of consciousness and are not merely degrees of a state of relaxation.

Valentine studied the performance of nineteen concentrative and mindfulness meditators (aged twenty-four to forty-three years) on a test of sustained attention and compared the results with those of thirty-four controls. Both groups of meditators demonstrated superior performance on the test of sustained attention in comparison with controls (Valentine and Sweet, 1999). Long-term meditators were superior to short-term meditators, suggesting the progressive gain that can occur with increased practice.

How can the simple, group-based intervention of having patients attend to their experience, one thing at a time, nonjudgmentally, and without attempting to alter the course or intensity of their experience, result in such subjective and objective treatment effects? Brown might argue that mindfulness meditators increase their observational powers, per se (Brown, Forte, and Dysart, 1984a). He conducted an experiment with more limited and objective experimental variables, testing visual sensitivity differences using tachistoscopic presentation of light flashes in thirty-nine practitioners (in three groups) of Buddhist mindfulness meditation and ten nonmeditator controls. Results showed that meditation practitioners were able to detect light flashes of shorter duration than the nonmeditators. There were no differences among practitioner and control groups in ability to discriminate between closely spaced successive light flashes. Brown suggests that a lower detection threshold for single light flashes reflects an enduring increase in sensitivity, the long-term effects of the practice of meditation on certain perceptual habit patterns. The lack of differences in the discrimination of successive light flashes, Brown suggests, reflects the resistance of other perceptual habit patterns to modification. He reports that his results support the statements found in Buddhist texts on meditation concerning the changes in perception encountered during the practice of mindfulness.

In another study with a similar design, Brown tested visual sensitivity before and immediately after a three-month retreat employing intensive Buddhist meditation for twenty-one retreatants at the Insight Meditation Society (IMS) and eleven

IMS staff members, who were controls (Brown, Forte, and Dysart, 1984b). Retreatants practiced mindfulness meditation for sixteen hours per day, while staff meditated about two hours per day in addition to their work at the IMS. Visual sensitivity was defined by a detection threshold, presented tachistoscopically and of fixed luminance, based on the duration of simple light flashes and a discrimination threshold based on the interval between successive simple light flashes. Results show that after the retreat, practitioners could detect short, single-light flashes and required a shorter interval to differentiate between successive flashes correctly. The control group did not change on either measure. While this study examines the effect of intensive mindfulness meditation on experienced practitioners of the technique, it clearly suggests that mindfulness enabled practitioners to become aware of some of the pre-attentive processes involved in visual detection. Mindfulness-based strategies appear to change the scope and accuracy of attention.

While there is no reason to believe that a shorter and extremely less intensive intervention, such as those that are being conducted in the U.S. (Baer, 2003; Bishop, 2002; Davidson et al., 2003; Kabat-Zinn, 1984; Kabat-Zinn et al., 1985, 1986, 1992, 1998; Kaplan, Goldenberg, and Galvin-Nadeau, 1993; Reibel, Greeson, Brainard, and Rosenzweig, 2001; Segal et al., 2002; Speca, Carlson, Goodey, and Angen, 2000; Williams, Kolar, Reger, and Pearson, 2001; Wiser and Telch, 1999), would produce similarly dramatic changes in the ability to attend to simple visual stimuli, the fact that both experienced mindfulness meditators (when measuring simple objective criteria) and patients (when measuring global psychological criteria) experience changes is powerful experimental evidence for the effectiveness of mindfulness-based procedures. But the evidence and the number of experimenters producing the data are much larger than those yet reviewed.

Twenty-two patients with generalized anxiety and panic disorder were administered the same mindfulness-based group meditative practice used with chronic pain patients (Kabat-Zinn et al., 1992), and significant improvements in several measures of anxiety and depression were found at posttreatment as well as at a three-month follow up. A three-year follow-up of the same participants showed that the treatment gains had been maintained (Miller et al., 1995).

Kaplan assessed the effectiveness of a ten-week mindfulness meditation–based stress reduction program in the treatment of seventy-seven patients with fibromyalgia (Kaplan et al., 1993). Although the mean scores of all subjects completing the program showed improvement, only the 51 percent who showed at least a 25 percent improvement in 50 percent of the outcome measures were counted as treatment responders, again showing the clinical utility of the intervention.

Kabat-Zinn studied thirty-seven psoriasis patients treated with mindfulness meditation in combination with phototherapy or photochemotherapy treatment (Kabat-Zinn et al., 1998). The patients scheduled for medical treatment were randomly assigned to one of two conditions: a mindfulness-based stress-reduction intervention guided by audiotaped instructions during light treatments, or a control condition consisting of the light treatments alone with no taped instructions.

Psoriasis status was assessed by direct, unblinded inspection by clinic nurses, direct inspection by blinded physicians (tape or no tape), and blinded physician evaluation of photographs of psoriasis lesions. Four sequential indicators of skin status were monitored during the study, with the mindfulness-treated group showing significantly more rapid response to treatment than those in the no-tape condition for both medical treatments. The authors conclude that a brief mindfulness-based stress-reduction intervention delivered by audiotape during ultraviolet light therapy can increase the rate of resolution of psoriatic lesions.

There is even evidence that meditative techniques, including mindfulness, can extend longevity of life and increase psychological well-being (Alexander, Langer, Newman, Chandler, and Davis, 1989). Alexander took seventy-three residents of eight homes for the elderly (mean age of eighty-one years) and randomly assigned them among no treatment and three treatments highly similar in external structure and expectations: the Transcendental Meditation (TM) program, mindfulness training (MF), or a relaxation (low-mindfulness) program. A planned comparison indicated that the "restful alert" TM group improved most, followed by MF, in contrast to relaxation and no-treatment groups, on two measures of cognitive flexibility, on mental-health measures, and on a physical measure (systolic blood pressure). The MF group improved most on perceived control, followed by TM. After three years, the survival rate was 100 percent for TM and 87.5 percent for MF in contrast to lower rates for simple relaxation groups.

Kutz early noted the beneficial effects of adding meditative practices to traditional psychotherapy techniques (Kutz, Borysenko, and Benson, 1985). He studied the effect of a ten-week meditation program on twenty patients (mean age of thirty-eight years) undergoing long-term individual dynamic-explorative psychotherapy. The length of the psychotherapy ranged from one to ten years. Their diagnoses varied from severe narcissistic and borderline personality disorders to anxiety and obsessive neuroses, thus showing great variability in their symptom picture. While the patients continued their weekly individual psychotherapy sessions, they also met weekly as a group to meditate and discuss meditation, and meditated for forty-five minutes daily at home. Home meditation consisted of meditation through attention to breathing, body awareness meditation, and mindfulness meditation. The patients' improvement was rated by themselves and their individual psychotherapists. Both the therapists and the patients identified similar areas of improvement on measures of anxiety and depression. Therapists reported marked improvement in the development of insight. Kutz concludes that meditation can be an important adjunct to even dynamically oriented psychotherapy in that it reduces arousal and thus improves insight. He sees these benefits as complementary rather than competing therapeutic technologies.

Mindfulness has been shown beneficial in nonpathological samples (premed and medical students) as well (Shapiro, Schwartz, and Bonner, 1998). The experimenters examined the short-term effects of an eight-week meditation-based stress-reduction intervention on seventy-three students using a wait-list control group as a comparison group. The Empathy Construct Rating Scale, the Hopkins Symptom Checklist 90 (Revised), the State-Trait Anxiety Inventory (Form Y), and the Index of Core Spiritual Experiences were used as pre-post measures. Findings indicated that participation in the intervention effectively reduced self-reported state and trait anxiety, reduced reports of overall psychological distress (including depression), increased scores on overall empathy levels, and increased scores on a measure of spiritual experiences assessed at the termination of the intervention. These results were replicated in the wait-list control group later, and have held across different experiments. Astin conducted a similar study over an eight-week period with twenty-eight undergraduate students and found similar results (1997). Mindfulness has thus been shown effective with "normal" populations. Results such as these have been interpreted in light of control theory or self-awareness (Barbieri, 1996).

The frequency of mindfulness research has increased recently as the effect sizes and variety of patient populations on whom they are found effective has increased. A great deal of research has been published just in the last three to four years. Carlson and her colleagues investigated the relationships between an eight-week mindfulness-based stress-reduction meditation program for forty-nine early stage breast cancer patients and ten prostate cancer patients and quality of life, mood states, stress symptoms, lymphocyte counts, and cytokine production (Carlson, Speca, Patel, and Goodey, 2003). Significant improvements were seen in overall quality of life, symptoms of stress, and sleep quality. Biological changes in cell production were measured. The authors conclude that their results are consistent with a shift in immune profile from one associated with depressive symptoms to a more normal profile.

Cancer patients were also studied by Speca (Speca et al., 2000). They assessed the effects of mindfulness on mood disturbance and symptoms of stress in ninety cancer outpatients (ages twenty-seven to seventy-five). The study is significant in demonstrating not only decreased symptoms, but that the symptom relief was consistent across gender, age, type, and stage of illness. Subjects completed the Profile of Mood States and the Symptoms of Stress Inventory both before and after the intervention. The intervention consisted of a weekly meditation group lasting one and a half hours for seven weeks, plus home meditation practice. After the intervention, patients in the treatment group had significantly lower scores on total mood disturbance and subscales of depression, anxiety, anger, and confusion and more vigor than control subjects. The treatment group had fewer overall symptoms of stress, fewer cardiopulmonary and gastrointestinal symptoms, less emotional irritability, lower depression, less cognitive disorganization, and fewer habitual patterns of stress. Overall reduction in total mood disturbance was 65 percent, with a 31 percent reduction in symptoms of stress.

Sleep-related complaints were investigated by Shapiro and colleagues following treatment with mindfulness-based stress reduction (Shapiro, Bootzin, Figueredo, Lopez, and Schwartz, 2003). Sixty-three women between thirty-eight and seventy-seven years old who had been diagnosed with stage II breast cancer were administered questionnaires before, during, and after intervention. Subjects who reported greater mindfulness practice improved significantly more on the sleep quality measure, which was most strongly associated with distress.

The effects of mindfulness have been tested on binge eating disorder (Kristeller and Hallett, 1999). These experimenters use an even shorter intervention period (six weeks rather than the eight weeks used by most researchers) but use eating-specific mindfulness meditation exercises as well as standard mindfulness instructions developed by Kabat-Zinn. A single-group extended-baseline design assessed all variables at three weeks before and after intervention. Binges decreased in frequency, from 4.02 per week to 1.57 per week, and in severity. Scores on the Binge Eating Scale and on the Beck Depression and Anxiety Inventories decreased significantly, while a sense of control increased. Time using eating-related meditations predicted decreases on the Binge Eating Scale.

Demonstrating the robust effectiveness of mindfulness-based interventions, Riebel and colleagues examined an heterogeneous 136 patients on health-related quality of life and physical and psychological symptomatology after an eight-week intervention (Reibel et al., 2001). The patients were aged twenty-three to seventy-six years old and were required to practice twenty minutes of meditation daily, in addition to participation in the structured treatment intervention. Pre- and postintervention data included the Short-Form Health Survey (SF-36), Medical Symptom Checklist (MSCL), and Hopkins Symptom Checklist 90 (Revised; SCL-90-R). Health-related quality of life increased, as demonstrated by improvement on all indices of the SF-36, including vitality, bodily pain, role limitations caused by physical health, and social functioning. Physical symptoms were reduced, as shown by a 28 percent reduction on the MSCL. Decreased psychological distress was indicated on the SCL-90-R by a 38 percent reduction on the Global Severity Index, a 44 percent reduction on the anxiety subscale, and a 34 percent reduction on the depression subscale. Follow-up after one year revealed maintenance of improvements.

While she reports no data, Logsdon-Conradsen argues for the utility of mindfulness-based treatment for individuals with HIV/AIDS, given their increased susceptibility to illness and disease progression as a result of the immunosuppressive effect of stress (Logsdon-Conradsen, 2002). Winiarski and colleagues (Wagner, Miller, Greene, and Winiarski, 2004) have done just that, describing modification of DBT skills training to include HIV treatment adherence (again, no data reported as yet). Marlatt (2002), well-known in the relapse model for prevention of substance abuse, argues that mindfulness-based procedures and Buddhist philosophy can be applied in the treatment of individuals with substance-abuse problems (alcohol, smoking, and illicit drug use) and other addictive behaviors (like compulsive eating and gambling).

Some of the most powerful research showing, in neuroanatomical terms, the power of a simple eight-week mindfulness-based stress-reduction program was recently conducted by Davidson, Kabat-Zinn, and colleagues (Davidson et al., 2003). A randomized and controlled study on the effects on brain and immune function were applied in a work environment with healthy employees. They measured brain electrical activity before and immediately after the eight-week training program in mindfulness meditation, and then again four months later. Twenty-five subjects were tested in the meditation group, while sixteen subjects in the wait-list control group were tested at the same points in time as the meditators. At the end of training, subjects in both groups were vaccinated with an influenza vaccine. They reported significant increases in left-sided anterior activation (a pattern previously associated with positive affect) in the meditators compared with the nonmeditators. They also found significant increases in antibody titers to influenza vaccine among subjects in the meditation group compared with those in the wait-list control group. Meditation thus instigates changes in neurobiology affecting the immune system directly. It can lead to brain changes consistent with more effective handling of negative emotion under stress (Kabat-Zinn, 2003).

Almost all of the reports in the literature of using mindfulness-based interventions have positive findings. Of course, if it's too good to be true, it's probably not true. McMillan studied 145 traumatic brain injury patients, ages sixteen to sixty-five (McMillan, Robertson, Brock, and Charlton, 2002). While an earlier pilot study indicated improvement in self-reported cognitive impairment, the later randomized and controlled clinical study found no differences on objective or self-report measures of cognitive function, mood, or symptom reporting. The authors conclude that brief exposure to mindfulness meditation cannot be recommended as a treatment technique for patients with traumatic brain injury.

Wells discusses the theoretical aspects of mindfulness with generalized anxiety disorder and proposes that mindfulness activates a metacognitive mode of processing, disconnects the influence of maladaptive beliefs on information processing, boosts flexible responding to threat, and strengthens metacognitive plans for controlling cognition (2002). While Wells offers theoretical reasons why mindfulness may be effective in the treatment of patients with generalized anxiety disorder, he offers caution that mindfulness cannot always be counted upon to challenge anxiety-generating thoughts.

Teasdale and colleagues present one of the most interesting applications of mindfulness (1995). They attempt to use mindfulness as a prevention strategy with recurrent depression. Experimental subjects had to have several prior episodes of depression but not be currently depressed in order to participate in this multisite study. In patients with three or more episodes of depression (77 percent of the total sample of 145), what they term mindfulness-based cognitive therapy (MBCT) significantly reduced relapse compared to treatment as usual; in patients with only two prior episodes of depression (23 percent of the total sample), there was no difference in relapse rates between patients receiving MBCT and treatment as usual. More episodes of depression predicted greater effect from the MBCT program. The treatment-as-usual control group showed a 66 percent relapse rate over the total sixty-week study period, whereas those who received MBCT showed a relapse rate of 37 percent. Adding MBCT to treatment as usual had the effect of reducing the risk of relapse almost by half for those patients who had more than two prior episodes of depressive disorder.

What is particularly interesting in this study is that very little of the intervention is designed around known aspects of depression (loss of interest in pleasurable activities, disputing depressing thoughts, increasing hope and behavioral activity level, increasing reinforcer effectiveness, etc.). Instead, the authors use psychoeducation (cognitive therapy) to encourage mindfulness practice both during group treatment interventions as well as daily (forty-five minutes) between treatment sessions.

In a treatment manual subsequently published, the authors present one of the most comprehensible explanations of how to lead mindfulness-based interventions (Segal et al., 2002). The authors emphasize that the stance of the mindfulness approach is one of welcoming and allowing. It is invitational. It encourages "opening" to the difficult and adopting an attitude of gentleness to all experience rather than engaging in problem solving that reinforces rumination. Nonreactivity, kindly awareness, gentleness, curiosity, a sense of adventure, and a willingness to observe are noted as essential characteristics of mindfulness. "[W]herever your mind may be, you can always start again the next moment. The essence of mindfulness is the willingness to begin over and over and over again" (p. 134).

The aim is not to prevent mind wandering "but to become more intimate with how one's mind behaves. . . . If your mind wanders a hundred times, then simply bring it back a hundred times" (p. 168). Staying present and being nonreactive or nonstriving to what you observe is reinforced. "Participants are encouraged to notice the change during the practice from focusing attention (gathering) in the early stage to expanding attention in the later stage" (p. 197).

The authors note: ". . . people find themselves preoccupied with avoiding harm or achieving reward in unhelpful ways that add to the negativity of the unwanted object or event, or to the frustration of not having the object of desire or affection" (p. 201).

Attachment and aversion are noted to be antithetical to mindfulness. "Note, again, that the aim of the practice is not relaxation or even happiness. Rather, it is freedom from the tendency to get drawn into automatic reactions to pleasant and unpleasant thoughts, feelings, and events" (p. 193). Linehan goes even further and states that "mindfulness is conceptualized as attitudes and behaviors that the therapist emits, as opposed to behaviors that the therapist teaches the client to do" (Dimidjian and Linehan 2003, p. 169).

Segal, Williams, and Teasdale specifically note the role of negative thoughts in mindfulness-based approaches: Unlike cognitive behavior therapy, mindfulness invites us not to gather evidence for or against our thoughts, to dispute them as if they are the enemy, but rather to bring a different quality of awareness to our thoughts such that we relate to them in different and new ways (2002).

Baer reviews the literature on mindfulness and finds twenty studies that meet her criteria for experimental soundness (2003). She interprets mindfulness as involving exposure, cognitive change, self-management, relaxation, and acceptance. Of the twenty studies, she notes that nine used pre-post designs with no control group. Nine used treatment as usual or waiting-list control groups. A meta-analysis of the twenty studies found effect sizes that ranged from 0.15 to 1.65, which she interprets as medium-sized effects "with some effect sizes falling within the large range" (p. 135). She concludes that "mindfulness training, on average, may bring participants with mild to moderate psychological distress into or close to the normal range" (p. 137). However, it should be noted that the studies she reviews primarily use the mindfulness-based stress-reduction program developed by Kabat-Zinn regardless of the patient population or disorder being treated. The mindfulness exercises are not combined with disorder-specific interventions. A standardized eight- to ten-week mindfulness practice program is provided no matter what the diagnosis or patient population. In spite of this nonspecific intervention, the noted statistically significant effects were shown.

The Segal study (Segal et al., 2002), as mentioned, relies substantially upon the mindfulness-based stress-reduction program developed by Kabat-Zinn. It has been suggested that the powerful nonspecific effects of this program may be due to deep breathing, which may increase parasympathetic activity and vagal tone, thus facilitating attention and affect regulation (Thayer, Friedman, Borkovec, Johnsen, and Molina, 2000). These powerful effects, however, might be substantially increased if mindfulness-based meditative strategies were combined with disorder-specific psychotherapeutic interventions (as suggested in this book).

The addition of mindfulness and acceptance-based interventions have radically altered the direction of much behaviorally oriented research and practice. For a very thorough, book-length scholarly review recently published, the reader is directed to *Mindfulness and Acceptance: Expanding the Cognitive-Behavioral Tradition* (Hayes, Follette, and Linehan, 2004).

DIALECTICAL BEHAVIOR THERAPY

The final strand of research to be reviewed is conducted on the dialectical behavior therapy model itself. Rather than having simple behavioral or acceptance-based strategies, this line of research evaluates outcomes on patient populations using the fuller dialectical framework developed by Linehan (Linehan, 1993b, 1993c). This DBT research differs from the acceptance-based research reviewed above due to the inclusion of dialectic analysis (including the core dialectic of psychotherapy itself that demands movement along the change versus acceptance continuum), psychoeducation including mindfulness skills, emotion regulation skills, distress tolerance skills, and interpersonal effectiveness skills. While different experimenters may vary their therapeutic intervention depending on the patient population addressed, they all adhere to one degree or another with Linehan's treatment manual (Linehan, 1993c).

Linehan began her academic career in the study of suicidal behavior, which led naturally to the study of borderline personality disorder (BPD). Borderlines frequently engage in suicidal and what Linehan describes as "parasuicidal" behavior

(behavior that may result in death, although the intent or purpose of the patient may not in the moment be to destroy their lives). Obviously such individuals are emotionally aroused, and the intensity of their affect is one of the defining characteristics of the BPD disorder. However, as the research below demonstrates, many disorders have the same core characteristics identified by Linehan in the BPD spectrum of symptoms (high emotional arousal, slow return to emotional baseline following threat, impulsive behaviors designed to reduce arousal, and emotional escape and avoidance strategies). Patients who demonstrate the same spectrum of symptoms that DBT was designed by Linehan to treat include those with eating disorders, generalized anxiety disorder, post-traumatic stress disorder (PTSD), panic disorder, agoraphobia, depressive disorder, impulse-control disorder, and many of the personality disorders, as well as those suffering various addictions to substances.

Linehan compared one group of twenty-two females (ages eighteen to forty-five) with BPD who underwent DBT for one year and twenty-two matched females with BPD who underwent treatment as usual in the community (Linehan et al., 1991). The subjects were assessed before treatment and at four, eight, and twelve months after treatment. There was a significant reduction in the frequency and medical risk of parasuicidal behavior among subjects who received DBT compared with subjects who received treatment as usual. The number of days of inpatient psychiatric hospitalization was fewer for subjects who received DBT than for controls, resulting in greater cost-effectiveness for DBT in spite of DBT's intensive treatment design, which includes both individual and group psychotherapy, as well as accessibility for telephone consultation between sessions, for one year. While DBT was not shown differentially effective in improving patients' depression, hopelessness, suicide ideation, or reasons for living, the reduced parasuicidal behavior intensity and frequency, together with fewer psychiatric hospitalizations (lower cost and greater ability to sustain patients in the least restrictive environment) is impressive.

Linehan reported on a naturalistic follow-up of her initial DBT experimental and control patients one year following the termination of her initial one-year study (Linehan et al., 1993). She analyzed thirty-nine women who met criteria for borderline personality disorder. Efficacy was measured on parasuicidal behavior (Parasuicide History Interview), psychiatric inpatient days (Treatment History Interview), anger (State-Trait Anger Scale), global functioning (Global Assessment Scale), and social adjustment (Social Adjustment Scale—Interview and Social Adjustment Scale—Self-Report). Subjects were assessed at six and twelve months into the follow-up year (after one year of DBT treatment). Comparison of the two conditions revealed that throughout the follow-up year, DBT subjects had significantly higher Global Assessment Scale scores. During the initial six months of the follow-up, DBT subjects had significantly less parasuicidal behavior, less anger, and better self-reported social adjustment. During the final six months, DBT subjects had significantly fewer psychiatric inpatient days and better interviewer-rated social adjustment. Swenson and colleagues report on the same application of DBT principles to BPD in psychiatric inpatient hospitalizations (Swenson, Sanderson, Dulit, and Linehan, 2001).

Verheul studied sixty-four women with BPD in the Netherlands (Verheul et al., 2003). They were randomly assigned to either a year of DBT (thirty-one patients) or treatment as usual (TAU; thirty-three patiens) in a randomized controlled study. Patients assigned to DBT received twelve months of both psychosocial skills education, for two to two and a half hours per week, as specified in the Linehan manual (1993c), as well as cognitive behavioral individual psychotherapy on a weekly basis. It is not clear from the research report if the individual therapy was truly dialectical, since it is described as "Individual therapy focus[ed] primarily on motivational issues, including the motivation to stay alive and to stay in treatment" (p. 135). Balancing acceptance and change as a therapeutic target is clearly deployed, with median adherence score on a five-point Likert scale achieving 3.8. Patients in the TAU group attended no more than two sessions per month with a psychologist, psychiatrist, or a social worker, clearly indicating that treatment intensity in the TAU was not as great as in the DBT intervention group.

The Netherlands study assessed recurrent parasuicidal and self-damaging impulsive behaviors at eleven, twenty-two, thirty-three, forty-four, and fifty-two weeks after randomization using the Borderline Personality Disorder Severity Index and the Lifetime Parasuicide Count (modified) to measure self-mutilating behavior such as cutting, burning, and pricking. Significantly more patients who were receiving DBT (63 percent) than those patients in the TAU group (23 percent) continued in therapy with the same therapist for the entire year. Treatment retention thus favored DBT. Self-multilating behavior for the DBT group diminished over the treatment year, while the TAU patients engaged in more self-mutilating behavior. At week fifty-two, 57 percent of the TAU patients reported self-mutilating at least once the in the previous six-month period, compared to only 35 percent of the DBT group. Impulsive behavior was consistent across both the DBT and TAU groups, with no significant differences between the two. The greater improvement of the DBT group could not be accounted for by use of medications, baseline severity of symptoms, or any other measured pretreatment and during-treatment difference. DBT tended to be more successful when symptoms were more intense, in that DBT was found more effective in the high-symptom-severity group but no difference from TAU was found in low-symptom-severity groups.

Verheul and colleagues conclude that DBT is an effective form of treatment for BPD, noting that TAU actually resulted in significant deterioration of the patient's symptom picture over time (Verheul et al., 2003). They note that DBT is effective regardless of substance-abuse issues and offer the alternative notion that DBT is not targeted for BPD patients per se, but may be appropriate for patients with severe impulse-control disorders other than BPD as well.

Bohus reports a pilot study of twenty-four female patients who were compared at their admission to the hospital and again at one month after discharge with respect to psychopathology and frequency of self-injuries after receiving inpatient-based DBT (Bohus et al., 2000). Significant improvements in ratings of depression, dissociation, anxiety, and global stress were found. A highly significant decrease in the number of parasuicidal acts was also reported. Analysis of the average effect sizes shows a strong effect, although they acknowledge the lack of a randomized controlled design.

Hawton reviews the literature on self-harm (parasuicidal behavior) to identify and synthesize the findings from all randomized, controlled trials that have examined the effectiveness of treatments (Hawton et al., 2000). Only randomized clinical control studies were included in the review. Both psychotherapy and psychopharmacological treatments were included. In order to qualify for the reviews, patients must have engaged in deliberate self-injury. The outcome measure was parasuicidal or suicidal behavior. A total of twenty-three trials were identified in which repetition of deliberate self-harm was reported as an outcome variable, with modest data indicating that DBT-type treatment was differentially effective. The reservations of the reviewers are based mostly on insufficient numbers of patients in trials as a limiting factor. They conclude that there is a need for larger trials of treatments and that such trials must also be replicated.

A study of incarcerated women with histories of childhood sexual and/or physical abuse indicated DBT effectiveness. The intervention group used DBT and writing assignments (Bradley and Follingstad, 2003). Researchers randomly assigned twenty-four participants to DBT-based group treatment (thirteen completed) and twenty-five to a no-contact comparison condition (eighteen completed). The Beck Depression Inventory, Inventory of Interpersonal Problems, and Trauma Symptom Inventory were administered, with the data demonstrating significant reductions in PTSD, mood, and interpersonal symptoms in the DBT group.

Evans explores the use of DBT-based treatment manuals in parasuicidal patients (Evans et al., 1999). This pilot study is significant in that patients are provided with six DBT brochures or self-help manuals rather than receiving the full and intensive DBT treatment as prescribed in the Linehan treatment manual (1993c). Thirty-four patients (ages sixteen through fifty) with histories of self-harm within the prior twelve months were randomly assigned to six sessions of DBT-informed short-term treatment linked to the booklets, and the remainder of the subject pool were assigned to treatment as usual. Assessment of clinical symptoms and social function were made at baseline and repeated by an independent assessor masked to treatment allocation at six months. The number and rate of all parasuicide attempts, time to next episode, and costs of care were also determined. Thirty-two patients (eighteen in DBT; fourteen in TAU) were seen at follow-up, and ten patients in each group (56 percent DBT and 71 percent TAU) had a suicidal act during the six months. The rate of suicidal acts per month was lower with DBT (median 0.17 per month DBT; 0.37 per month TAU; $P = 0.11$), and self-rated depressive symptoms also improved ($P = 0.03$). The treatment involved a mean of 2.7 sessions and the observed average cost of care was 46 percent less with DBT ($P = 0.22$). Although the authors acknowledge that this short-term treatment is not DBT as defined by Linehan (1993b, 1993c), they conclude that DBT-informed treatment is efficacious in the typical clinical setting in reducing parasuicidal behavior.

One of the issues facing DBT dissemination into traditional clinical practice is the complexity of DBT theory itself, especially when applied to the complex (and frequently comorbid with other disorders) conditions of BPD. Many state departments of mental health have adopted DBT as the treatment of choice for BPD, and DBT enjoys wide acceptance in the public mental-health system, since the experimental evidence strongly suggests higher efficacy and lower costs. But can the complexities of DBT be effectively taught to therapists who have widely varying theoretical backgrounds and experience? Hawkins and Sinha used a detailed examination of DBT knowledge and evaluated the conceptual mastery of 109 clinicians trained through a state department of mental health initiative (1998). Performance on the examination correlated specifically with DBT training. Prior education or background in behavior therapy accounted for little variance in mastery of the concepts, indicating that therapists occupying diverse roles acquired reasonable intellectual mastery over DBT with training. While DBT is a complex model of service delivery, it is teachable and learnable.

Examining the degree to which some of the specific elements of DBT contribute to lowered parasuicidal behavior, Linehan investigated the influence of the patient-therapist relationship in reducing suicidal behavior in DBT (Shearin and Linehan, 1992). Subjects were four therapist-patient dyads. Weekly patient and therapist relationship ratings were measured over seven months with a short form of the Structural Analysis of Social Behavior. Dialectical techniques balancing acceptance and change were more effective than pure change or acceptance techniques in reducing suicidal behavior. Therapist ratings consistent with nonpejorative conceptualization (seeing behavior as attempts to operate on the environment rather than as manipulative or pathological) were also associated with less suicidal behavior.

The applicability of DBT to addictions was shown in a study of comorbid BPD and addiction (Linehan et al., 1999). A TAU regimen for drug-dependent suicidal women displaying borderline personality disorder was compared to DBT. Twenty-eight women (ages eighteen to forty-five) were randomly assigned to DBT or TAU groups. TAU subjects were either referred to alternative substance-abuse or mental-health counselors and community programs or continued with their own psychotherapists. Results show a dropout rate of 36 percent from DBT compared with a rate of 73 percent from TAU. Urinalysis showed a significant reduction in substance abuse among the DBT subjects, and DBT subjects showed significant improvements in social and global adjustment at the sixteen-month follow-up. Linehan concludes that DBT is an effective treatment for severely dysfunctional drug-dependent patients.

Although DBT was designed for the treatment of BPD and suicidal patients, Linehan notes that research has expanded to more diverse populations, including comorbid substance dependence and BPD and inpatient treatment for BPD, as well as antisocial behaviors in juveniles and adults (Rizvi and Linehan, 2001). The current review shows that DBT has been expanded well beyond these areas.

Linehan (Linehan et al., 2002) compared the effects of the use of DBT with twenty-three heroin-dependent female BPD patients to the results of comprehensive validation therapy in conjunction with a 12-step program (CVT + 12S). During a twelve-month period, patients received either DBT or CVT + 12S, a manualized approach that provides DBT in combination with participation in a twelve-step program. All patients concurrently received the opiate agonist therapy with levomethadyl acetate hydrochloride oral solution. Subjects were assessed for drug use through urinalyses, interviews, and self-reports. Results showed that both treatment conditions were effective in reducing opiate use relative to baseline, but at four months following treatment termination, all DBT subjects exhibited a low proportion of opiate-positive urinalyses. Subjects assigned to DBT maintained reductions in mean opiate use through twelve months of active treatment, while those assigned to CVT + 12S treatment significantly increased opiate use during the last four months of treatment. In contrast to other studies of DBT (that show that DBT-treated patients tend to sustain involvement in treatment and demonstrate lower dropout rates during study), in this experiment DBT-treated patients showed an increased dropout rate compared to the 12S subjects: all twelve CVT + 12S subjects completed the twelve months of treatment, while only 64 percent of DBT-treated subjects completed the clinical trial.

Agras and Linehan (Telch, Agras, and Linehan, 2001) report a study of the use of DBT for binge eating disorder (BED). Forty-four women with BED were randomly assigned to group DBT or to a wait-list control condition and were administered the Eating Disorder Examination in addition to measures of weight, mood, and affect regulation at baseline and posttreatment. DBT-treated women evidenced significant improvement on measures of binge eating and eating pathology compared with controls, and 89 percent of the women receiving DBT had stopped binge eating by the end of treatment. Abstinence rates were reduced to 56 percent at the six-month follow-up. Although comparative measures of weight, mood, and affect regulation were not significant between the DBT treatment group and controls, the authors suggest their results support further research into DBT as a treatment for BED.

Linehan reports the efficacy of DBT on interpersonal outcome variables for patients diagnosed with BPD. In a one-year clinical trial, twenty-six female patients with BPD were randomly assigned to either DBT or a TAU condition (Linehan et al., 1994). All subjects met criteria of *DSM-III-R* and diagnostic interview for BPD disorder and were chronically suicidal. In both the TAU and DBT completion groups, DBT subjects had significantly better scores on measures of anger, interviewer-rated global social adjustment, and the Global Assessment Scale and tended to rate themselves better on overall social adjustment than TAU subjects. Linehan and her colleagues interpret these results as suggesting that DBT is a promising psychosocial intervention for improving interpersonal functioning among severely dysfunctional patients with BPD.

In a more recent study, Koons took twenty women veterans who met criteria for BPD and randomly assigned them to DBT or TAU for six months (Koons et al., 2001). The DBT-treated subjects, in comparison to TAU subjects, had significantly greater decreases in suicidal ideation, hopelessness, depression, and anger expression.

DBT subjects showed significant decreases in number of parasuicidal acts. "Strong trends" (those factors not statistically significant but showing strong differences between DBT and TAU) included anger experienced but not expressed, dissociation, and number of psychiatric hospitalizations. Both DBT and TAU groups showed significant decreases in depressive symptoms and BPD-like behaviors. Neither the DBT group nor the TAU group showed substantial decreases in anxiety. The authors note that the DBT can be successfully implemented independent of the developer (Dr. Linehan did not participate in this study).

Of course, not all experimenters fully adhere to the DBT manual, given the clinical population of interest, diagnosis, and previous theoretical orientation of the experimenters. However, studies conducted by experimenters not coming from the behavioral tradition but adopting some of the aspects of DBT have also shown substantial patient improvement. For example, a study by Barley with 130 mostly female subjects (age range from sixteen to fifty-seven years) psychiatrically hospitalized for an average of 106 days (range of hospitalization from 3 to 629 days) presents interesting results (Barley et al., 1993). The inpatient unit was psychodynamically oriented, and psychodynamically informed case formulations and treatment continued with the gradual introduction of DBT. The nonrandom study divided assessment periods into three broad segments: no DBT, introduction of DBT into the unit treatment regimens, and a full DBT program. Results across the three time intervals were compared with parasuicide rates in another unit in the hospital not introducing DBT. The results indicate that following the introduction of DBT, parasuicidal behaviors significantly declined compared to the no-DBT psychiatric unit also treating personality disorders. While the lack of a randomized control group limits the degree to which findings can be generalized, this naturalistic study demonstrates that DBT-informed treatment (even when administered by professionals who have a psychodynamic theoretical orientation) can substantially decrease patient parasuicidal behavior.

Linehan's training corporation (Dimeff, Koerner, and Linehan, 2001) reports an unpublished study (Miller, Rathus, Leigh, and Landsman, 1996) where 111 suicidal teens were assigned to DBT or TAU based upon the severity of their symptoms (the more severe teens receiving the DBT treatment). Twenty-two percent of the sample was male (most studies to date have primarily female participants). DBT treatment was modified from the treatment manual in several substantial ways: the treatment lasted only twelve weeks rather than the standard one year, treatment handouts were modified to be more appropriate to a teen population, and the number of skills modules taught were reduced. Family therapy was included in addition to individual psychotherapy. Mindfulness skills were taught only three times in the twelve-week psychoeducation program.

Although this was only a quasi-experimental study without randomization, the results are impressive. Subjects in the DBT group completed treatment significantly better than TAU subjects (62 percent versus 40 percent) and had significantly lower psychiatric hospitalizations (0 percent versus 13 percent). No significant differences were found between the two groups on parasuicidal behaviors, although Dimeff and colleagues note that since patients were assigned to DBT based upon the severity of their symptoms, the lack of a difference between conditions is noteworthy. Moreover, pre- and posttreatment measurement within the DBT group showed substantial changes over the following measures: decreases in suicidal ideation, reductions in Global Severity Index of symptoms and distress, and (on the SCL-90-R) decreases in anxiety, depression, interpersonal sensitivity, and obsessive-compulsive symptoms. Trends in positive directions not meeting statistical significance included decreases in paranoia, confusion about self, impulsivity, emotion dysregulation, and interpersonal difficulties.

In another unpublished study (Dimeff et al., 2001), DBT is substantially altered from the original treatment manual by reducing treatment from the initially studied one year of intensive treatment to six months (Stanley, Ivanoff, Brodsky, and Oppenheim, 1998). DBT again was compared to TAU (all subjects having BPD and being female). Reported results show statistically significant reduction in self-mutilation behavior and urges and suicidal ideation and urges. No suicide attempts occurred in either the DBT or TAU groups during the six-month study. This finding is significant in that it demonstrates that even shorter-term DBT interventions can be effective, even with borderline patients.

An early study by Springer (Springer, Lohr, Buchtel, and Silk, 1996) is especially significant because these experimenters deleted the acceptance-based module traditionally seen as a core skill of DBT (Linehan 1993b). They eliminated the mindfulness module that teaches patients to attend to their feelings, even when painful, but taught patients improved psychological coping skills (the remaining three modules of Linehan's BPD program—emotion regulation, distress tolerance, and interpersonal effectiveness). The results of the DBT-informed treatment were compared to a wellness discussion group that included TAU. This general inpatient unit population included only short-term treatment (subjects in both conditions attended an average of six sessions during their hospital stay). The results were not encouraging in that, although patients in the DBT-informed group felt that they had better skills to handle their difficulties after discharge, increased self-mutilative behaviors were observed. Linehan comments that perhaps "contagion effects" (discussing parasuicidal behavior in a group context) explain the results (Dimeff et al., 2001), but perhaps the excessively short treatment episodes (an average of six sessions) and the absence of acceptance-based technologies are equally important factors.

Although patients with BPD tend to engage in the highest frequency of parasuicidal acts due to their high emotional arousal, other personality disorders can also profit from DBT. While most DBT studies have occurred in either outpatient or inpatient treatment settings, DBT has been adapted for use in forensic settings (McCann, Ball, and Ivanoff, 2000). Patients in the criminal justice system tend to have violent histories and multiple diagnoses, including BPD and antisocial personality disorder. In this study, where the authors report that half of their subjects have BPD and half antisocial personality disorder, they also report a high frequency of axis

I psychotic and mood disorders. This is thus a complex diagnostic group to treat. Twenty-one DBT patients were compared to fourteen TAU patients over a twenty-month period. While DBT was altered somewhat to include the violent acting-out behavior (externalizing behavior in addition to internalizing behavior), the fundamental theoretical framework of DBT was maintained. Results showed that DBT patients, in comparison to TAU patients, had a significant decrease in depressed and hostile mood, paranoia, and psychotic behavior. DBT patients were shown to have fewer interpersonal coping difficulties on the forensic unit compared to TAU patients, and DBT therapists reported a lower staff burnout rate compared to TAU therapists. This study is thus significant in several respects. First, DBT is found to be effective for antisocial personality disorder as well as for patients who have axis I mood and psychotic disorders. Second, it should be noted that, unlike those in other studies, these are not voluntary patients. They are incarcerated patients within an intermediate security ward of a prison. DBT is thus found effective even for highly resistive patients. Third, increased support is offered for the DBT model since the TAU group is highly monitored. Since the TAU group is also incarcerated, increased information is available about medication compliance and treatment adherence. The TAU group was compliant with treatment, and when compared with the compliant DBT group, additional improvement is noted with the DBT group.

In a randomized, controlled trial involving twenty-four outpatient suicide attempters, DBT was compared to client-centered therapy (Turner, 2000). Blinded, independent rater evaluations and a battery of patient self-report measures were completed at baseline, six months, and one year during the course of treatment. Measures of suicide attempts and self-harm episodes were collected on a weekly basis. The number of psychiatric hospitalization days per six-month period was also measured. Outcomes showed that the DBT group improved more than the client-centered group on most measures. Subjects in the DBT group showed statistically significant improvement at both the six- and twelve-month follow-up in suicide or self-harm behavior. At the twelve-month follow-up, the DBT group showed significantly less anger, impulsivity, and depression, while showing improved global mental-health functioning compared to the subjects receiving client-centered treatment. The DBT group showed significantly reduced hospitalization rates at both six- and twelve-month follow-up periods. The quality of the therapeutic alliance accounted for significant variance in patients' outcomes across both treatments. Remarkable is that the DBT treatment included psychodynamic techniques, and that psychosocial skills training occurred during the individual psychotherapy sessions, a clear departure from Linehan's recommendation that skills training occur separately from the individual psychotherapy session.

Another recently published study with juvenile female offenders in a mental-health facility compared one cottage in the correctional facility using DBT with a comparable cottage using treatment as usual (TAU) (Trupin, Stewart, Beach, and Boesky, 2002). The study compared TAU to twice-weekly DBT groups together with coaching the use of DBT skills throughout the four-week study period. The authors report that aggression, parasuicide, and class disruption were lower in the DBT group, and decreased progressively during the intervention period. The DBT group therapists had to use fewer restrictive, punitive responses compared to the TAU therapists during the intervention period. Following DBT treatment, the experimental group participants showed significantly improved transition to off-cottage but on-campus services compared to TAU participants.

A study of elderly depressed patients using DBT was recently published (Lynch, Morse, Mendelson, and Robins, 2003). This randomized controlled trial of thirty-four patients compared DBT to TAU plus clinical management in a twenty-eight-week treatment. DBT included only group skills training, not individual dialectically based psychotherapy. Both DBT and TAU included antidepressant medication. Both groups were assessed at baseline, twenty-eight weeks, and at a six-month follow-up. While analysis of the groups showed few differences between them at the termination of treatment, at the six-month follow-up the DBT-treated group showed greater improvement on the Beck Depression Inventory. On the Hamilton Depression Rating Scale (HAMD), 67 percent of the DBT patients met criteria for being improved and asymptomatic at posttreatment, while only 50 percent of the TAU group met such improvement. At the six-month follow-up, 73 percent of the DBT patients and 40 percent of the TAU patients were in the asymptomatic range. DBT patients showed greater functional status and coping compared to TAU patients.

In reviewing the research to date on the use of DBT, Koerner and Linehan note that DBT can be adapted to patients with comorbid substance-abuse disorders as well as other disorders (2000). They note that across studies, DBT seems to reduce severe dysfunctional behaviors that are targeted for intervention (for instance, parasuicide, substance abuse, and binge eating), enhance treatment retention, and reduce psychiatric hospitalization. Evidence suggests that additional research is warranted to examine which components of DBT contribute to positive outcomes. They believe that skills coaching seems to be a crucial ingredient in producing reductions in parasuicidal behavior, and specific strategies (like validation and balance of change and acceptance interventions) may play an important role in positive behavioral change.

They note ongoing and as yet unpublished studies that are evaluating the efficacy of DBT. Asberg and colleagues at the Karolinska Institute in Sweden have begun a randomized clinical pilot study comparing DBT for women who have made multiple suicide attempts to Kernberg transference-focus psychotherapy, also using a TAU control group. Van den Bosch has completed a randomized clinical trial for women who met criteria for BPD and substance abuse, comparing DBT with TAU. They note that results from these studies should become available over the next several years, providing further empiric evidence by which to evaluate the efficacy of DBT.

PERSONAL OBSERVATION

How can these research findings be interpreted? Note that these findings from various researchers in different settings treating different patient populations with different diagnoses all show promise using DBT-informed treatment principles. The exact treatment manual developed by Linehan (Linehan, 1993c) is frequently departed from, with continued treatment gains shown. My own experience in using DBT in both inpatient and outpatient settings is consistent with the above research findings.

For example, during an eighteen-month period, every patient admitted to Monterey Psychiatric Health Facility (over 150 patients), which I directed, was treated with DBT, regardless of diagnosis. Patient diagnoses included major depressive disorders, anxiety disorders, eating disorders, impulse control disorders, obsessive-compulsive disorders, schizophreniform disorder, addictive disorders, and personality disorders.

What was remarkable was that these varied patient problems were treated together, without patient segregation, and the DBT principles were found applicable and relevant by most patients. Treatment staff were multidisciplinary, including psychiatrists, psychologists, clinical social workers, psychiatric nurses, and paraprofessional staff. The acute psychiatric inpatient unit never had to use seclusion or restraint procedures against any patient, due to the respectful and validating nature of the treatment process. Furthermore, only one patient discontinued treatment (against medical advice) and only one patient was discharged prior to completion of treatment (for use of drugs within the facility). While we have no formal data to present from this eighteen-month period, staff (who came from other, more traditional acute psychiatric inpatient programs but were all formally trained in DBT prior to opening of the new freestanding psychiatric facility) reported that patients were more involved in their own treatment process. The staff experienced less patient resistance to treatment interventions, and high patient-satisfaction ratings with both treatment staff and treatment procedures were found. High patient-satisfaction ratings appear to be the rule rather than the exception when deploying DBT (Cunningham, Wolbert, and Lillie, 2004), even when such ratings are collected by researchers independent of the deploying facility. In fact, our facility obtained accreditation with commendation from the Joint Commission on the Accreditation of Healthcare Facilities, indicating that the Commission's independent peer review ratings placed the facility in the top 10 percent of hospitals rated. While many hospitals (10 percent) can claim such commendation, few obtain such ratings during their first six months of operation. DBT is thus a powerful, robust, and effective treatment orientation worthy of consideration.

My subsequent experience applying DBT in outpatient private practice as a psychologist suggests that DBT-informed strategies of treatment are equally effective in solo practice settings.

In teaching therapists both dialectic approaches to psychotherapy and the psychological coping skill sets (mindfulness, meaning making, emotion regulation, distress tolerance, strategic behavior, and interpersonal effectiveness), I have found that professionals from a variety of theoretical orientations (dynamic, cognitive behavioral, and eclectic) easily learn the DBT approach to treatment. Subsequent to training, they report that they actually use some, if not all, of the principles in their practices, whether in solo private practice, public mental-health settings, or hospital-based settings. DBT has much to offer the professional who treats patients in acute emotional pain.

Chapter Summary

Behavior therapy research clearly demonstrates the role of avoidance and escape in promoting psychopathology and the power of exposure in treating such maladies. While much of the early research was on avoidance and escape of environmental events, more recent research makes it clear that experiential avoidance (avoiding one's own emotions and internal experience) is no different. Private practitioners tend to discount the role of learning theory since most behavioral contingencies are internal, delayed, or intermittent. DBT invites the therapist to attend to these variables, even though their assessment is difficult and time-consuming. Acceptance-based research, especially with mindfulness meditation, demonstrates dramatic and unexpected benefits to patients with a variety of both physical and emotional disorders. Clinically significant gains are found with patients who practice mindfulness just a few minutes each day for just a few weeks' duration, and the benefits are found to be sustained months and even years after the brief interventions. Adding acceptance and mindfulness interventions is supported with many randomized controlled experiments covering a variety of mental disorders. DBT is a sophisticated set of technologies developed by Linehan (1993b, 1993c)—dialectic individual psychotherapy, group psychosocial skills education, exposure therapy, behavior therapy, and acceptance—that combines many of the successful treatment interventions found critical in the treatment of acute disorders. Research suggests that using the DBT framework is effective with a variety of patient populations, and studies suggest that clinically significant improvement is seen in some populations even when the full (original) treatment protocol is not deployed.

CHAPTER 3

Pathogenesis: Emotion Regulation as a Core Therapeutic Target

While in the first chapter we reviewed DBT as a new school or theoretical orientation, and in the second chapter we reviewed the research literature for the clinical findings about how successful DBT has been with various disorders, in this chapter we will review literature and theory about the pathogenesis of disorders that DBT is designed to treat. An argument will be made that general and high emotionality or arousal accounts for most acute mental disorders. This "single-factor" model of emotional sensitivity, it will be argued, accounts for the various successful results of many psychotherapy techniques, despite their differing theoretical assumptions. Psychological factors (history) that predispose patients to high emotionality will be reviewed, including issues of attachment, trauma, loss, and invalidation of affect. Genetic and neurobiological substrates underlying emotional sensitivity will then be discussed. The kindling effects that serve to increase and sustain emotionality will conclude this chapter.

It will be proposed that the combined or separate effects of psychological factors (such as attachment, trauma, and loss, including the critical factor of emotional invalidation), together with genetic factors (the neurobiological substrates underlying emotionality), predict emotional sensitivity (high baseline emotional arousal, slow return to baseline following threat that increases arousal, and inappropriate scanning of the environment for potential sources of threat). Patients with such emotional sensitivity, regardless of diagnosis, are ideally suited for DBT treatment interventions.

PSYCHOLOGICAL FACTORS PREDISPOSING PATIENTS TO EMOTIONALITY

While increasingly available research has focused on genetic or pharmacological issues involved in treatment, there is ample evidence that genetic or neurological issues alone do not account for arousal and emotionality found in many acute disorders. Psychological factors also play a critically important role in the development of the pathotopology noted with acute mental disorders. Bowlby was perhaps the first and most prolific investigator-clinician to describe the sequence of protest, despair, and detachment in children separated from their mothers for long periods (1969). Of course, separation is only one among several factors that predict attachment disorder, and this is the first of the psychological factors explored that tend to result in high emotionality.

Attachment Issues

Attachment can be defined as the process of trust in a caregiver as providing an adequate environment that produces safety and predictability. In this sense, the kind of attachment I refer to in this section is quite different from the attachment that is discussed in DBT theory, that of "holding on" to pleasant experiences. Here, attachment is about a relationship between a dependent and an adult, a form of process-oriented safety net for those who have the inability to protect themselves. This form of attachment is about a relationship born of dependency and the need for consistency. Unavailability of the mother during the prime bonding year after birth has fairly consistently shown deficits in the attachment process (Field, 1994). Primary caregivers (typically the mother) support affect regulation through mirroring (Field, 1994). Mothers tend to follow their children's behaviors and affects in a way that gives the impression that these behaviors and affects are shared. The mother is both a behavioral and physiological regulator, providing optimal stimulation from a sensitive reading of her infant's signals (Bradley, 2000). The infant can then be alert, attentive, and receptive to interactions with the mother, can seek out optimal stimulation, and can avoid or avert their attention from nonoptimal stimulation. (Early avoidance behavior in infants who experience intolerable distress has been noted by child psychologist researchers, who note "gaze aversion." See Bradley, 2000, for a complete discussion and review.) Absent the affect mirroring of the mother, infants are unable to regulate their alertness in an adaptive way. The result, if consistent mirroring is not present, is a lack of stimulation regulation and resulting dysregulation of the child's own emotions.

Interventions to attempt to influence speech development, attachment, and intelligence are now beginning as early as ten months after birth in attempts to promote healthy development (Waidhofer, 2004).

The attachment system has been conceptualized as a system for affect regulation (Bradley, 2000). The categories of attachment can been seen as generalized reaction patterns for regulating feelings in the company of a caregiver. The securely attached child can express both negative and positive emotions and perceives the caregiver as appropriately responding to their happiness and distress. With the avoidantly attached child, the child is conditioned to avoid negative affect, and this may interfere with their experiencing, labeling, and learning about feelings. These children may be less likely to develop solution-focused strategies and more likely to use emotion-focused coping, exhibiting what Bradley refers to as pseudodisplays of positive affect to cover up negative affect. This is central to the DBT notion of affect dysregulation, where the individual no longer trusts their own emotional experience and instead looks to the environment to tell them how to respond. Such dependence on the environment (looking to others and to situations to predict how they feel rather than directly processing their experience itself) can lead to profound changes in the typical emotional information-processing process.

The unpredictability of the caregiver's response will produce confusion, difficulty deploying attention, and problems with self-soothing. A lack of a stable pattern (called disorganized attachment) is more likely to produce extremes of affect, which make development of solution-focused coping responses more difficult.

Sometimes the mother is available but not appropriate in her emotional mirroring. The most common attachment pattern associated with rejection or lack of warmth is that of avoidance. It is also the most common reaction displayed by inhibited or reactive children in situations of novelty or uncertainty. The avoidant attachment style is thus a defensive strategy in response to parental rejection (Cassidy and Kobak, 1988). The result is avoidance of attachment and avoidance of affect, predicting the stereotypical emotionality syndrome (high emotionality, slow return to emotional baseline, and inappropriate scanning of the environment for additional sources of threat) characteristic of DBT-appropriate patients.

Maternal responsiveness is thus a key psychological variable in the development of emotional sensitivity. Mothers of securely attached infants respond to both positive and negative affect in their infants, in contrast to mothers of avoidant infants, who tend not to respond to negative affect, and mothers of resistant infants, who respond more to negative than to positive affect. Infants learn that certain affects are more acceptable to their mothers and consequently develop a style of responding that allows them to be more acceptable (Goldberg, MacKay-Soroka, and Rochester, 1994). As noted in the literature on the development of borderline personality disorder, one characteristic feature is that those suffering from BPD rely more on the validation of the external environment (looking to others to validate their feelings) rather than trusting their own emotional responses as valid sources of information about their experiences (Linehan, 1993b). The fact that insecurely attached infants display evidence of arousal despite their use of affect-suppressing strategies indicates that these strategies, although effective in the short term, may have a longer-term negative impact on levels of arousal and styles of interpersonal relating (Spangler and Grossmann, 1993).

The maternal caregiver appears to be a physiological regulator of the infant, assisting the child to learn which cues to pay attention to and which to ignore (Hofer, 1995). The caregiver becomes a physiological regulator by modulating the arousal level itself. This is critical in attachment theory, since an information-processing model of "awareness" is thus invoked. The typically attached infant looks to the mother for validation of their arousal, but other sources of information become overly important when such attachment is insecure or is not evident at all (Hofer, 1995).

In a more theory-driven article than those cited thus far, Main proposes that the environment affects formation of mental representations that guide behavior (1995). Security of attachment is related to the development of psychopathology. The lack of attachment in the infant is directly related to the later development of affect dysregulation.

Empirical work supporting the relationship between attachment, security, and styles of affect regulation comes from examination of mother-child interaction (Bradley, 2000). Bradley has been the most recent and thorough investigator to examine the role of attachment and affect regulation. She identifies four types of disordered attachment that are labeled insecure, avoidant, resistant, or ambivalent, and that are associated with either hostility or fearfulness. Avoidant individuals are seen as suppressing affect, in contrast to resistant individuals, who exaggerate affect. Sensitive caregiving has been associated with emotional openness and with a child's capacity to label and share feelings (Greenberg, Kusche, and Speltz, 1992).

The evidence from the attachment literature suggests that insecure attachment is a vulnerability factor that may interfere with the development of optimal affect regulation and predispose children to the development of psychopathology. These processes can be presumed to affect neural development, potentially leading to a decrease in behavioral and affective flexibility with prolonged adversity (Bradley, 2000).

The same dynamic can be seen much later in life with the role of expressed emotion in the family of origin, especially in the case of schizophrenic patients. High emotionality in the family well predicts psychiatric relapse (Vaughan and Leff, 1976). Three components in the attitude or behavior of the significant adult toward the patient were identified: critical comments, hostility, and emotional overinvolvement. The less patients are able to identity with and use their significant others as cues to how to regulate their own arousal, the less they are able to stabilize their own out-of-control affect spiraling. The more emotionality in the home, the greater the likelihood that the adult schizophrenic will relapse and become rehospitalized. The role of expressed emotion in adult schizophrenics thus mimics the role of attachment in the infant.

Kraemer presumes that attachment may act at a psychobiological level, at the level of social learning, and also at the level of the development of internal working models or schemata (1992). It appears that insecurely attached individuals are more vulnerable to difficulty in managing stress (Kraemer, 1992). Whether this vulnerability is best explained as a neurotransmitter supersensitivity, a failure to learn adequate coping strategies, a deficit in internal working models, or a combination of all three will have to await more empirical tests of the various theories, according to Kraemer.

Kraemer notes that the attachment system plays a role in the development of affect regulation, and that individuals with insecure attachment have a greater likelihood of experiencing prolonged arousal when under stress, one of the core issues DBT is designed to treat (high emotional arousal under baseline conditions).

One important psychological element in the pathogenesis of emotional sensitivity that DBT is designed to treat is thus inadequate attachment between infant and primary caretaker during the first year or so of life. Lack of attachment during infancy has repercussions throughout the course of life. Without early attachment, the child is left with inadequate psychological coping resources on a fundamental level. The child distrusts their own affect as providing reliable cues about how their distress can be cured, about how the environment will react to their distress, and about how to focus attention, either internally or externally, in order to optimize problem solving. Solution-focused coping decreases, and emotion-focused coping tends to increase. While research data are not entirely consistent about the longevity of attachment issues throughout the life cycle (beyond adolescence) due to the paucity of long-term research, clinical observations from those who work in adoption and child protective service agencies tend to support the notion that failure to form attachment quite early in infancy can have long-term catastrophic consequences on a psychological level for the child as they mature.

Trauma

While adequacy of attachment with the primary caregiver in infancy can predict emotional sensitivity (high emotional baseline arousal and slow return to baseline following threat) and inadequate solution-focused coping, attachment is only one among many factors that can challenge an individual's capacity to appropriately regulate their affect. Trauma can also disrupt the emotion regulation process. Trauma can occur at any age. Broadly, trauma can be divided into two categories: first, short-term but intense emotional experiences of threat, which tend to be processed in the hippocampus rather than the cerebral cortex, as discussed below under neurobiological substrates; and second, prolonged and inescapable emotional arousal (chronic stress) that sets into motion kindling effects on a neuronal basis. The experience of trauma as a factor in the development of affect dysregulation can thus be considered separately from the avoidance and escape strategies that patients use for traumatic experiences that unintentionally increase the longevity and severity of their emotional arousal. Trauma, even without avoidance or escape, disrupts the optimal ability of the individual to regulate their affect.

In a multisite study of schizotypal, borderline, avoidant, and obsessive-compulsive personality disorders, more trauma (especially sexual trauma) was found with BPD than with other personality disorders (Yen et al., 2002). However, trauma was found positively correlated with severity of traumatic exposure, as indicated by earlier trauma onset, trauma of an assaultive and personal nature, and more types of traumatic events for all personality disorders. Patients with childhood abuse or neglect have been found to be four times more likely than those without such trauma to be diagnosed with personality disorders during early adulthood (Johnson, Cohen, Brow, et al., 1999). Frequent negative life events (trauma) predispose one to a personality disorder (Zimmerman, Pfohl, Stangl, and Corenthal, 1986).

A complete review of the role of trauma in producing emotional disorders is unnecessary for any experienced mental-health professional, who readily correlates the revelations of their patients who frequently have had multiple, if not chronic, traumatic experiences in their lifetime. A history of trauma, abuse, or loss is a feature common to many disorders, including anxiety and mood disorders, eating disorders, conduct disorder, and many personality disorders (Kessler, Davis, and Kendler, 1997). While genetic factors can modestly predict both lifetime traumas and recent stressful life events (Kessler et al., 1997), there is little reason to assume that genetics alone, absent environmental threat, could produce the disability frequently seen in clinical practice.

The fact that prolonged states of hyperarousal are evident from physiological studies of individuals who have been victims of trauma and abuse alone is evidence of the long-term and pervasive effects of trauma upon our patients' lives (van der Kolk, 1996). Anecdotal evidence is strong that DBT treatment is effective for patients with history of trauma (Simpson et al., 1998).

Trauma can come in many forms, including threat to life, physical abuse, sexual abuse, emotional abuse, and neglect. Perhaps at this point most research has focused on post-traumatic stress disorder, due to its chronicity and high potential for severe disability. Neurobiologists and neuropsychologists (van der Kolk, 1996) believe that in PTSD, the amygdala, thalamus, and hippocampus fail to extinguish their effects in the absence of further trauma, representing the failure of the sensory cortex to inhibit a kindling-type reaction in the amygdala (see the section below on kindling effects). Interference with hippocampal function has been demonstrated with high levels of glucocorticoids (part of the physiological response to stress) and with high-intensity stimulation from the amygdala, and this effect is thought to represent one pathway that produces deficits in concentration, attention, and memory (Charney, Deutch, Krystal, Southwick, and Davis, 1993). Since glucocorticoid receptors play a role in mediating the action of the three main monoaminergic neurotransmitter systems—

the serotonergic, noradrenergic, and dopaminergic systems—prolonged emotional stress can have substantial and wide effects on both psychological and physiological experiences (Bradley, 2000). Extended release of glucocorticoids during episodes of repeated and severe major depression, as well as during post-traumatic stress disorder, have resulted in hippocampal atrophy that helps explain explicit (conscious, factual) memory deficits in psychiatric disorders (Sapolsky, 2000). When secreted transiently, as during normal, short-term stress, the glucocorticoids mobilize energy, increase cardiovascular tone, suppress unessential bodily functions, and potentiate aspects of immunity (Sapolsky, 2000). However, excessive glucocorticoids cause atrophy of dendritic processes in the hippocampus, preventing consolidation of short-term memory into long-term explicit memory, as well as increasing the risks of hypertension, insulin-resistant diabetes mellitus, amenorrhea, impotency, ulcers, and immune suppression.

Psychological experiences of threat, especially if prolonged, thus change the brain chemistry in ways that keep neuronal patterns signaling threat going long after the threat has been removed. The result is the high emotional sensitivity and poor solution-focused coping found to be effectively treated with DBT interventions.

Trauma has much more profound effects than simple experienced distress. It produces longer-term neurochemical and neurobiological changes that decrease the individual's ability to effectively regulate affect in the future (see the discussion below on the neuroanatomical aspects of trauma).

Loss

Although loss is essentially another form of trauma, it is covered separately because many individuals present for treatment who can identify no past trauma in their life. Loss of a loved one, although a normal and expected part of life, is traumatic. Loss during infancy produces the stages of protest, despair, and detachment in children separated from their mothers for long periods (Bowlby, 1969). Note that the loss need not be permanent. Early adversity, including loss, predisposes an individual to anxiety, and anxiety is frequently a precursor to depression (Brown and Harris, 1993). Anxiety is a vulnerability factor in many disorders and is typically evident before the first episode of depression. Brown and Harris report that there is considerable overlap in distortion of cognitions between anxiety and depression (1993). The similarity of loss in depression and danger in anxiety is noted.

In the U.S. National Comorbidity Study, Kessler found that loss was a frequent correlate for many emotional disorders (Kessler et al., 1997). Loss probably results in many of the same physiological changes noted for traumas above but certainly decreases the ability of the individual experiencing loss to deploy existing psychological coping resources.

Invalidation of Affect

A final psychological factor in the development of affect dysregulation is invalidating environments, as described by Linehan (1993b). An invalidating environment is described as one where a person's inner experiences are denied, trivialized, or punished. When an individual describes their internal experience as painful, intolerable, hurtful, or intense, and important others (family members, spouse, friends, or other authority figures in the person's environment) tell the person in pain that they should not experience such pain or intense emotion, affect is invalidated. Linehan notes that such experiences of invalidation have two primary effects. First, it tells the person that they are wrong for having those emotions. Second, it tells them that they have negative and socially undesirable personality characteristics for having the affect in the first place. Invalidating environments typically are intolerant of negative affect (anxiety, anger, guilt, shame, depression, and hurt) and demand only strong or resilient responding (feelings of triumph, competence, confidence, and the will toward success, even in the face of adversity).

Consequences of such invalidation are either an unwillingness, based upon previous punishment and disapproval, to display negative emotions or an inability to do so due to previous negative reinforcement conditioning. An individual growing up in a highly invalidating environment does not learn the cues to label and describe affect or to tolerate negative affect when it occurs, and thus they are encouraged to engage in impulsive and urgent attempts to decrease negative affect immediately before the environment has an occasion to punish them for having it.

The negative consequences of invalidation of affect are not simply theoretical. Data from a community-based longitudinal study found that patients who experienced verbal abuse during childhood were three times more likely to develop borderline, narcissistic, obsessive-compulsive, and paranoid personality disorders during adolescence or early adulthood (Johnson et al., 2001). Significantly, the authors found that such verbal abuse accounted for subsequent personality disorder development independent of such factors as offspring temperament, childhood physical abuse, sexual abuse, neglect, physical punishment during childhood, parental education, parental psychopathology, and co-occurring psychiatric disorders. Verbal abuse is thus a powerful predictor of the development of later psychopathology.

One of the most pernicious consequences of emotional invalidation is that the person learns to distrust their own emotions. Affect no longer serves as sensual input. The person no longer looks to their feelings to tell them about their values, safety, and meanings in the here and now. In order to compensate for this lack of information, the person turns instead to others to tell them how they should feel and what they should do. Of course, the environment cannot adequately inform such individuals about issues of safety, meaning, and desire because the environment can't adequately read and predict the reinforcement history and needs of the individual. Each individual, having different needs and wants, will predict a different response and provide different demand characteristics. So using the environment exclusively to tell the person what they should or could feel provides a psychologically paralyzing situation.

Often, individuals who have experienced high-frequency invalidation of affect become self-invalidating. Over time, the person no longer waits for invalidation from the environment because the punishment has become internalized. They begin to question their basic identity each time they experience negative affect. To avoid the possibility that they may have cause to demonstrate negative affect, they're subject to increased scanning of the environment for potential sources of threat. Such negative-seeking behavior is anticipatory. By identifying threat before it occurs, the individual seeks to terminate negative affect before it occurs so that they do not experience either the negative affect or the subsequent self-punishment.

The psychological factors of attachment, trauma, loss, and invalidation of affect have substantial and long-lasting effect upon the person. While current psychopathology theories emphasize the consequent effect of the development of mental disorders (that anxiety and depression interrupt attention, concentration, memory, and problem-solving abilities), such theories tend to rely upon diagnostic-specific explanations. It is here argued, consistent with other reviewers (Bradley, 2000), that neurobiological data predict a single-factor (general emotionality or arousal) account for most acute mental disorders. Our discussion thus turns to the neurobiological substrates of emotionality.

NEUROBIOLOGICAL SUBSTRATES OF EMOTIONALITY

Our discussion of neuroanatomy and neurochemistry substantially follows the presentation and data by Bradley, who excellently reviews child, adult, and animal research on the effects of emotional arousal on physiology (2000).

The following table reviews the current theory regarding brain-behavior relationships.

Table 2: Neuroanatomic Functions

Brain Area	Functions	Source
Orbitofrontal and ventromedial cortex	Complex higher reasoning; essential site of the regulation (inhibition) of affect from "lower" areas due to its dopaminergic and noradrenergic innervation, sensory input from all modalities, and control over sympathetic and parasympathetic output to the hypothalamus	Davidson and Irwin, 1999 Shore, 1994
Left frontal hemisphere	Language in right-handed individuals; associated with positive emotions; damage produces depressive reaction (overregulation of affect)	Bradley, 2000 Goleman, 2003
Right frontal hemisphere	Processing nonverbal material (face identification, spatial distribution of attention, emotional aspects of communication); damage causes euphoria or lack of emotional concern; associated with negative emotions	Bradley, 2000 Goleman, 2003
Right anterior hemisphere	Display of emotions	Bradley, 2000
Limbic structures	Essential sites of the perception and experience of affect	Mesulam, 1985
Amygdala	Activation of negative affect; generation and detection of fear; detection of emotional relevance of information; damage causes aggression or rage; controls the release of ACTH hormone (stress response); stores "emotional" memories; interfaces with autonomic, endocrine, and immunological responses	LeDoux, 1993
Hippocampus	Memory and generation of affect; stores spatial and temporal aspects of memory and categorization of information (important for conscious retrieval and learning)	Johnson, Kamilaris, Chrousos, and Gold, 1992
Hypothalamus	Controls the autonomic nervous system	Kagan, 1994
Heteromodal areas	Integration of input across modalities (sensory, emotional, and motor channels); motivation; initiation of movement; response inhibition, attention, planning	Mesulam, 1985
Paralimbic areas	Memory and learning, regulation of drive and affect; higher control of autonomic response	Bradley, 2000

Frontal cortex areas have long been known to involve complex higher reasoning and planning activities. For example, the inability of schizophrenics to increase frontal activity in response to task demands has been suggested as evidence of the central feature of thought disorder in schizophrenia (Carter et al., 1998). However, neuroanatomy does not appear to distinguish between thought and emotion, as every region of the brain that has been found to play a singular role in emotion has also been connected with cognition. The circuitry for emotion and for cognition are intertwined (Davidson and Irwin, 1999), as the limbic system (long known to control emotional responses) has interconnections with many areas of the frontal cortex (allowing recognition, processing, and planning activities subsequent to perception of emotional danger). Such data support the central presumptions of cognitive behavioral therapy: by engaging more activation in the frontal cortex (enhancing the use of cognitive skills), the patient is able to improve the neural feedback loop between limbic, paralimbic, and frontal cortex areas, thus improving affect inhibition. Recent findings of PET scans clearly show a distinction between the effects of cognitive behavior therapy, which produce more effects on the neocortical areas of the brain, and antidepressants, which produce more effects on the limbic areas of the brain (Goldapple et al., 2004). The fact that both behavioral (cognitive behavioral psychotherapy) and psychopharmacologic interventions show similar but reverse PET-scan results suggests that medications perform a "bottom-up" function (directly controlling affective experience), while psychotherapy performs a "top-down" function (controlling the inhibitory functions of the cortical areas over affect). There is some evidence that the top-down function of psychotherapy results in lower recidivism or reoccurrence rates posttreatment (Goldapple et al., 2004).

There does not appear to be a continuous feedback loop between the rational (frontal cortext) and the emotional (limbic, amygdala, and hippocampal) areas of the brain. The presense of feedback systems accounts for our adaptive abilities. The lack of such feedback loops between these two areas accounts for many emotional disorders. Underactivation of the frontal areas (hypofrontality), is found in mood-disordered patients (Ketter, George, Kimbrell, Benson, and Post, 1996). When the connective pathways between the limbic structures, amygdala, or hippocampus are impaired, the ability to inhibit emotional responses decreases. The central role of the frontal cortex regions of the brain are inhibitory. While they do not produce emotional responding, they can inhibit it. Modulation of cortical-limbic pathways through cognitive behavioral therapy has been shown to produce longer-lasting effects (presumably due to the lasting power of inhibitory thought processes) compared to medication-oriented interventions (Goldapple et al., 2004). The ventromedial cortex, and especially the right orbitofrontal cortex, is the center of affect regulation (Shore, 1994).

Broadly, "left-sided cerebral damage generally produces a depressive reaction (suggesting overregulation of affect), in contrast to right-sided damage, which produces a lack of emotional concern and sometimes a euphoric reaction (suggesting an underregulation of affect)" (Bradley, 2000, p. 7). The amygdala plays a key role in the circuitry that activates emotion (important in both the detection of signals of fear as well generation of fear itself), while the prefrontal cortex does much of the regulation.

Bradley reviews the critical role of the limbic system in emotion perception, experience, and regulation (2000, pp. 111-118). The limbic system is the main area for the experience and control of feelings. The amygdala has many connections within the limbic system. It is the amygdala that stores experiences that predispose individuals to PTSD. This is understandable since the amygdala has few if any direct connections to the cerebral cortex, so hippocampal-stored and amygdala-stored memories are not available for conscious processing. They are "monkey-brain" memories, primitive and not under conscious control. While there has been a raging debate in psychology about the notion of "visceral memories" (Loftus, 1993, 1994, 2003; Thomas, Bulevich, and Loftus, 2003), which are memories that reside in the muscles and monkey brain and are not available to the cerebral cortex, neuroanatomical mapping of brain-behavior relationships suggests that indeed some memories may be stored in areas that have fewer pathways to the frontal cortex. This does not support the cognitive behavioral perspective in psychology. Instead, it suggests that affect regulation itself may be a separate system from cognition, especially when emotionally intense experiences have not been processed (or available for processing) by the cerebral cortex.

The amygdala and the hippocampus are adjacent to one another. The amygdala is importantly involved in negative emotion, the hippocampus in aspects of memory. Goleman (2003) suggests that it's not an accident that our brains were constructed in such a way that these two structures are right next to each other with very extensive interconnections. Negative emotions and memory are tightly connected for survival purposes. Strong sources of threat are to be remembered and avoided. This promotes survival in instinctual ways.

Bradley suggests that "dysfunction of circuits connecting to limbic areas such as the amygdala or hippocampus may produce interference in distinguishing real from unreal or inner-generated from outer-generated information" (2000, pp. 259-260). Bradley reminds us that the limbic areas, which are the structures in closest association with the hypothalamus, regulate functions critical to the survival of the individual and species: "memory and learning, the modulation of drive, the affective coloring of experience, and the higher control of hormonal balance and autonomic tone" (Mesulam, 1985, p. 9).

Brain-behavior relationships have thus been substantially but incompletely mapped. It should come as no surprise that we, as biological entities, have anatomical substrates that not just mirror but control our experience. In addition, the chemistry within the brain has far-reaching consequences for experience. Prolonged arousal may have an influence on the development of neurotransmitter systems, but withdrawal from arousal may also influence a person's opportunities to learn about affects and coping strategies. Withdrawal deprives the person of opportunities to learn adaptive strategies for conflict resolution and can interfere with the development of social skills. Prolonged stress (such as that which may occur in emotionally sensitive individuals exposed to high levels of stress) may actually impair hippocampal development and functioning, as high levels of corticosteroids are known to produce hippocampal cell loss (Bradley, 2000). This may render such exposed individuals more vulnerable, as cognitive strategies for dealing with their distress may be impaired through hippocampal damage (O'Brien, 1997).

The Nobel Laureate in Physiology or Medicine in 2000, Eric Kandel, explicitly links the role of psychological experience and brain physiology:

> Insofar as psychotherapy or counseling is effective and produces long-term changes in behavior, it presumably does so through . . . [alteration of the] anatomical pattern of interconnections between nerve cells of the brain. . . . Stated simply, the regulation of gene expression by social factors makes all bodily functions, including all functions of the brain, susceptible to social influences. (Kandel, 1998, p. 460)

The Role of Neurotransmitters

Much work has been done to map the role of neurotransmitters in emotional functioning. The following table shows the role of some neurotransmitters in functioning (Bradley, 2000; Panksepp, 1993).

Table 3: Neurotransmitters and Their Functions	
Neurotransmitter	**Effect**
Glutamate	Excitatory function
Cortisol	Key role in stress; high chronic levels result in hippocampal cell loss
Gamma-aminobutyric acid (GABA)	Inhibitory function
Glucocorticoids	Prepare for action on short-term basis; interfere with attention, focusing, and remembering new information when chronic
Norepinephrine	General alertness; increases signal-to-noise ratio in the cortex
Dopamine	Anticipatory eagerness and positive emotionality

Serotonin	Inhibitory control over emotions; Constrains information flow; prevents sensitization to threatening stimuli
Acetylcholine	Mediates arousal and attentional processes

Obviously, under normal circumstances, our biochemistry provides us with the adaptive capacity to modulate and reciprocally influence the environment in goal-directed ways. But what happens under trauma or chronic stress? When glucocorticoids are placed into brain ventricles of rats over several days, increased corticotropin-releasing hormone (CRH) activity is evident in the amygdala. This activity, which may correlate with activation of both the central and peripheral catecholamine systems, can produce fearful and hypervigilant behaviors. Chronic activation of the central nucleus of the amygdala through CRH, whether related to stress or the effects of elevated glucocorticoids, produces a state of what Schulkin and colleagues call "allostatic load" or "arousal pathology" (Schulkin, McEwen, and Gold, 1994). They define allostatic load or arousal pathology as the state of chronic anticipation of negative events. The cognitive behavioral tradition of focusing on negative thoughts thus has a specific neurochemical basis following trauma.

The environment can affect the development of neurotransmitter systems (Kraemer, Ebert, Scmidt, and McKinney, 1989). Unfortunately, chronic high emotionality has predictive negative effects upon recovery. The reverse is true for people who have lower levels of chronic high emotionality.

The person who is able to recover quickly has a lower level of cortisol, which plays a key role in stress. Cortisol is a hormone released by the adrenal glands but controlled by the brain. When cortisol is present at high levels over a long period of time, it may kill cells in the hippocampus.

People who recover quickly also have higher immunity; they have higher levels of natural killer-cell activity, a primary defense that the immune system uses to fight off many kinds of foreign antigens that enter the body, from cancerous tumor cells to the common cold (Goleman, 2003, pp. 197-198).

Disruptions in attention, concentration, and memory are frequently noted in acute disorders. The biochemical substrate of such difficulties appears to be serotonin (5-HT), which acts to constrain information flow, reducing interference from irrelevant stimuli and from sensitization to potentially threatening stimuli (Bradley, 2000). Although primate studies show that 5-HT facilitates social behavior (increases in approach behavior and decreases in avoidance, vigilance, and social solitude), the relationship with changes in 5-HT is not direct. Depletions of 5-HT may change an animal's sensitivity to signals that normally suppress social behavior, resulting in inappropriate social behaviors (Bradley, 2000, p. 225).

Self-regulation is dependent on attention. Bradley notes that there are three attentional networks: first, norepinephrine projections from the locus coeruleus to the cortex, responsible for general alertness; second, a posterior system involving the superior colliculus, the pulvinar nucleus of the thalamus, and the parietal lobe, regulating engaging and disengaging of attention; and third, the anterior cingulate, located in the frontal regions and conceptualized as providing effortful control, a way of moderating more reactive posterior systems. Some form of guidance from the frontal cortex (positioned on the right) assists in the development of mature coping (Derryberry and Reed, 1996).

Effects of Stress on Neurotransmitters

Stress induces secretion of epinephrine and norepinephrine from the adrenal medulla and norepinephrine from terminals in the sympathetic nervous system. Corticotropin-releasing hormone, released by the paraventricular cells of the hypothalamus, stimulates secretion of adrenocorticotropic hormone (ACTH) by the pituitary, which in turn induces release of glucocorticoids from the adrenal cortex. Typically, with reduction of the stress, the hypothalamus-pituitary-adrenal (HPA) stress response is turned off through a negative feedback process in which the effect appears to occur largely through glucocorticoid effects on receptors in the hippocampus and hypothalamus. The release of adrenergic substances tends to be more immediate and short-lived, in contrast to the glucocorticoids, which appear within minutes to hours and tend to have a longer-lasting impact on the system (Johnson et al., 1992).

The short-term effects of increased glucocorticoids prepare the organism for action by changing the normal homeostatic balance in a number of physiological systems. These changes have a negative impact on the organism when the stress becomes chronic. The negative physiological effects of chronic or sustained stress appear to result more from the glucocorticoids than from epinephrine or norepinephrine (Bradley, 2000, pp. 84-85). For example, recent neurochemical research suggests that prolonged stress increases body fat cells and increases hunger for what are commonly known as comfort foods that, over time, can result in obesity (Dallman et al., 2003).

These physiological processes will most probably be "mapped" to both psychopathological and personality disorder syndromes in the future. For example, three interactive systems determine a person's response tendencies: harm avoidance (serotonergic), novelty seeking (dopaminergic), and reward dependence (noradrenergic) (Cloninger, 1987). So, antisocial personality disorder would be seen as the result of high novelty seeking, low reward dependence, and low harm avoidance. Impulsivity is due to high novelty seeking and low harm avoidance, and oppositional behavior is due to low reward dependence and low harm avoidance. Experience, as well as interaction of physiology, determines psychopathology (Bradley, 2000).

Prolonged vs. Acute Stressors

The frontal lobes, the amygdala, and the hippocampus change in response to experience. They are the parts of the brain dramatically affected by our emotional environment and by repeated experience (Goleman, 2003). The left frontal cortext is generally associated with positive emotions, while the right frontal cortext is generally associated with negative emotions. Goleman reports that people who have higher left frontal cortical activity describe their feelings as generally vibrant, optimistic, and pleasurable. Goleman notes, "We each have a characteristic ratio of right-to-left activation in the prefrontal areas that offers a barometer of the moods we are likely to feel day to day. That ratio represents what amounts to an emotional set point, the mean around which our daily moods swing" (p. 12). Perceived unpredictability or lack of control provokes or sustains physiological stress responses.

Elevated levels of glucocorticoids appear to interfere with attention and focusing as well as with remembering new information.

Healthy newborns show elevations of cortisol in response to noxious stimulation, but with handling show increases in quiescence and other self-regulatory behaviors. They also show greater habituation and sensitization to repeated stimuli. Babies with some obstetrical complication that causes them to experience chronic stress not only cry in response to both types of stressors but show a breakdown of normal self-regulatory behaviors at high levels of HPA activity. They fail to show habitiation or sensitization to handling or nociceptive stimulation (Bradley, 2000).

Having control over a noxious stimulation tends to buffer the stress response: monkeys raised with some control over their environment were less fearful, were more willing to explore, and showed a smaller HPA response to stress when given drugs to induce anxiety (Bradley, 2000). So, brief and moderately intense stresses can organize and promote adaptive functioning, while more prolonged or highly intense stresses are likely to be maladaptive.

The elevation of corticosterone with exposure to stress can be normalized with antidepressant pretreatment, which is thought to up-regulate glucocorticoid receptors, enhancing the control over the stress response. Once an individual has been exposed to high levels of glucocorticoids, the capacity to regulate the stress response may become dysfunctional. Burnout related to norepinephrine depletion or to cognitions of hopelessness may lead to retardation, apathy, and low mood (Gunnar and Barr, 1998).

Prolonged states of stress or exposure to high levels of corticosteroids may damage the hippocampus, potentially interfering with prefrontal-hippocampal connections and possible regulatory mechanisms (Kiraly, Ancill, and Dimitrova, 1997; O'Brien, 1997).

Since glucocorticoid receptors play a role in mediating the action of the three main monoaminergic neurotransmitter systems—the serotonergic, noradrenergic, and dopaminergic systems—prolonged emotional stress can have substantial and wide effects on both psychological and physiological experiences (Bradley, 2000).

Psychological experiences of threat, especially if prolonged, thus change the brain chemistry in ways that keep neuronal patterns signaling threat going long after the threat has been removed. The result is the high emotional sensitivity and poor solution-focused coping found to be effectively treated with DBT interventions.

While mental-health professionals are knowledgeable about the outward dysfunctions of patients who experience prolonged trauma (fear, social isolation, impulsivity, hopelessness, pessimism, etc.), there is substantial evidence that trauma results in neuroanatomical changes that can be persistent and even permanent (Sapolsky, 1994). In her excellent review of the literature on the neural basis of prolonged stress, Bradley notes adverse life events increase physiological stress responses, and that if stresses are prolonged, there is increased vulnerability to the development not only of psychopathology but also of cardiovascular and other medical problems (2000). Some of the medical effects appear to be mediated through elevations of catecholamines as well as through activation of the HPA axis and elevated levels of corticosteroids. People who come back to emotional baseline quickly are those who have less activation in the amygdala and whose activation is shorter in duration. They are people who also show more activation in the left prefrontal cortex, the area correlated with positive emotion.

Psychopathology can result from the individual's inability to terminate the stress response, since chronically high levels of glucocorticoids have a negative effect on many bodily systems (Kiraly et al., 1997), including the brain, especially the hippocampus. In the hippocampus, prolonged elevation of glucocorticoids results in shrinking of dendrites and loss of neurons that regulate the HPA axis (O'Brien, 1997). These effects are profound in that they can affect not only the individual, but in the pregnant woman, can even affect the fetus. Elevation of maternal glucocorticoids produces reduction of glucocorticoid receptors in offspring, which in turn is related to less effective HPA responses to stress in rats and monkeys. There is no reason to assume that the same is not true for humans, given the data on recovery from stressors in infants (Strelau, 1994).

The Kindling Effect

Knowledge of neuroanatomical activation thus demonstrates that prolonged emotional arousal results in changes in both neuroanatomy and neurochemistry, no doubt producing powerful experiential changes in patients. Above and beyond such dynamics, kindling effects predict that high emotional arousal, especially when sustained, predicts continued high emotional arousal. Kindling is essentially a permanent change in the sensitivity of the brain to a stimulus (Robertson and Cottrell, 1985).

The notion of kindling comes from a model of epilepsy whereby repeated administration of brief, low-intensity electrical stimulation comes to elicit seizures. Even in the absence of overt tissue damage, an animal that has been kindled is subsequently in a permanent state of increased susceptibility to seizures. The kindling paradigm is that repetition of initially subconvulsive stimulation can lead to a progressive and permanently enhanced epileptic susceptibility (Le Gal La Salle, 1982). A number of persistent biochemical and physiological alterations in function accompany kindling, including loss of synaptic dendrites (Nishizuka, et al., 1991). Some of these alterations impact upon behavior for a long period of time despite the absence of further seizure activation (Gilbert, 1994). Importantly, kindled reactions result in increased emotional behavior in animals (Kalynchuk, et al., 1997), dramatically increasing fearful behavior that does not sensitize over time as do behaviorally precipitated fear reactions (Kalynchuk et al., 2001).

Experimental kindling reactions have been produced not just with artificial electrical stimulation but also with central nervous system stimulants and other chemical compounds (Post and Kopanda, 1976), demonstrating that such kindling reactions are not simple experimental effects but may have direct applicability to human psychopathology, such as recurrent affective disorder (Post, 1992). Post notes that "stress-induced brain changes sensitize the individual such that subsequent episodes can be triggered by a relatively minor event through both intracellular chemical changes affecting proteins and neurotransmitters and neuroanatomical changes (synaptic number and density). Preventing early adverse experiences in order to prevent difficulties at the level of brain development is thus important" (p. 999).

It has been proposed that perhaps kindling is the reason that antiseizure medications work as mood stabilizers in bipolar disorder (Post et al., 1998).

The limbic structures, responsible for emotion generation, are especially susceptible to kindling in animal models of experimentation. The increased proclivity for seizure disorders that characterizes kindling is not restricted to the initial kindling stimulus, but generalizes to other agents with convulsive properties (Gilbert, 1994). Experimenters obtain increased natural firing of neural pathways following experimental stimulation of such areas (Adamec and Stark-Adamec, 1983). Long-lasting synaptic potentiation and increased suspectibility to synaptic failure is noted following such artificial stimulation. Since the discovery of the kindling effect in 1969, even mild periodic electrical stimulation to any one of many brain sites leads to the development and progressive intensification of elicited motor seizures (Barnes and Pinel, 2001).

For our purposes, the kindling effect has far-reaching consequences for psychopathology. Essentially, the kindling effect predicts that while psychological life events may have an initial, powerful effect upon brain chemistry and anatomy, producing psychopathology, later episodes of psychopathology may be less predicted by major life events (psychological processes) and more by simple increased susceptibility to neural pathway firing (Hlastala et al., 2000). Major psychosocial stresses may thus play a diminishing role over the course of psychiatric illness over time as neurological kindling takes over and produces increased neural pathway firings independent of external precipitants. This would explain the emotional sensitivity model of psychopathology: that some individuals, independent of genetic propensity, are more prone to arousal and thus emotional disorders.

For example, while stressful life events have been shown to be critically important in the development of the first episode of major depression, subsequent episodes of depression in the same person appear less related to new psychosocial stressors (Kendler, Thornton, and Gardner, 2000), which the researchers conclude provides results consistent with the kindling hypothesis applied to human psychopathology. A subsequent study showed that genetic risk factors for depression provided a prekindling effect, requiring little environmental stress or trauma to trigger depression. Even in individuals not genetically predisposed to depression, previous depressive episodes (the kindling) result in subsequent depressive episodes with little environmental provocation (Kendler, Thornton, and Gardner, 2001).

Kindling produces effects far beyond the induction of seizure activity in animal experimentation. Kindling in the centromedial amygdala facilitated the subsequent development of restraint-induced stomach ulcers in rats. It was suggested that the neuronal hyperexcitability produced by the kindling procedure led to an increased susceptibility to gastric pathology in response to stress (Henke and Sullivan, 1985). This is consistent with the clinical observation of therapists that patients who are in emotional distress have greater somatic manifestations of their emotional arousal in many bodily systems.

Kindling effects have not only been invoked to explain recurrent depression, bipolar disorder, addictive behavior, chronic anxiety, and obsessive-compulsive disorder (Post and Weiss, 1998), but have also been used to explain self-injurious behavior (Russell and John, 1999).

The dramatic and far-reaching psychopathological processes that may be kindling-related are noted by Pontius (1993):

> It appears that in humans the influence of specific external stimuli that revive the memory of repeated past experiences may "kindle" a transient episode of limbic overactivation. Thereupon the normal balance between the limbic and frontal lobe systems is disturbed (for a few minutes) as are normal human decision making and control of action. Linked with such a transient frontolimbic imbalance is out-of-character behavior, psychosis (hallucinations or delusions), autonomic activation, and severe distortion of affect and of action . . . (p. 615).

The pervasive consequences of the kindling effect have been interpreted as due to, on a neurochemical basis, constriction of information flow. The person is less capable of differentiating relevant from irrelevant stimuli and shows increased attention to potentially threatening stimuli (Spoont, 1992). This results in increased avoidance behavior due to heightened emotional arousal. The kindling effect is thus entirely consistent with the DBT notion that high emotional arousal, the slow return to emotional baseline following threat, and increased scanning of the environment for sources of threat produces many acute emotional disorders.

A "neural network" model for kindling is proposed by Mehta, who notes that a large number of excitatory synaptic connections are formed during learning (Mehta,

Dasgupta, and Ullal, 1993). Once a set of neural pathways are connected through innervation, that same set of pathways tends to fire together in the future. This neural network model thus predicts, again, that once emotional arousal occurs, it can be difficult to terminate those neural firings in the future. The "emotional pain threshold" has been reduced. It takes less provocation to result in the same intensity of firings in the future. "During kindling, pathological changes may occur at several organizational levels of the nervous system, from alterations in gene-expression in individual neurons to the loss of specific neuronal populations and rearrangement of synaptic connectivity resulting from sustained stimulation of major excitatory pathways" (Mody, 1993, p. 395).

Segal and colleagues note that "kindling and sensitization at a neurobiological level may activate interlocking negative associations such that once activated they are difficult to contain; their continuing activation may spiral into psychopathology such as depression. The neural networks are thus more readily accessed each time they are activated" (Segal, Williams, Teasdale, and Gemar, 1996, p. 371).

The kindling effect thus predicts that initial high emotional arousal causes neuroanatomical, neurochemical, and neural net (firing pathway configuration) changes such that lower psychosocial stressors (life events) are required for subsequent increases in emotional arousal. High emotionality is kindled. External psychological factors take on increasingly negligible roles, and neurological processes take on increasingly potent roles following initial psychological trauma. DBT is designed to treat this dysfunctional process.

Unfortunately, there is an additional psychological overlay to the kindling effect. When affect is high and there are no external precipitants, people search cognitively for explanations of their arousal. They begin to develop identity-based shame and guilt responses when they are unable to explain their arousal by immediate environmental events.

THE SINGLE-FACTOR THEORY: AROUSAL AND MENTAL DISORDERS

The major result of our discussion on physiological aspects of emotional disorder is the conclusion that high emotional arousal itself is the cause of much subsequent emotional disorder. Decreasing the arousal (changing the emotional state) will assist to change the neural net pathways that fire. Simply decreasing physiological arousal (apart from dealing with the negative thought process or associations that current environmental triggers evoke) can have a substantial therapeutic effect.

Support for this position is strong. Longitudinal studies have found that emotionality accounts for most of the variance in later symptom reporting (Levenson, Aldwin, Bosse, and Spiro, 1988). Comorbidity of anxiety and depression disorders suggests a shared vulnerability (Clark and Watson, 1991) that predicts high levels of such comorbidity (Marra, 2004). The National Institute of Mental Health (NIMH) collaborative study comparing psychotherapy to psychopharmacology in the treatment of depression and anxiety (Elkin et al., 1989) found that cognitive behavioral therapy produced therapeutic outcomes equivalent to those for antidepressant treatment. Furthermore, tricyclics, selective serotonin reuptake inhibitors (SSRIs), and benzodiazepines were found roughly comparable in their effectiveness. How can such interventions, having very different modes of action, produce similar results? The general factor of emotion regulation was suggested by the experimenters as accounting for treatment outcome in all successful therapies.

The nonspecific effects of many therapeutic interventions suggest the common element of treatment may be an anxiety- or distress-relieving mechanism (Bradley, 2000). Emotional reactivity is reduced with effective treatment.

Moreover, studies examining the high prevalence of anxiety across most mental disorders have suggested a common factor in psychopathology: emotionality (Garvey, Noyes, Anderson, and Cook, 1991). The ability to modulate emotional arousal (whether produced through psychosocial stressors or the kindling effect produced from prior arousal) is thus predicted to be the most powerful factor to influence in order to produce therapeutic outcomes for our patients. This is clear in the case of mood or anxiety disorders, where the internalizing effects of arousal are readily reported by the patient, but it's perhaps less evident (but just as true) with personality disorders.

In a paper on the autonomic nervous system factors underlying disinhibited, antisocial, and violent behavior, Raine (1997) examined the effects of underarousal. Raine proposes that individuals vulnerable to externalizing disorders are more inclined to engage in pathological sensation-seeking behaviors. Physiological underarousal is theorized as the basis for such novelty seeking, the purpose of which is to increase arousal to normal levels. The same dynamic is used to explain internalizing personality issues, where inhibited children exhibit higher levels of arousal to stressful stimuli compared to noninhibited controls (Kagan, Reznick, and Snidman, 1987). Children show a pattern of withdrawal or avoidance when confronted with new or challenging situations. Inhibition in avoidant children produces more intense arousal and greater prolongation of arousal once it is initiated (Kagan et al., 1987). Bradley reviews research indicating that behaviorally inhibited children show greater increases in salivary cortisol than do uninhibited children. She predicts that this difference is a predisposing factor to anxiety and mood disorders (2000). Over-emotionality or underemotionality (arousal homoeostasis) is thus proposed as a major mediator of subsequent psychopathology, even in personality disorders.

There is a neuroanatomical basis for this conclusion. The affect-generating regions of the brain, the amygdala and its projections, play a key role in fear conditioning and regulation. The connections of the amygdala to the hippocampus are involved in emotional memories. Arousal in these limbic circuits are high in all acute disorders. Such arousal will not differentiate one emotional disorder from another (Bradley, 2000), although Bradley proposes that "psychotherapy may bring about more changes in the prefrontal cortex, hippocampus, and amygdala, where medication may have a greater influence on overall modulating systems, such as dopaminergic or serotonergic systems" (p. 268). All effective interventions decrease emotional arousal. And the reverse is also true. Those with heightened emotional arousal are more likely to develop an emotional disorder.

Arousability is shown to be directly related to attachment and temperament in studies of children (Strelau, 1994), supporting our initial discussion of the role of attachment in producing the emotional dysregulation DBT is designed to treat. Prolonged states of hyperarousal are also seen in physiological studies of individuals who have been victims of abuse and trauma (van der Kolk, 1996), integrating the roles of both psychological and physiological factors in emotionality.

Successful interventions will thus help patients to regulate affect. There are several aspects to such affect regulation. First, patients must be able to recognize and label emotion cues in self and others. Such recognition demands emotion-focused attention. Second, the patient must develop strategies to control uncomfortable levels of arousal (switching back and forth between an emotion-focused and a solution-focused attention) and to mediate interpersonal difficulties if they are involved in the stress response (solution-focused coping). Problem-focused coping is difficult when emotional distress is high (Lazarus and Folkman, 1984), but acceptance-based strategies have been shown to decrease such emotionality (Linehan, 1993b). DBT offers a technology of affect regulation designed to ameliorate the pathological features of dysfunctional arousal here proposed as the major single factor in most mental disorders.

Chapter Summary

There are many causes of emotional sensitivity (the label for the pathotopology DBT is designed to treat: high emotional arousal, slow return to emotional baseline following threat, and hypersensitivity to threat cues that keep the process going). Some of them are psychological (attachment, loss, trauma, and invalidation of affect), but most of them are beyond the control of the patient who experiences them. For example, attachment issues occur in infancy , and loss, by definition, is beyond the person's influence. Other causes of emotional sensitivity are neurobiological, where there is fairly clear clinical evidence that emotional experiences are not always modulated by our cognitive processes. For example, memories stored in the hippocampus and amygdala are not available for conscious processing due to the paucity of connections between the amygdala and the cerebral cortex. There is reason to believe that the areas of the brain that developed emotionality developed separately from the areas of the brain that developed rationality (LeDoux, 1996). Negative emotion (predominating in the amygdala) and emotional memory (predominating in the hippocampus) are neuroanatomically programmed for permanence. And for good reason, as this arrangement promotes survival in instinctual ways.

While the role of neurotransmitters has understandably been well studied (since they can be manipulated with medication less intrusively), the role of prolonged arousal has been less attended to. Prolonged stress results not only in the development of hyperarousal to environmental threat but also in release of biochemicals that result in the shrinking of dendrites (reducing neural pathways) and actual loss of hippocampus cells. Prolonged stress thus has neurochemical, neuroanatomical, and psychological consequences that predict the emotional sensitivity that DBT is designed to treat. There is also ample evidence that once high emotional arousal occurs, the kindling effect predicts that the patient will have an increased susceptibility to high emotional arousal in the future, meaning that it will take less to set the person off. The kindling effect is neurochemical and neurological, thus beyond the control of the individual. These issues can be subsumed under a neural-network model that basically predicts that past emotional intensity lowers the threshold for future emotional intensity.

The conclusions are fourfold. First, emotionality is controlled primarily by neurochemical, neuroanatomical, and neural net firings. What might be considered the emotional systems of the brain are related to, but separate from, the cognitive or rational systems of the brain. Second, psychological factors can either enhance or inhibit emotional arousal. Third, once emotional sensitivity occurs, the probability of traumatic psychological factors eliciting emotional disorders decreases. It takes less and less provocation from the environment to elicit highly emotional responses. Fourth, all of these processes are beyond the conscious control of the person; they are not doing it to themselves or engaging in secondary gain.

Emotionality is thus defined as the single most important factor causing mental-health disorders.

CHAPTER 4

Pathotopology: Dialectic Conflict as a Core Therapeutic Target

In preceding chapters we reviewed the theoretical foundations of DBT, the psychological and physiological causes of major acute disorders DBT is designed to treat, and concluded that emotionality per se accounts for the greatest proportion of variance in causation of acute disorders. In this chapter we turn our attention to dialectic conflict and its role in sustaining disorders. We also explore general treatment strategies designed to reduce dialectic conflict and thus to reduce suffering in our patients.

COMORBITY

High emotional arousal, defined by muscular tension, short and rapid breathing, increased heart rate, increased perspiration, negative and pessimistic thoughts, and intensity of affect itself all have interactive consequences upon the psychological adaptability of the individual. Current nosologies, such as the *Diagnostic and Statistical Manual of Mental Disorders*, fourth edition (American Psychiatric Association, 1994), attempt to divide disorders into broad classifications (psychotic, mood, anxiety, somatoform, eating, sleeping, impulse control, sexual, personality, adjustment, etc.) based upon symptom clusters. Clearly, psychotic conditions differ substantially from personality disorders in terms of causation, topography, and treatment. There is thus good reason to categorize mental disorders based upon major symptom clusters and theorized pathogenic factors.

Nevertheless, major mental disorders frequently have overlapping features that make the nomothetic criteria less relevant to the idiographic application to a specific patient. In fact, there is tremendous evidence that the majority of major mental disorders involve comorbidity. The powerful influence of comorbidity is not currently addressed by most studies. For example, Zimmerman found that, using typical Food and Drug Administration (FDA) protocols for antidepressant drug trials, 85 percent of consecutive patients who were from typical private practice and were diagnosed with unipolar major depression would be excluded due to comorbidity issues (Zimmerman, Posternack, and Chelminski, 2002). In other words, if each of your unipolar depressed patients—as they presented for treatment intakes—were evaluated for inclusion in an FDA study, 85 percent would be excluded because they exhibit symptoms that go beyond simple unipolar depression. Boyd and colleagues found that patients with panic disorder have chances nineteen times greater of suffering from their disorder if they also experience depression than are patients who are depression free (Boyd et al., 1984). Depression frequently is comorbid with anxiety disorders. Simple phobias are nine times greater if the person is depressed. Obsessive-compulsive disorder (OCD) is eleven times greater if the person is depressed, according to Boyd. Depression is frequently comorbid with OCD (Abramowitz et al., 2000); anxiety and depression are almost always comorbid when either disorder is chronic or even just lengthy (Brown and Harris, 1993; Clark and Watson, 1991; Garvey et al., 1991; Hudson and Pope, 1990); panic and agoraphobia are frequently comorbid (Rosenbaum et al., 1988); the frequency of substance abuse coupled with many mental disorders has been noted (Linehan et al., 2002); and the fact that personality disorders coexist with major mental disorders is validated by our current multiaxial classification system. As previously argued, while there is statistical and heuristic value in our classification system, many emotional disorders can be explained by high emotionality and emotional sensitivity.

EMOTIONAL SENSITIVITY

"Emotional sensitivity" is the label used to describe arousability. The emotionally sensitive person requires less environmental prompting to elicit high emotionality; needs less threat before they become intensely anxious, depressed, experience a sense of urgency, or become hyperaroused; and tends to scan the environment for threat cues, and thus is more likely to "find" threat in the environment. This keeps emotional arousal high.

After environmental threat ceases, the emotionally sensitive person takes longer to return to their set point or baseline arousal level.

High Emotional Arousal

If we define emotional arousal not just as mental and physical symptoms of anxiety but also as depressed affect, negative appraisals, anticipation of danger and threat, excitability or the lack thereof, and general existential dis-ease, then most mental disorders are appropriate for DBT treatment. While certainly the dementias, schizophrenias, and mental disorders due to general medical conditions are not treatable using DBT, all disorders having high emotional arousal as a central feature can profit from the DBT approach.

What happens when our patients experience high emotional arousal over lengthy periods of time? Not only do they experience despair, but a number of critical and adaptive information-processing capabilities begin to deteriorate. Concentration and attention skills decline as the individual becomes increasingly distracted by their own proprioceptive cues that something is dramatically amiss. Attention is frequently turned inward, and the individual attends to bodily processes, thoughts, and affects rather than environmental events. The tendency toward self-absorption is frequent with most major mental disorders.

Self-absorption predicts that critical environmental events will be ignored. The ability to differentiate salient from irrelevant variables in the environment decreases. Without appropriate cues to prompt solution-focused coping with environmental changes, the person instead expends major psychic energy in attempting to deal with the high emotional arousal itself. As the biopsychosocial model predicts, a negative spiral occurs where increased arousal causes the patient to turn their attention inward toward their arousal, attempting to identify its source and impact. As we reviewed in chapter 3, frequently neural nets begin automatic firing, predicting kindling effects; the patient will find no source of current emotional threat because the source and genesis of such arousal is long gone. The cause is so distant that even an intelligent and reasonable person cannot identify the source. The lack of predictability and understandability of distress increases emotional arousal, since a lack of control over our situation increases any sense of threat. The more the patient attends to their arousal, the more it increases. The increased arousal can be experienced physiologically (as anxiety symptoms), cognitively (as mood symptoms), or affectively (frequently the comorbid condition we find in clinical practice).

Another interesting variable is that the high arousal need not be experienced as especially distressful. Some individuals are so skillful at not accessing their affective responses that they define their arousal as boredom. Such people feel underaroused and engage in impulse-driven behaviors to increase perceived arousal. This is especially true of individuals who engage in substance abuse as a method to increase perceived arousal. The notion that arousal per se is involved in such substance abuse is confirmed by the fact that such individuals will rely either on sedatives or stimulants to create a change in arousal level; it is change of arousal level rather than specific increases or decreases in stimulation that such individuals appear to be seeking. The DBT therapist must therefore be sensitive to the notion that the patient may not report high experiential arousal and may instead report underarousal, but their behavior belies such an understanding of their condition.

In addition to concentration, attention, ineffectual self-focus, and problem-solving deficits, individuals who experience high arousal engage in more emotion-focused and less problem-focused coping. The tendency is to place more effort and strain on reducing the immediate emotional stimulation rather than attending to long-term strategies to decrease arousal. Increased focus on short-term relief, at the expense of long-term objectives, frequently occurs with individuals experiencing chronic high arousal. This is thus one of the central dialectics to which the DBT therapist attends: assisting the patient to balance short-term with long-term objectives. The therapist helps the patient to redeploy attention away from themselves (their emotions, their physiology, and their thoughts) at times and to expose themselves to the emotionally painful symptoms at other times. The dialectic is to move the patient between modes of responding (focus on self vs. focus on others, people vs. environment focus, emotion vs. cognition focus, avoidance vs. acceptance focus, short-term vs. long-term objectives, idealized vs. practical responsiveness, and so forth), as the ability of the individual to shift from one mode of responding to another has been impaired by the high emotional arousal.

Slow Return to Emotional Baseline

In addition to high emotional arousal, many individuals with major mental disorders have a difficult time recovering from threat. Not only does the person feel intensely, but even when the perceived threat has terminated, their ability to relax is impaired. This can be due to several factors. First, the individual (engaging in ruminative self-focus) may continue to attend to physiological cues of arousal (muscle tension, blood pressure, breathing rate, parathesias) and fail to redirect their attention to the increased safety that the environment now predicts. Second, they may similarly attend to the lingering emotional consequences of previous threat and not allow feelings of relief to be generated. Third, the individual may internalize the source of threat (judging themselves as inadequate, shameful, guilty, or bad) and thus intensify previous negative affect over time. Linehan refers to this as secondary emotional response (Linehan, 1993b, 1993c). Fourth, thoughts about the injustice or unfairness of the previous threat may create a new source of threat (that of being the unacceptable victim of abuse) such that threat cues, rather than safety cues, are attended to. Lastly and perhaps most importantly, the individual's psychological coping responses may not be involved at all in sustaining emotional arousal. Kindling effects on a neurobiological level, totally beyond the control of the individual, may explain continued high arousal. Most of us don't want to admit that painful experience is beyond our control, so we continue to engage in trial-and-error attempts to decrease the emotional arousal. When each such attempt fails, arousal increases due to frustration and feelings of failure. The result is impulse-driven behavior (impulsiveness), often seemingly erratic and counterproductive.

Since shifting attention between affect, cognition, physiology, behavior, and environment is difficult, the resulting behavior of the individual can appear illogical. However, such attempts should be seen as attempts to operate on the environment. As Linehan comments (Linehan, 1993b) regarding borderline personality disorder (but applicable to many acute mental disorders), such frantic attempts to control experience should be viewed as attempts to control the internal experience of chaos rather than as manipulative or pathological attempts to gain attention from others. A central principle of DBT is thus that the therapist should assume that the experience of the patient and their attempt to improve their situation is operant behavior. A nonpejorative assumption regarding our patient's experience and behavior is critical to the success of therapy; otherwise, we become another invalidating experience in the patient's life, increasing rather than decreasing their emotional arousal.

Understanding the general but predictable course of many mental disorders will help the therapist design intervention strategies. While patients may present chief complaints indicating depression, anxiety, impulse control, sleep, or any of a number of difficulties, if the therapist attends to the big picture of emotional arousal, frequently the following pattern will be found.

In figure 1, emotional arousal is subjectively measured from very low (0) to intolerably high (100). Prior to the occurrence of a threatening situation a normal individual would have a moderately low level of emotional arousal (perhaps 20 on our scale of 1 to 100, reflecting typical situational stressors of having daily task demands placed upon them). When a stressful event occurs (being rejected by a valued other, having a failure at work, having an intense argument with a spouse, etc.), the normal individual's arousal may double (to 40 on our scale). This is clearly

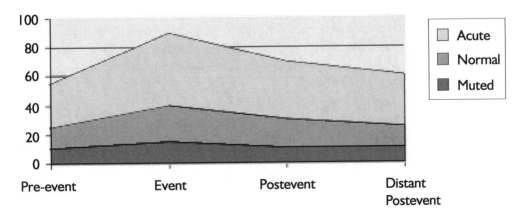

Figure 1: Slow return to emotional baseline following threat

uncomfortable for the individual, but it is manageable and doesn't lead to catastrophic predictions by the person that their situation is intolerable or their future hopeless. Gradually, the typical person's arousal will decrease as both the effect of time and use of psychological coping resources allows new experiences to prompt improved emotions. Eventually, the emotional arousal from the event will be fully dissipated, and the person's arousal will be close to baseline again.

In acute disorders, the same general pattern of emotional arousal is not found. Even prior to stressors occurring, emotionality is high. This is due to previous psychological factors discussed in chapter 3 (attachment difficulties, previous trauma, loss experiences, and history of emotional invalidation) or to neurobiological kindling effects. Having an already high baseline arousal, it takes less-powerful triggers to further increase emotional arousal. Emotional sensitivity thresholds are lower. Reactivity of the individual is higher. Moreover, recovery over time occurs more slowly. The result is that the person never fully recovers from psychological stressors, and each new stressor over time has an accumulative effect, slowly but steadily increasing baseline arousal levels.

An emotionally muted individual, one who is emotionally insensitive, follows the opposite pattern. Compared to normal, they have low levels of arousal functioning, prior to the occurrence of stressors, and psychological stressors are ignored or effectively distracted against. Arousal does not vary greatly as a result of events that typically cause most of us distress, either during the stressor or at points across time following the potential stressor.

There are, of course, advantages and disadvantages to each response style. Emotionally sensitive people are prone to emotional pain and agony but are highly influenced by the environment. They tend to be highly responsive to others, thus more easily form emotional attachments to others, and since emotions are easily accessed, they rarely have a difficult time identifying their immediate goals and preferences. Their lives are colorful, and meaning is more easily identified by them. The emotionally muted individual experiences less emotional pain and agony but is also less influenced by the environment. It takes more to get them "up" just as it takes more to get them "down." Once negative affect begins, the gradual lowering of their mood is less changeable since they are less influenced by the environment. The emotionally muted individual has a more difficult time putting their finger on what is meaningful in life, and their values are less readily apparent either to themselves or to others. They tend to be seen as predictable and less interesting by others who know them.

Emotional sensitivity is independent of depression per se. The flat affect noted in depression is different than the arousal levels addressed here. Depressed affect is an anticipatory, fear-based response to frustration, strain, failure, or emotional pain. There is an active defense against affect in clinical depression rather than the enduring threshold of arousability here described.

Hypervigilance

The slow return to emotional baseline for acute disorders predicts several consequences. First, greater anticipatory fear will occur about stressors for the emotionally sensitive individual because the consequences of the stressors are more severe and longer lasting. Second, greater anticipatory fear predicts stronger avoidance responses. Third, once stressors occur, the person will engage in greater escape responses attempting to lower the emotional load experienced. Lastly, hypervigilance is likely to occur as a method to avoid threat in the first place. The person scans the environment for sources of threat, and the world is perceived to be an increasingly dangerous place to live. Threat may be anticipated or perceived where no threat exists.

EMOTIONAL AVOIDANCE OR ESCAPE REPLACES EMOTION REGULATION

Individuals who are not prone to acute mental disorders regularly and naturally engage in emotion regulation strategies. People naturally seek out experiences of joy, amusement, and meaning to counterbalance experiences of stress, strain, and trauma. Typically, no one has to coach them to engage in experiences that prompt positive affect; these people engage in reinforcing activities simply because they feel good. The pleasure and pain principles so well described by Freud work without effort or conscious thought by the person. Having some amount of balance between negative and positive experiences occurs naturally. Internal prompts, such as novelty seeking, provoke the person to achieve such balance. External prompts, such as interpersonal requests of family and friends, also serve to achieve the balance between positive and negative life experiences.

Other emotion regulation strategies, such as the ability to identify and label affect (thus engaging cognition to the affective load of the experience) are less threatening to the typical person because there is not the anticipation of doom through experience (recognition and labeling) of affect. Fewer secondary emotional processes (guilt, shame, or anger) follow primary emotional experiences since affect is not followed by the punishment of lingering emotional arousal following a stressor. Feelings under normal circumstances are identified as natural and even helpful human responses to living rather than as treacherous processes to be avoided. People not prone to acute emotional disorders tend to be less ruminative (less "in their heads"), because they are not constantly scanning the environment for sources of threat. They are less self-absorbed, and thus there is a natural movement between focus on self and focus on environment. This permits the person to more fully use their senses of touch, sight, taste, hearing, and aroma to embellish life's experience.

New experiences, substantially based upon senses, replace old ones in memory. New, pleasant neural net pathways fire, replacing older, painful ones. Obstacles to improved mood are identified, and appraisals of success in overcoming such obstacles lead the person to persevere in the face of such difficulties.

Avoidance Replaces Emotion Regulation

For those who are emotionally sensitive, avoidance tends to replace emotion regulation skills. Why? The torment of high emotional arousal prompts the individual to try to terminate such arousal quickly (escape) or to avoid the arousal altogether (avoidance). Anticipatory processes (to avoid pain) are difficult to extinguish due to mediating thoughts; it is difficult to convince someone that the behavior they used did not prevent something that has not happened. Moreover, anxiety is typically lowered once a negative event is avoided and this lowering of anxiety is reinforcing. The avoidance is thus reinforced by reduced anxiety. It is difficult to assist our patients to understand that the lowered anxiety is an empty achievement (since the negative anticipation is the very source of anxiety that is being reduced by the avoidance).

The self-absorption and rumination characteristic of high emotional arousal paradoxically heightens sensation thresholds. The person is no longer easily able to enjoy the senses of touch, taste, smell, hearing, and vision. They are thus less influenced by the environment, and fewer new experiences are available to replace older (typically negative) ones. If the environment offers little hope to prompt joy, amusement, or stimulation, why seek it? The pain principle thus supersedes the pleasure principle. Avoiding further harm takes precedence over seeking further pleasures in life. The balance between positive and negative life events slowly begins to swing in the negative direction.

Feelings themselves become the culprit to be avoided, since they are perceived as the source of pain. Fewer discriminations between mild and intense feelings are made as anticipatory avoidance of affect becomes the goal. I am repeatedly amazed that patients present for treatment who experience lethargy, loss of meaning in their life, disturbed sleep, appetite changes, loss of libido, and other powerful symptoms and then are surprised when I suggest that they are depressed. Such individuals have avoided identifying and labeling their affect for fear it will increase it.

With high emotional arousal, the probability of mood-dependent behavior increases. Mood-dependent behavior is when the patient engages in behavior that is prompted by their affect rather than their goals or objectives. Irritability offers a good example. When frustrated, the person who verbalizes sarcastic and biting comments to a loved one who is not offering threat is engaging in mood-dependent behavior. Avoidance of affect is a high-probability behavior with high emotional arousal and is mood dependent. The paradox here is that affect prompts avoidance of affect. Likewise, the DBT dialectic intervention is paradoxically to assist the patient to more effectively avoid affect at times and to expose the patient more fully to affect at other times.

Escape Replaces Emotion Regulation

While the anticipatory nature of avoidance encourages patients to use it as a strategy (to avoid the anticipated harm), escape offers even more powerful and immediate cues: to terminate emotional pain that has already begun. Dr. Kabat-Zinn's book title *Wherever You Go, There You Are* (1994) is relevant here. Escape from emotions is difficult, because the act of running from them generates anxiety. Escape is a natural response tendency, but when what you are attempting to escape is within you rather than an external threat, the process can be interminable.

With emotional escape, attention is directed at threat cues that can become increasingly amorphous. Anxiety increases and exacerbates other conditions (depression, impulse control, oversleeping, insomnia, overeating, undereating, addiction, and characterological issues). The breadth of attentional focus shrinks, thus limiting information input and memory retrieval, concentration is impaired, and problem solving turns more exclusively to emotions rather than solutions.

The acceptance-based strategy of mindfulness used in DBT is designed to reduce emotional escape behavior. Acceptance is differentiated from approval. By accepting emotional arousal, the patient is invited to remove the anxiety and agony surrounding the more fundamental and primary emotion (removing the anxiety of being depressed, the fear of weight gain with eating disorders, the anticipatory strain of abstinence for addictions, and so forth). Acceptance is a form of exposure, and with exposure anxiety is reduced. Freedom of response results, as the person is no longer mood dependent but can use both solution-focused and emotion-focused coping in designing a response to a particular situation.

The dialectic conflict with avoidance and escape procedures is thus between safety and freedom. If the patient engages in avoidance or escape they feel safe, but they have lost freedom. If the patient chooses acceptance, they gain freedom but sacrifice safety in the here and now. The role of the DBT therapist is to help the patient more skillfully navigate this dialectic so that they are not always using the same strategy regardless of the outcome.

SELF-MANAGEMENT OF AFFECT RATHER THAN COGNITIONS

Traditional cognitive behavioral therapy presumes that much emotional dysfunction results from cognitive distortions of various sorts: overgeneralization, emotional reasoning, reasoning from faulty assumptions, depressing schemas, arbitrary inference, selective abstraction, dichotomous thinking, and the like (Beck et al., 1979). While some cognitive therapists would argue that thoughts define feelings, most would simply endorse the notion that thoughts, affect, and physiology have interactive effects upon one another (the biopsychosocial model of disease). Change the cognitions, and the feelings will soon follow. While DBT would not totally disagree with this presumption, a strong caveat is offered: Telling a patient that their thoughts are wrong, no matter how palatably delivered, is invalidating and may result in increased rather than decreased emotional arousal.

The following therapeutic dialogue demonstrates how a DBT therapist might respond to a patient's affect rather than their thoughts.

Patient: I just feel broken. I work so hard to get everyone's approval, but I never get it. I wish I could give up this sense that everyone should love me. I feel so lousy all the time.

DBTherapist: Can you focus on feeling lousy and broken?

Patient: What do you mean?

DBTherapist: Rather than telling me about why you feel broken and lousy, describe for me the feelings of being broken and lousy.

Patient: (*Pause*) Well, there must be something wrong with me, because I work so hard and I never get what I want.

DBTherapist: Stick with describing the feelings of being broken and lousy.

Patient: I'm broken because I'm always hurting. I feel broken because you want me to describe my feelings, and all I can think of is what is causing my feelings. I feel broken because . . .

DBTherapist: Please don't tell me the reasons, the "becauses." Describe the feelings of broken and lousy.

Patient: It feels inadequate, inferior . . . less than, shameful, disgusting.

DBTherapist: Can you feel it in your body, too?

Patient: My chest feels heavy and tight, and I'm trying not to cry.

DBTherapist: Allow yourself to cry. Welcome the crying, if that expresses the broken feeling.

The DBT therapist thus does not reinforce the explanations and multiple examples the patient may offer about why they think what they think (the cognitions). Instead, the therapist focuses on affect that is being avoided with this rationality. The purpose is to discourage affective avoidance and escape and to normalize the experience of strong affect. Once the patient begins to experience emotional intensity, the therapist encourages the patient to "stick with it" for a few seconds beyond what they would normally permit themselves. The therapist explains to the patient that sustaining attention to affect just a few seconds longer each time decreases the fear of their emotions.

One of my favorite metaphors to use with patients is the bogeyman under the bed. Almost everyone had the experience as a child of believing that something horrible and menacing, frequently a monster of some sort, was in their bedroom at night after their parents left the room. The bogeyman was surely there. The bedroom was dark and scary, making the perfect environment for a bogeyman to come kidnap or devour the helpless child. The typical childhood response is to either close their eyes and hope the bogeyman does not notice them (avoidance) or run frantically to their parents screaming for help (escape).

I ask the patient, why does the child assume that closing their eyes helps protect them from the bogeyman? Why does the child expect that the bogeyman will not grab them as they run from the room? Every patient gives essentially the same reasonable response: fear is the operating principle. The only true way out of the bogeyman-under-the-bed experience is to actually look under the bed—even when you're terrified—to confirm that the bogeyman is not actually there. Otherwise, the fear will continue. The goal of DBT is management of affect rather than management of thoughts.

One study examining well-trained cognitive therapists found a negative correlation between the frequency of therapist comments about patients' cognitive processes and the quality of the therapeutic alliance (Castonguay, et al., 1996). While thoughts are frequently a therapeutic focus because they are the most easily manipulated in conversational psychotherapies, DBT proposes that, though cognitive reframing is a minor rather than a major intervention, it is worthy of application with most mental disorders. We nevertheless turn our attention to DBT-style cognitive interventions and note how such reframing of thoughts can occur while minimizing the effects of invalidation.

DBT-Style Cognitive Reframing

DBT assumes the primacy of emotion rather than cognition in generating and sustaining acute mental disorders. Rather than cognitive distortions establishing high emotional arousal, DBT assumes the reverse. Having high emotional arousal (caused by the psychological, neuroanatomic, and neurochemical processes outlined in chapter 3), the person searches for explanations of their high arousal. "I must be unlovable, since I feel that everyone rejects me" is a response to feelings of strong inadequacy and dependency spawned by the pathogenic factors previously reviewed.

The following clinical dialogue illustrates how a DBT therapist deals with cognitive issues in therapy.

Patient: My mother told me I was a failure, most of my girlfriends told me I was a failure, and now my wife is telling me I'm a failure, too. No wonder I feel like a failure.

DBTherapist: I'd feel like that, too, if I focused on all those negative messages from others.

Patient: You'd feel like a failure?

DBTherapist: Yes, I'd feel like a failure if I started collecting all the instances where people were mean and angry with me.

Patient: But my mother was constantly critical. She never had a good word to say to me.

DBTherapist: Yes, I've heard your previous disclosures about how abusive and rejecting your mother was to you. I'd feel rejected too.

Patient: Listen, Doc, you're not making me feel any better here. You're telling me you would feel the same way I do.

DBTherapist: Exactly, I'm telling you that your feelings are right. You feel rejected when someone hurts you. I'd feel rejected if someone hurt me. That's normal.

Patient: So what am I supposed to do with all these feelings of inadequacy and failure?

DBTherapist: Can you accept them for what they are? They're normal responses to rejection amplified by the fact that you had a crappy relationship with your mother, someone you reasonably expected to be loving and supportive.

Patient: My mother really was crappy to me.

DBTherapist: Yes, she was.

Patient:	But I still hurt. It's not just about my mother. I could let that go, but it keeps happening. My wife is telling me that I'm lazy and that she shouldn't have married me. We've been in marriage counseling for practically as long as we've been married, and nothing has helped.
DBTherapist:	You said you could let go of your feelings about your relationship with your mom. Instead, for just this moment, can you really get into those feelings?
Patient:	Of my mom hurting me?
DBTherapist:	Yes, of your mom hurting you. Describe the hurt. You've already told me about the events, about what caused the hurt. Now describe the hurt rather than the reasons.
Patient:	I felt like it was my fault. If I'd been good enough, she'd love me. I wanted to be loved so badly—I wanted to please her.
DBTherapist:	Stick with wanting to be loved.
Patient:	(Cries)
DBTherapist:	Stick with the sadness for just a few seconds with me. I'd feel sad too. It's okay to cry.

Rather than telling the patient that they are wrong for having the thoughts they have, DBT suggests that we help to explain to the patient why it is totally understandable and reasonable that they have developed the thoughts they have, given their strong emotionality and history of dialectic failures. We suggest to them that their thoughts are reasonable conclusions, given their history, experience, and emotional pain. We also suggest to them that modification of certain thoughts can decrease their emotional suffering.

The dialectic conflict here is between emotion-focused and solution-focused coping. While their thoughts may be reasonable conclusions, given the emotional data that has been torturing them for long periods of time, it hurts them. The reason to modify the thoughts is not because they are wrong but because those very thoughts hurt them. This is not invalidating and in fact offers the suffering individual the opportunity to decrease rather than increase pain. It offers understanding without approval of their issues, another important dialectic conflict that the therapist is charged with helping the patient to navigate.

Let's continue with the same therapeutic dialogue to illustrate how the acceptance versus approval issue is put into practice in therapy.

Patient: It's been a long time since anyone made me cry.

DBTherapist: Made you cry?

Patient: Well, you know what I mean. A long time since I've cried in front of anybody.

DBTherapist: I'm glad you trust me enough to do that in front of me.

Patient: But I'm not sure how getting into my feelings about my mother is really going to help me in my marriage.

DBTherapist: You've been telling me that your feelings of failure as a person started with your mother. Then others, now including your wife, have brought on those same feelings.

Patient: (Nods yes)

DBTherapist: Can you accept that feeling sad and lousy when people criticize you is normal and even healthy, even though you don't like it?

Patient: I guess so. Are you telling me just to tough it out?

DBTherapist: No, I'm telling you to allow yourself to have the feelings you have, to notice them and experience them, *before* you try to change the situations that are prompting them.

Patient: But I know that I feel lousy.

DBTherapist: You told me you don't allow yourself to cry in front of others. This includes your wife?

Patient: (tears up again) Yeah.

Table 4 shows a comparison of traditional cognitive behavioral reframing and DBT-style reframing to cognitions. Note how DBT-informed reframing connects the thought process to underlying affect, thus providing validation through demonstrating to the patient that the therapist understands the foundation for the thought process. DBT attempts to stay closer to the affect generating the thoughts rather than attacking the thought process itself.

Table 4: Comparison of CBT and DBT Cognitive Reframing Strategies		
Dysfunctional Thought	CBT-Style Reframing	DBT-Style Reframing
Everyone must love me, or I'll feel horrible.	It is impossible for everyone to love anyone. Rejection and disapproval are a part of life. Having just a few people love you is more important than striving for the impossible goal of having uniform and unending love from everyone you encounter.	Of course you want everyone to love you. That would increase your sense of safety and security. We all want that. You've felt rejected so often, and it hurts so much, desiring universal approval would go a long way toward reducing your pain. But it hurts you to want this love because it sets you up for disappointment.
Negative feelings are bad and destructive. I should avoid them at all costs.	Negative feelings like sadness and disappointment are a part of life. You can't avoid them, so you might as well accept them as normal aspects of human living. You can't have the good without the bad.	You're right. Negative feelings like sadness and disappointment hurt badly. We all want to avoid them. No one has found an acceptable way to throw out the bad feelings, and trying puts tremendous pressure on you.
Others don't approve of my feelings. I shouldn't feel the way I do.	Seeking others' approval makes you dependent on others for your happiness. Values and opinions vary so greatly from person to person, seeking their approval will lead to frustration and disappointment. Revise your "should" rules and you'll feel better. Say to yourself, "It would be nice if others approve, but I can't expect others will always agree with me."	Of course you seek the approval of others for the feelings you have. Most of us do so. We want to be affirmed—this is natural. But when you begin to negate your feelings because the approval you want doesn't come, it makes you feel bad. Your feelings are yours, and just because others don't have the same feeling does not mean that your feeling is wrong.

Dysfunctional Thought	CBT-Style Reframing	DBT-Style Reframing
The world is a very dangerous place. People can be cruel and hurtful. I need to avoid them.	The world is neither dangerous or supportive. It is neutral. Sometimes we get what we want, sometimes we don't. Sometimes people can be nice, sometimes hurtful. It depends on the situation. Avoiding others or stressful events deprives you of what possible good could come your way. So say to yourself instead, "The world is neutral. It is my job to avoid harm while seeking pleasure. I deserve as much as is available to me."	You're right. The world can be a dangerous place, and your depression and anxiety are results of this danger. No one wants to feel that kind of hurt. I certainly don't. I try to avoid hurt, too. But you also feel lonely when you avoid people. It's a balancing act between avoiding hurt yet not feeling alone and afraid. Compromises must be made between being safe and being happy. And that is hard for all of us.
I must be bad because I frequently don't get what I want. There is something wrong with me.	Just because you don't get what you want does not mean that you're bad. You may be frustrated, but that doesn't mean that you're bad. It may be the tools and strategies you are using that keep you from accomplishing your goals, and that doesn't mean that there is anything fundamentally wrong with you. We just need to improve your tools and strategies. Then you will more frequently accomplish your objectives.	I can understand why you feel that there is something wrong with you. Your feelings are so intense and seemingly unending. You try so hard to change what's going on. But it hasn't yet worked. Most of us would feel bad, given what you've experienced. Blaming your self hurts, though. It adds to your pain rather than relieving it.

Dysfunctional Thought	CBT-Style Reframing	DBT-Style Reframing
I'll be humiliated in public if others see how vulnerable I feel.	Most people are so self-absorbed that they don't see or even try to see what you are experiencing. They are concerned with themselves. Why try to please people you don't even know? Focus on your own objectives, and stop worrying what others think and feel.	You feel vulnerable and concerned about others' judgments of you. Most of us want approval, and when we feel vulnerable this need increases. Of course you're anxious. Let's work at decreasing your sense of vulnerability, then others' judgments of you will be less important.
I'm hopeless, and I'll never get well.	Nobody is hopeless. There is tremendous evidence that (depression, phobias, PTSD, BPD, bipolar, GAD. . .) is curable with the appropriate treatment strategy. There is hope. You can get better. Stick with our treatment plan and look for improvement in small increments.	Of course your hope is low. You have been feeling (depression, phobias, PTSD, BPD, bipolar, GAD. . .) for a long time. Most people with this problem feel just like you do. How could you feel any differently? What we will do together is change strategies so that different feelings occur.

The goal in cognitive behavioral therapy is to change dysfunctional thought processes. The goal in DBT is not simple agreement with the patient but rather assisting the patient is see how their underlying thought process is a natural consequence of their underlying strong emotional arousal. By connecting the thought process to the underlying emotional process, the therapist aids the patient to understand their emotion-focused rather than solution-focused strategies. The patient is not wrong in having the thoughts they have—these thoughts are predictable outcomes of strong affect. However, they lead to strategies that increase rather than decrease emotional pain. DBT strategies work on changing the cognitive schemas, rather than because of logic, in order to reduce functional outcomes of pain. Validation of emotion and affect allows the patient to accept new ways of coping without increasing underlying feelings of inadequacy.

Major Emphasis on Affect Rather than Cognitions

While the DBT therapist may focus on thoughts that increase emotional pain in their patients, this is not the primary focus of treatment. Dialectic conflict (compromise formations, in Freud's language) results in heightened emotional arousal. A primary focus of DBT is assisting the patient to increase emotion management. The major emphasis is on self-management of affect rather than cognitions. Affect self-management can occur through acceptance-based technologies such as mindfulness skills (more fully explored in chapter 5) or through dialectical analysis, which we'll discuss next.

DIALECTIC FAILURES CONTRIBUTE TO HIGH AROUSAL AND LOW PROBLEM SOLVING

Dialectics is the art of logical discussion, but unlike cognitive behavioral strategies, the focus is not on logic at all but on dialogue. The DBT therapist develops a dialogue about meaning and purpose in life. The dialogue centers on the fundamental nature of reality, which involves thesis and antithesis, balance and imbalance. Each imbalance offers an opportunity for rebalance (Linehan, 1993b). Psychological dialectics involve conflict and opposition (compatible with psychodynamic theory), as the needs and desires of the person are frequently in conflict with the demand characteristics and contingencies of the environment at the moment.

Let's take one last example from our unhappily married man who had an emotionally abusive relationship with his mother and subsequent repetitive failure experiences with women.

Patient: I don't know what I'm doing wrong. I try so hard to please my wife, but nothing works.

DBTherapist: Remember how we discussed your fear of disapproval? How your horrible experiences with your mother made you fearful of doing the wrong thing?

Patient: Yeah.

DBTherapist: That fear of disapproval is controlling you. You don't want to disappoint your wife, so you do as little as possible. You're behaviorally and emotionally paralyzed. It makes you passive.

Patient: My wife says I'm more than passive. She says I'm unavailable.

DBTherapist: Perhaps because you're paralyzed?

Patient: I'm afraid of disappointing her.

DBTherapist: How often do you take risks in the relationship? When do you really do what your heart tells you to do?

Patient: Probably never.

DBTherapist: So you have a dialectic going on here. On the one hand, you have a sincere desire to please your wife. On the other hand, you have a deep fear of doing anything that will increase conflict. You want to be absolutely safe, but you also want to have a great marriage. You can't have both.

Patient: There you go with that compromise stuff again!

DBTherapist: You don't see it?

Patient: Yeah, I see it. I just don't like it. I don't like the idea that I have to give up my safety in order to have a good relationship. I don't like conflict. In fact, I hate it. You're right, it brings up all those feelings I had with my mom. I know Shirley is not my mom, but the feelings are the same.

DBTherapist: You're trading safety for satisfaction in your marriage.

Patient: Yeah, and I don't like the compromise I've been making.

DBTherapist: I wouldn't either. It's a choice, but a hard one in face of all that fear.

DBT therapy is thus unlike traditional cognitive or behavioral approaches in that attention to affect is not simply symptom focused but involves recognition of the substantial strain being placed on the patient to form compromises between competing and frequently contradictory demands of the environment and personal wishes and wants.

How do dialectic issues increase high arousal? As discussed in chapter 3, patients who present for treatment have powerful and frequently early experiences of emotional pain. Issues of attachment primarily occur in early infancy. Trauma, loss, and emotional invalidation can occur throughout the life cycle. Once these psychological issues occur, the person is predisposed toward high emotional arousal. Neurological and neurotransmitter neural net firings then take over, sustaining high emotional arousal over long periods of time. The central dialectic between one's own experience and comparison with the experience of others (who are fortunate not to have the attachment, trauma, or loss experience, or genetic predisposition toward negative kindling effects) results in conflict. "I don't seem to experience the world in the same way as others who are happy and carefree" is a frequently unarticulated but fundamental conclusion of the person in chronic emotional pain. This dialectic conflict between self-experience and comparison with others increases arousal as the patient blames themselves (as inadequate, faulty, depraved, or defective) for the very problems they wish to solve. Shame, anxiety, fear, and anger frequently result from this dialectic, adding additional emotional load to the problems these people face. The environment itself (healthy others) becomes invalidating as the person compares their own experience to the perceived experience of others. One result of this dialectic is that the patient is less likely to use reward rather than punishment in facing life's difficulties. The self-hatred or self-blame following failure to achieve goals results in this self-punitive response, further increasing already high emotional arousal.

Over time, the self-invalidation (comparison of others' level of comfort with one's own lack of such comfort) leads to invalidation of emotional experience itself. "I shouldn't be feeling what I'm feeling, since others aren't feeling this way." Distrust of one's own emotional experience and looking to others (or to the environment) to define what one *should* be feeling is inherently invalidating. The inherently unrealistic goal of having oneself feel what others feel (or what one perceives others feel) results in increased emotional arousal.

Rather than a cognitive focus, the DBT therapist targets the high sensitivity to emotional stimuli resulting in emotional vulnerability, in order to decrease emotional intensity, speed return to emotional baseline, and decrease need for emotional avoidance (Linehan, 1993b). The DBT therapist increases solution-focused coping and decreases emotion-focused coping that fails to recognize the role of dialectic failure in our patient's lives.

According to Linehan (1993b), the process is for the DBT therapist to increase emotion modulation abilities. This involves assisting the patient to more effectively navigate dialectic conflict, inhibit behavior related to strong affect (decrease mood-dependent behavior), self-regulate physiological arousal associated with strong emotionality, and organize one's self for strategic behavior (solution-focused coping).

Problem solving is difficult with high emotionality. The role of the DBT therapist is to compare the dialectics of the treatment process itself (see chapter 7), involving movement along the dimensions of skill enhancement versus self-acceptance, problem solving versus problem acceptance, and affect regulation versus affect tolerance, to the dialectics of the patient's specific emotional disorder (see chapter 6).

SUMMARY OF DIALECTIC THERAPEUTIC TARGETS

Table 5 summarizes the general issues to which the DBT therapist attends. The general therapeutic goals with all acute mental disorders are to reduce emotional arousal by assisting the patient to shift attention to new cues, to refocus between emotion-focused and solution-focused coping, and to reduce emotional escape and avoidance behaviors. Below are general DBT strategies independent of diagnosis. In chapters 6 and 7 we will deal with interventions and dialectic conflict depending on the specific mental disorder with which the patient presents.

Table 5: Summary of DBT General Strategies	
Pathotopology	**DBT Strategies**
High emotional arousal	Identify and label affect.
	Mindfulness (acceptance).
	Stress-management and self-soothing techniques. Redeploy attention to external rather than internal cues.
	Redeploy problem solving to long-term objectives.
Slow return to emotional baseline	Shift attention between affect, cognition, physiology, behavior, and environment.
	Decrease mood-dependent behaviors.
	Reduce arousal through stress management.
	Identify secondary emotional reactions and reframe.
Emotional sensitivity	Mindfulness (acceptance).
	Redirect to solution-focused strategies.
	Move between short-term and long-term objectives.
Hypervigilance	Reduce avoidance and escape strategies.
	Cognitive reframing.
	Attend to safety cues.
Emotional avoidance and escape	Exposure (acceptance).
	Identify and label affect.
	Mindfulness (acceptance).
	Reduce mood-dependent behavior.
	Teach emotion regulation and distress tolerance skills.
	Coach application of skills to daily living (generalization).
	Increase solution-focused coping.

Chapter Summary

Emotional sensitivity (defined as high emotional arousal, slow return to emotional baseline, and hypervigilance to threat cues) leads to emotional avoidance or escape. Such avoidance or escape replaces emotion regulation activities. Under high emotional arousal, patients have a difficult time shifting their strategies from being self-focused to being environment-focused, from being emotion-focused to being solution-focused, or from being mood-dependent to being strategic about their long-term goals and wants. DBT attempts to undo this process through emotional exposure. Acceptance of emotions and the willingness to experience them demands that the therapist focus on management of affect rather than cognitions. DBT assumes that dialectic failures, defined as the unwillingness to form compromises between competing and contradictory wants and demands, decreases problem solving and increases emotional arousal over the long term.

CHAPTER 5

Dialectic Psychotherapy: Balancing Acceptance with Change

In the preceding chapter we reviewed how the experience and process of acute mental disorders (pathotopology) leads to dialectic conflict as the patient compares their own experience to the experience of others or their own experience to desired experience. Self-invalidation of their own emotional responses results. Dialectic psychotherapy's goal is to help patients make conscious and strategic decisions about navigating the dialectic conflicts as they arise. By articulating the conflicts and normalizing their occurrence and consequences, invalidation of affect is decreased and the patient is better prepared to respond to the multifactorial nature of human problem solving. In this chapter we focus on the general dialectic of the psychotherapy process itself, balancing acceptance of emotional problems and emotional pain with strategies to change them.

DIALECTICS OF THE PSYCHOTHERAPY RELATIONSHIP

The process of psychotherapy itself can be viewed as a dialectic between self-reliance (independence) and the need for assistance (dependence). Patients entering therapy frequently feel badly that they have not been able to solve their own problems by themselves. Placing oneself in the care of another person (a stranger), even a professional, can challenge the patient's sense of self-esteem and their need to view themselves as independently adequate. The DBT therapist openly acknowledges the dialectic conflict between independence and dependence, and the introductory conflict of seeking help can thus frequently be the first opportunity to discuss the role of dialectics in life (compromises between competing and frequently contradictory wants and needs). The assumption of DBT is that skillful dialectic problem solving involves shifting strategies, sometimes meeting the demands of one end of the polemic and at other times sacrificing those demands and meeting the needs and wants of the opposite end of the polemic. Recognizing one's limitations and taking action to resolve those very limitations (help-seeking behavior) is thus a strength since it recognizes the long-term goal of improving one's independence while simultaneously engaging in dependent behavior in order to move closer to independence. Seeking psychotherapy increases vulnerability through the admission of inadequacy while decreasing the sense of threat that comes through anticipation of continued emotional pain due to stasis. Getting help from a professional is also the triumph of hope over hopelessness, another dialectic frequently seen in acute mental disorders. This dynamic presents an opportunity for the DBT therapist to validate the patient, affirming that even establishing the first appointment indicates the strength of the patient to be able to skillfully navigate the dialectics of daily living.

Meta-analysis of therapist effects in psychotherapy outcome studies indicate consistent and robust effects, anywhere from 5 to 9 percent of the total variance in patient outcome, are determined by the characteristics of the therapist rather than the therapeutic interventions themselves (Crits-Christoph et al., 1991). An analysis of thirty years of empirical research on psychotherapy effectiveness suggests that the emerging therapeutic relationship between patient and therapist is a more powerful predictor of success than is the technique or school of psychology deployed by the therapist (Henry, 1998). While DBT invites the therapist to attend to special aspects of the patient's psychology (affect arousal, dialectics, varying attention deployment between self and environment, exposure to affect, and acceptance), certainly the outcome studies are just as powerfully conclusive that the factors of attentiveness, attitude, stance, and empathy of the therapist, independent of their techniques and interventions, are critical (Luborsky et al., 1986). The DBT therapist must show warmth, understanding, tolerance, and acceptance of the patient and the compromises they make along their dialectic journeys in life. The DBT therapist accepts the patient, understanding the homeostasis of competing dynamics. The DBT therapist communicates this understanding directly and unambiguously to the patient rather than relying upon the patient's observational skills to discern such acceptance and understanding.

The high emotional arousal experienced during acute mental disorders is painful. The DBT therapist must thus be nurturing, supportive, and emotionally available. Therapists are trained to identify problems. I must admit that I am more comfortable when a patient brings to the table a variety of problems to be addressed, since this validates my role as helper. However, another dialectic of the psychotherapy relationship is the need to balance focus on problems versus focus on strengths. The patient in acute emotional distress is already focusing on deficits and difficulties, frequently to the exclusion of attention to strengths and capabilities. The DBT therapist can unintentionally reinforce this depression-causing focus on inadequacy. It is the responsibility of the DBT therapist, not the patient, to attend to the dialectic of strengths versus limitations and to do so in a manner that recognizes the role of invalidation of affect. The feelings of the patient should never be disputed. The patient's feelings are always correct approximations to understanding their world as experienced. Rather than negating affect, the DBT therapist helps the patient to understand the genesis of their current feelings and assists them to shift their attention to other dialectics where strengths and skills are evident.

The dialectics of the psychotherapy relationship are thus no different from the dialectic analysis employed to solve specific issues presented by the patient for resolution. The role of the therapist is to identify opposites and find the truth and wisdom involved in both extremes along polemics. In table 6 are frequent dialectics of the therapy relationship (Linehan, 1993b) to which the DBT therapist attends.

Table 6: Dialectics of the Psychotherapy Relationship		
Acceptance	◄———————►	Change
Flexibility	◄———————►	Stability
Nurturing	◄———————►	Challenging
Skills and capabilities	◄———————►	Limitations and deficits
Problem acceptance	◄———————►	Problem solving
Affect regulation	◄———————►	Affect tolerance
Independence	◄———————►	Dependence
Transparency	◄———————►	Privacy
Trust	◄———————►	Suspicion
Watching	◄———————►	Participating
Focus on self	◄———————►	Focus on environment
Contemplation	◄———————►	Action

The dialectic of acceptance versus change is perhaps the most difficult for the DBT therapist to adequately implement. The therapist must simultaneously accept the patient just as they are in the moment as well as identify the changes that must occur in order for the patient to achieve their objectives. Acceptance involves understanding the dynamics and needs of the patient, including the useful role their defenses are serving for them, without approval of those defenses or absolute approval of the needs. The role of the therapist is to identify other needs and wants that are compromised by the current synthesis of competing urges, thus introducing the need for change. The therapist must move along the acceptance and change dimension, just as they invite the patient to do so. Let's look at a clinical vignette to see how this plays out in psychotherapy

This woman is a thirty-eight-year-old who lives with her mother and has never lived on her own. While she works part-time, her mother basically supports her. She enters therapy with the chief complaints of depression, lack of initiative, low self-esteem, and boredom.

Patient: My mom does her best. I know she cares, and she is trying to put up with me. But she keeps reminding me that I'm not doing anything with my life. I'm so tired of being reminded that I'm not living up to my potential.

DBTherapist: Tell me why it's tiresome to have your mom remind you of your potential.

Patient: Well, of course she's right. I mean I already know that I'm bright and capable of supporting myself. I'm scared of going out on my own. I haven't made a new friend since high school, and I'm afraid if I get a good-paying job mom will ask me to move. I imagine being miserably lonely if I had to live on my own. And what if she's wrong? What if I'm not as capable as everyone tells me I am? What if I get a job, have to move, then fail miserably? I'd be out on the street, proving to everyone that I was right all along—I'm incompetent. I get anxious just thinking about it.

DBTherapist: So you've told me that you're bored out of your head living with your mom, but you're terrified of risking the security you have by testing your capabilities. You're sacrificing potential happiness for security.

Patient: When you put it like that, it sounds even worse. My mom would hate me if she thought I was making a choice.

DBTherapist: Aren't you making a choice?

Patient: It doesn't feel like a choice. It feels like terror versus depression.

DBTherapist: Absolutely a choice about emotions.

Patient: I'm getting anxious again.

DBTherapist: Can you allow yourself to stick with the anxiety, just for a few moments?

Patient: If I have to. (*Pause*)

DBTherapist: Do you feel overwhelmed?

Patient: No, but I don't feel comfortable either.

DBTherapist: Of course you don't. Thinking about failure and disappointing others naturally leads to anxiety.

Patient: What if it doesn't go away? What if, like my depression, this anxiety stays for years?

DBTherapist: It won't. The depression has stayed for years because of the compromise you've been making, sacrificing happiness for safety. I just wonder what would happen if you allowed yourself to experience some of the anxiety, to compromise more in the direction of risk and give up just a little bit of that safety you've given yourself all these years.

Patient: That's what you think I should do?

DBTherapist: No. I think you should identify what is really important to you. What would give you the inspiration to get up in the mornings actually looking forward to your day rather than dreading it?

Patient: I've told you, I don't have any energy.

DBTherapist: Don't you think the lack of energy is related to how you've narrowed your life, depriving yourself of experiences in order to maintain the safety your mother provides to you?

Patient: (*Tearful*) I just have no confidence.

DBTherapist: It's okay that this is sad. I don't think you need a lot of confidence right now. You need to focus on your wants and desires. Right now, there doesn't seem to be anything in your life that has the pull to affect your depression.

Patient: I don't let myself want anything because then I'd have to make a choice between safety and happiness.

DBTherapist: Right.

Validation

The therapist nurtures the patient by offering compassion, understanding, and support. A major implementation of support is to validate the patient. We tell them that their behavior and feelings make sense. If the DBT therapist can't identify how the patient's behavior and feelings make sense, then they have not adequately understood the patient's dialectic conflicts. The therapist must broaden their knowledge of the patient's needs and history in order to identify what needs are being fulfilled by their current behavior. Behavior and feelings are not random, and it is the therapist's skills and observational powers (not only the patient's) that must be deployed in order to identify the order that the patient is attempting to create out of internal chaos. Something in the current environment, even if it's internal thoughts or anticipations, is sustaining the patient's behavior.

Transparency

Psychotherapy involves asking very personal questions, questions that many patients have never had asked of them even by their most intimate family members, such as their mothers, spouses, or romantic partners. Patients may never have asked these questions of themselves. A patient in acute emotional pain may feel quite vulnerable allowing anyone else, including the therapist, to see these internal thoughts and emotions. Their sense of privacy and the intactness of their psychological boundaries can feel invaded. Being so transparent to another person can be threatening, so the DBT therapist respects the dialectic of transparency versus privacy by acknowledging the demands being placed on the patient and how difficult such demands can be. By acknowledging the stressor, the therapist is accomplishing several therapeutic goals. First, they are increasing their validation and understanding of the patient. Second, they are modeling transparency for the patient, a critical dimension of most intimate interpersonal relationships. Third, they are helping the patient to identify and label their feelings (the threat of being exposed). Fourth, they are encouraging the patient to move along the dialectic by acknowledging the difficulty but continuing to ask the intrusive questions anyway. The demand characteristics of the psychotherapy relationship itself and the therapist's persistence in asking questions while acknowledging the potential pain this causes is frequently sufficient support for the patient to become increasingly transparent with the therapist.

Patient: I've never done this before. In our first visit you said we would review history and set a treatment plan, which we did. Now you're not holding pen and paper in front of you, and I'm afraid you have some sort of expectations of me.

DBTherapist: Coming here was hard today?

Patient: Yes. I'm afraid of what might come up.

DBTherapist: I don't blame you. You don't know me, and you've never been in psychotherapy before.

Patient: What do we do now?

By simply acknowledging the anxiety, the patient is ready to move on and the probability of resistance is lowered.

Providing Nurturance vs. Challenging

The dialogue also provides an example of providing nurturance while simultaneously challenging the patient. By acknowledging the dialectic, the therapist is validating the suspicions of the patient while building trust through validating the threat. DBT interventions thus take into account the dialectics and move from one position on the polemic to another. Since the dialectics are operating simultaneously and are frequently incompatible with one another (trust and transparency go together, but suspiciousness and being challenged can conflict with the development of trust and transparency), the therapist must remain sensitive to their relative value to the patient and the urgency the patient feels to have each set of needs met in the current moment. By requesting change, challenging, and requesting action only when the patient's sense of safety and integrity are sufficiently intact in the moment, the DBT therapist is more likely to assist the patient to move in spite of resistance. Interventions are thus matched to the patient's strengths, and both verbal and behavioral tasks the therapist presents are limited to those the patient is likely to skillfully accomplish. In behavioral terms, the therapist uses successive approximations and shaping (small goals leading to a larger purpose) so that the patient has progressive successes in treatment.

Patient: I feel so ashamed talking about my sex life with a man.

DBTherapist: Tell me about the shame, and we'll return to the sexual issues in a moment.

Patient: I'm ashamed that I've had so many partners and about the dominance thing.

DBTherapist: Those are the sexual issues, but I want you to tell me about the shame that those topics bring up.

Patient: I'm ashamed that normal people are supposed to seek romance and commitment, and those things don't seem to be as important to me.

DBTherapist: You're ashamed that you not just like everybody else?

Patient: In the sexual area, yes. I'm also afraid that if any of this stuff got out, my career would be ruined.

DBTherapist: Most of us have secrets of some sort. I want to remind you about the agreement you signed. One of the most valuable reasons to have such a thing as a psychologist is that normal rules of gossip are forbidden. I will never share anything you tell me with anyone without your permission, unless it involves child abuse or danger, which the law compels me to report.

Patient: I know, but even having you know my secrets makes me feel shameful.

DBTherapist: You've never told anyone about these sexual issues?

Patient: No one. The only people who know are the strangers that I act out these weird needs with, and even then we don't talk about it—we just do it.

DBTherapist: Then I feel privileged indeed that you trusted me enough to make me be the first person you've discussed this with. Let's get back to the shame feelings . . .

The DBT therapist is thus sensitive to the dialectics of the therapy relationship itself. The therapist acknowledges the dialectics and consequent emotions they provoke and invites the patient to attend to these conflicts. The oppositional nature of those conflicts makes the patient's experience understandable, thus increasing the safety of the therapeutic relationship and offering a degree of freedom for the patient to make other (perhaps more adaptive) compromises.

BEHAVIOR AND AFFECT CHANGE VS. BEHAVIOR AND AFFECT ACCEPTANCE

Balancing acceptance with change strategies during the psychotherapy process is at the heart of how DBT differs from most other therapeutic approaches. Change and acceptance are opposites. With acceptance, we embrace that which exists. We don't attempt to struggle with it or change it. We don't necessarily approve of it, but the agony involved in disapproval is dissipated. We accept things as they are, for now.

Below is a brief therapeutic conversation where change and acceptance are explored.

Patient: I feel so guilty thinking this, let alone saying it. I sometimes wish my father would die in his sleep so I wouldn't have to take care of him any more.

DBTherapist: Guilty because you love him so?

Patient: Yes, and I know he would just be so blown away if he knew I had these feelings sometimes.

DBTherapist: Have you ever questioned exactly how important it is to you to take care of your father so well?

Patient: Never. He was so present and loving all during my childhood. He sacrificed for the entire family. You could see in all the family photographs how proud he was of me. There is not a day that goes by that I don't feel his love and devotion. That's why it's so disgusting that I would even have these thoughts about him dying so I can get off the hook for his care.

DBTherapist: You've accepted that his love for you and your love for him is worth all the effort and commitment.

Patient: I guess I haven't fully accepted it, or I wouldn't have these thoughts.

DBTherapist: How could you more fully accept this responsibility?

Patient: (*Pause*) I guess I just need to accept the inconvenience of the time commitment. I love my father. I could focus on that and accept that the hardships go along with the love.

DBTherapist: Acceptance is a process, and I can tell that you've been working on this one for a long time. I admire your devotion.

Dr. Linehan, during her presentation at a mindfulness workshop she conducted, created quite a stir among the primarily therapist audience when she announced the principle that everything is as it should be. She acknowledged that therapists in particular are bothered by such things as war, poverty, hunger, and injustices of all kinds. But the everything-is-as-it-should-be principle simply implies that war is understandable given politics as they now exist, that poverty is understandable given the greed and inefficiencies of government and culture, and that violence is a natural outcome of consequences that exist in cultures across the globe. We don't approve of or seek war, poverty, hunger, violence, or injustice. We do understand how these things come about, the obstacles to changing them, and how significant forces in the social order have an interest in sustaining them. Given our knowledge of how the world works, these consequences make sense. Everything is as it should be.

Acceptance of things that hurt us is difficult. It is difficult for a person who is being physically abused to accept that the only way out of the abuse is to lose the person who is abusing them. Change and acceptance are intimately connected. Acceptance is an acknowledgment of forces that we may not approve of and may wish didn't exist. Most of us would like to accomplish our objectives without sacrifice of any kind. We want change without acceptance. The role of the DBT therapist is to assist our patients to see the interconnectedness of acceptance and change. By accepting our emotional condition as it is in the moment, we are better prepared to engage in change. Unfortunately, everything is as it should be, so some things simply can't be changed. Acceptance of what can't be changed can paradoxically result in psychological change. At least the agony of struggle with reality as it is terminates.

The relationship between behavior and affect change is similar. Most of us would like our feelings to change without having to change our behavior, or we want our behavior to change without having to change our feelings. We know that, with many acute emotional disorders, the two systems of behavior and affect become disconnected. With high emotional arousal, behavior has less of an influence over our affect, and affect has less influence over behavior. This is especially true with depression, a frequent component of many major mental disorders that are chronic or acute. The role of the DBT therapist is to assist patients to overcome the behavioral inertia that their emotions have promoted through prompting, coaching, modeling, contracting, and support interventions. Helping the patient to redefine reinforcement contingencies and the relationship that their behavior may have upon their affect is thus a major focus of DBT.

MINDFULNESS AS EXPOSURE, DESENSITIZATION, AND ACCEPTANCE

Mindfulness is a simple yet complexly implemented intervention to decrease avoidance and escape responses. It's simple because it involves only three principles of attention: attending to only one thing at a time, adopting a nonjudgmental attitude, and describing from experience rather than through constructs or predefined categories. These simple notions are quite difficult to implement because they go against the grain of our typical observational processes. Most of us have been trained to multitask, to evaluate, and to categorize or analyze our observations simultaneously. To turn off the analytical skills that have been overlearned and the habitual parts of our observation process is quite difficult.

To nevertheless learn to precisely reorient our attention in a mindful way is a powerful strategy to decrease acute emotional disorders, as reviewed in chapter 2. Mindfulness can assist patients with several aspects of acute mental disorders. (Instructions for guiding your patients in mindfulness practice can be found in chapter 7.) Attention and concentration decrease with increased anxiety or depression, and mindfulness increases attention and concentration. Acute mental disorders predispose the individual to self-absorption; mindfulness increases attention to the environment. Acute mental disorders frequently involve a loss of attention to senses; mindfulness involves heightened sensual activity. The ability to shift attention away from thoughts and rumination is difficult with high emotional arousal; mindfulness is about turning the mind away from thoughts and to experience. Mindfulness is thus about increasing observational skills themselves, thus exposing the individual to their emotions (decreasing the avoidance and escape responses typically used in acute mental disorders). Mindfulness increases contact with the world in the moment, thus offering new environmental prompts to grow new emotions rather than focusing on old experiences that generated the negative affect. Mindfulness is thus about living life more experientially.

Teaching your patients how to be mindful can be easier and more effective if they understand the rationale for the practice. This rationale is to increase the scope and accuracy of attention, assist in shifting focus of attention, increase the effectiveness of the use of our senses in experiencing the world, become less ruminative and judgmental in our information acquisition, reduce the role of self-consciousness, decrease emotional escape and avoidance, and develop additional calm and inward peace by relinquishing aversion and attachment. Briefly reviewing some of the dramatic research findings in chapter 2 about the role of mindfulness in increasing pain tolerance, immune functioning, and longevity can increase the commitment and motivation of patients to engage in the necessary practice of mindfulness in their daily lives. Certainly an introduction should include the notion that all new skills feel weird or awkward in the beginning. Reminding them how it felt when they were first learning to ride a bicycle, play the piano, snow ski, touch-type, or drive a car can be helpful. In the beginning, each movement takes conscious effort and anxiety is higher than normal. Over time, the behaviors become natural and habitual as the skills are well learned. So too it is with mindfulness.

The role of the DBT therapist in teaching mindfulness to their patients is one of coaching, modeling, and shaping (as will be described further in chapter 7). The therapist can model mindfulness by taking an object in hand and beginning a verbal description of the object. You model using the senses rather than the intellect to describe the object. You can help them further by presenting the patient with a small bag full of objects and asking them to close their eyes and pull out one object from the bag. With their eyes closed, have them mindfully describe the object. This shaping intervention is to encourage them to use their senses (primarily touch) rather than simply naming the objects, to avoid evaluative labels ("I don't like the sharp edges; it feels yucky; I'm embarrassed to have my eyes closed"; etc.), and to sustain attention and description over time. The therapist coaches by providing gentle feedback to stay in the experiential mode rather than the rational (thinking) mode, to attend to one thing at a time, to sustain attention over time, and to increase involvement of the patient in the observational process.

Mindfulness can be so counterintuitive to the patient in acute emotional pain that encouraging outside reading as well as practice is helpful. My book *Depressed and Anxious* (2004), offers a rationale for mindfulness and a series of progressively demanding exercises to increase mindfulness skills. Also, the downloadable material (nhpubs.com/29064) includes instruction on mindfulness training. The therapist and patient together can assign homework exercises to practice between sessions and review the successes and obstacles the patient faced practicing the assignments during the next scheduled psychotherapy session. *The Miracle of Mindfulness* (Hanh, 1976) is an excellent bibliotherapy homework assignment.

Perhaps the most demanding aspect of teaching mindfulness to our patients is encouraging them to practice the exercise routinely. Frequent but gentle prompting is necessary. The skillful therapist can read Segal's book (*Mindfulness-Based Cognitive Therapy for Depression*, 2002) for excellent suggestions on how to gently and nonpunitively provide guidance on mindfulness, regardless of whether the goal is to prevent relapse to depression or not. Segal's language and style of presenting mindfulness are impressive. The patient can also be directed to Dr. Kabat-Zinn's mindfulness tapes and compact disks available from Stress Reduction CDs and Tapes, P.O. Box 547, Lexington, MA 02420. These audiotapes and CDs provide guided mindfulness practice the patient (and therapist) can use daily.

There is almost universal agreement in the literature that mindfulness cannot be effectively taught to patients unless the therapist practices mindfulness themselves on a regular basis. The struggle to incorporate yet another patient time demand cannot effectively be confronted by the therapist unless they themselves have mastered the routine of regular practice.

The process of engaging in mindfulness can serve several different functions. While mindfulness skills are generally treated in the literature as acceptance-based strategies, such skills can also serve as exposure and desensitization to strong affect.

Mindfulness as Exposure

While mindfulness is generally presented as a mode of "being" rather than "doing" (Segal et al., 2002) and as such is seen as effortless in the sense of being without a task or specific purpose, once mindfulness is placed on the emotions themselves the process serves as a form of exposure. The affect that has been avoided is experienced, and the experience is sustained over time. The result of such repeated and sustained exposure is that anticipatory anxiety surrounding experience of the emotion recedes. The secondary emotional reactions (emotional reactions to the initial affect), such as guilt, shame, anger, anxiety, frustration, and despondency decrease. Linehan (1993b, 1993c) describes these secondary emotional reactions as intensification of emotional arousal, prolonging the intensity and duration of emotional load on the patient. Mindfulness practice focused on emotions can decrease these secondary emotional reactions, decreasing both the intensity and duration of arousal.

As emotional intensity decreases, escape and avoidance of affect become increasingly unnecessary. Feelings no longer prompt a sense of urgency to escape, but can be attended to as useful sources of information. Mood-dependent behavior can decrease as arousal no longer interferes with information processing and problem-solving skills.

Mindfulness as Desensitization

Mindfulness can also be used as a more systematic form of desensitization. Having patients be mindful of their avoided affect, then mindful of pleasant sensations and memories, returning to mindfulness of the painful affect, then shifting to mindfulness of immediate sensations (such as breathing), then shifting back to mindfulness of the painful affect, and so forth, can serve as a form of emotional systematic desensitization. The result is decreased anticipatory avoidance and escape behaviors. Specific exercises for use of mindfulness as desensitization appear in Marra (2004). The role of the therapist is to coach and support the patient to tolerate the painful emotional affect for several minutes then support the patient to attend to pleasant stimuli. The therapist can verbally prompt attentional shifting back and forth between painful and pleasant experience, assisting the patient to both tolerate and sustain attention over increasingly lengthy periods of time. This serves to teach the patient to shift attention during intense affect, as well as to decrease fears of lingering and out-of-control affect once painful affect begins. It provides soothing within the context of emotional pain and teaches emotion regulation skills in vivo.

Mindfulness as Acceptance

For acute mental disorders, when emotional intensity is high and concentration is low, first training patients to be mindful of external events, objects, and processes (Marra, 2004) can be more tolerable than moving directly to mindfulness of self (the body, thoughts, and feelings). However, the goal is to eventually have the patient use their newly developed mindfulness skills to attend to their emotions. This is described as an acceptance-based strategy since the goal is letting go of aversion and attachment. The goal is no longer to hang on to positive experience and avoid negative experience. In fact, there is no specific goal with mindfulness. Letting go of goals, tasks, and effortfulness is central to the successful practice of mindfulness. No special state of emotion is sought; mindfulness is not relaxation. Instead, mindfulness of emotions is about accessing, understanding, experiencing, and describing what's there rather than changing what's there. Not being reactive to what is being attended to, the mindfulness meditator attempts to see and experience what is attended to rather than change it in any way. So the task, for example, would be to attend to the muscular tension involved in an anxiety reaction, to feel the location of this tension, its extent, how it's experienced, and the surrounding reactions of the body to the muscular tension. Unlike relaxation strategies, the goal is not to decrease the muscular tension but to notice and experience it. This results in a radical shift for most patients in acute emotional pain, because the relationship to pain is no longer to avoid and terminate but to experience and acknowledge. The abundance of psychic energy once needed to avoid and deny experience is no longer required.

Mindfulness as acceptance is thus about not trying to control our every experience but to control our attention itself (sustaining and intensifying attention through focus on sensations frequently ignored). The goal is no longer to attempt to think our way out of our feelings, but to feel fully. Mindfulness is about awareness and is characterized by gentleness, welcoming, curiosity, and a sense of adventure (Segal et al., 2002):

> So the issue is not learning how to switch thoughts off, but how best we can change the way we relate to them: seeing them as they are, simply, streams of thinking, events in the mind, rather than getting lost in them. (p. 134)

> The aim is not to prevent mind wandering but to become more intimate with how one's mind behaves. . . . If your mind wanders a hundred times, then simply bring it back a hundred times. . . . This approach is not about trying to suppress or control thoughts. (pp. 168–169)

With sensations of physical discomfort, the natural reaction to such discomfort is to tense or brace and push it away. Simply becoming aware of that tendency and bringing, as best we can, a friendly interest to it, and exploring it gently, provides a very useful practice. (p. 170)

Mindfulness approaches are not about thought control or substituting positive for negative images of the past, present, or future. Rather, they encourage people to allow these feelings of disappointment and regret to be there. (p. 189)

Note that the theme, which is never very far away from both attachment and aversion, is "wanting things to be different from how they are right now." By contrast, one of the first steps in dealing with our reaction to different mind states is simply to be present with them. . . . Learning that we can actually stop struggling and be present gives us the opportunity to see and relate to our circumstances with greater clarity and directness. With this insight comes the possibility of choosing behaviors that are more likely to deal skillfully with the situation before us . . ." (p. 202)

The point of mindfulness is to expand attention in a nonreactive way, without attachment or aversion. The goal is not relaxation or happiness but freedom from automatic reactions of the past. "The easiest way to relax is to stop trying to make things different" (Segal et al., 2002, p. 226). Mindfulness is about direct perception and observation, allowing new ways of navigating the world without habitual patterns of reacting.

Mindfulness as acceptance is about decreasing effort, strain, and goal orientedness. We accept that we need to understand and fully experience what is happening prior to making attempts to change what is experienced. Mindfulness is not strategic or purposeful. It is observation at its most elemental level. The research demonstrating robust improvement with mindfulness in patients experiencing a variety of emotional and medical problems suggests that mindfulness should be a central component of DBT treatment.

MEANING MAKING AS CHANGE AND AS ACCEPTANCE

The forgotten element in many behavioral strategies is meaning. In spite of the fact that behavioral technologies take full account of the role of reinforcement history and contingencies of behavior, the role of meaning in defining reinforcer effectiveness is absent. What makes complex human beings work hard to accomplish a purpose? What makes behavior difficult to extinguish? How do low-frequency consequences have such sustainable effects on human behavior?

Meaning, the interpretations and weight an individual places on certain events and processes, supplies the answer. When a child's sucker accidentally falls to the ground, it represents a loss, and the child hurts and cries. They know that the adult supervisor will not allow them to pick up the dirty sucker and continue to enjoy it. This causes sadness. The desire of the individual child (to suck the sucker) and the demands of the situation (to forgo the dirty sucker in spite of desire) create frustration and sadness. But the situation is temporary in that the frustrated child is distracted shortly after by other potential stimulations in the environment. Other equally reinforcing events occur or are promised, and the hurt dissipates.

Life can be less forgiving for an adult, who places greater weight on some reinforcers over others. Transient reinforcers (such as success at a game, interaction with a machine, obtaining a weekly paycheck, obtaining and enjoying a meal) pale in comparison to longer-term but more ambiguous reinforcers (to be seen as successful by society, feeling lovable, feeling safe and secure within the family system, feeling normal and like most others who are valued by the person). The long-term perceptions and needs of the person, which are total cognitive phenomena created over time by socialization experiences, will result in greater effort and emotional load on the person compared to the situational reinforcers that vary by circumstance and carry no long-term sense of meaning.

Meaningfulness of a reinforcer, more than its frequency and duration, better predicts emotional response and behavioral topography. Meaning predicts emotional intensity and duration and thus offers the best opportunity for clinicians to make substantial changes to an individual's suffering.

Meaning Making as Change

Assisting patients to identify, articulate, shift, and redefine meaning in their lives is thus among the most important interventions a clinician can make. Some theorists define this process as working with schemas (Blowers and O'Connor, 1995; Kraemer, 1992; Main, 1995), those general networks of ideas that provide overarching predictability and understandability to the world as we see it. A schema can involve ideas of safety, security, love, affiliation, success, permanence, survival, acceptability, goodness, spirituality, or any of a number of ideas of import to the person. The difference between a schema and an assumption is that an assumption has limited applicability across different situations, while a schema has far-reaching consequences across different situations. A patient assumes that the loss of approval of a specific individual matters and will result in hurt. However, this assumption is situation-specific. They do not necessarily assume that the loss of approval of the specific person will result in the loss of their lovability in general. A schema, on the other hand, might be that something in them makes them lovable to others, and that the loss of this attribute would result in their inability to loved by anybody. As you can see, the schema has perceived consequences across all situations. People will hurt more over the loss of lovability than they will from the loss of approval and love of a particular person.

Work with Values Rather than Thoughts

Working with our patients on meaning itself will thus have greater effect than working with their particular thoughts about a situation or event. Working with meaning creation is not that different for a therapist than working with cognitive reframing or reformulation. However, for the patient it can make all the difference in the world. Rather than working with their thoughts, you are working with their values. You work with what is important to them rather than what they happened to say about a particular situation in a particular moment.

While this shift in orientation may initially sound simplistic, it instead is profound both for the therapy interaction and for the material to be worked with. You don't listen for the assumptions the patient is making. You don't listen for errors in logic. You don't listen for cognitive distortions. Instead, you listen for needs, for wants, for how the patient's behavior is desiring something within dialectic conflict. You listen for conflict within chaos, and interpret the patient's behavior as compromise between conflicting wants and needs. As you look for needs rather than distortion, you'll more likely find different material that points toward frustrated meaning the patient seeks.

Paul is a thirty-three-year-old man with social anxiety disorder.

Patient:	. . . and then I had to wash my car before . . .
DBTherapist:	Wait a minute, Paul, you're giving me a rundown of how you spent your week and the pressure you felt to get everything done. But previously you told me how empty your life is, how you have no friends, and how ashamed you'd feel if others knew how friendless you were.
Patient:	Yeah.
DBTherapist:	Well, could you be trying to fill your life with activities so you don't feel your loneliness?
Patient:	(*Pause*) Yeah, but what am I supposed to do?
DBTherapist:	(*Pause*)
Patient:	Oh, you mean all the homework assignments you gave me to do? To attend some introductory social events? I thought

about it several times during the week, but there were all these other tasks I had to get done.

DBTherapist: Tasks that you were confident you could complete without anxiety. Things that kept you busy.

Patient: Okay, I know where you're going with this. I did what was comfortable for me rather than what was challenging.

DBTherapist: What do you think?

Patient: Of course you're right. I'm ashamed to go out by myself. Everyone will see that I'm alone. Everyone else goes with a friend, but I can't think of anybody to ask. If I only had one person I could go with, the situation would be totally different. I wouldn't feel so awkward.

DBTherapist: If you went alone, you'd have to experience your anxiety.

Patient: Yeah, I can't take the shame.

DBTherapist: The shame would hurt badly.

Patient: But you want me to do it anyway.

DBTherapist: How much do you want a social life?

Patient: More than anything I can think of. More than that stupid promotion I've been working my butt off to get.

DBTherapist: But not quite as much as you want to avoid the shame.

Patient: It's so hard.

DBTherapist: It is hard.

Patient: Avoiding the shame is important too.

DBTherapist: It's a compromise, avoiding shame versus having friends. Keeping busy avoids shame. Going out alone brings shame but increases the chances of making friends.

Patient: I'm not sure I can take the shame.

DBTherapist: But you already feel it. It's in the background, haunting you quietly but consistently.

Patient: Yes.

DBTherapist: So you're already taking it, right? Even without the behavior, even without going out, you're quietly experiencing the shame.

Patient: Yeah. I'm feeling it right now.

The shift, both for the therapist and the patient, is to move from short-term situations to long-term objectives. The therapist helps the patient to temporarily ignore the pain of in-the-moment frustrations and to compare many pains that have occurred over time with what they predict in terms of what is meaningful in general. Rather than disputing or arguing about assumptions, the role of the DBT therapist is to help the patient to identify the schemas that have been frustrated (to identify what is meaningful and what has lost meaning over time due to the anxiety and danger that frustrated situations have presented). This is a shift from specific to general, from thought to emotion, from reaction to need, and from immediate to epiphenomenal.

The reader may thus note another grand dialectic in DBT psychotherapy. On the one hand, through mindfulness we invite the patient to live in the world experientially rather than through preconceived notions and abstractions. In meaning making, we invite the reverse. With meaning making we invite the patient to return to their constructions of the world in very abstract ways and to identify the metacognitions that guide their activities through values and deeply held wants. Meaning making is the process of pointing to what is supremely important (through identification, articulation, extension, and even redefinition) to the person. This meaningfulness thus provides the point of reference to which the therapist returns in evaluating both the utility of behavior in specific situations and the general method or strategy to be deployed by the patient to accomplish the meaning.

Meaning making is difficult. Although self-help workbooks (Marra, 2004) attempt to take the patient through the process, this is where the skill of the therapist is most valuable in coaching the patient to persevere in using the simplistic, general formats offered in self-help manuals. The manual is the homework assignment between sessions, and within sessions the therapist asks probing questions both to broaden the patient's focus and to overcome a tendency to overlook interest and curiosity as unimportant. The therapist helps the patient to value activities and wants, to validate them, even as the patient tends to see their own desires and interests as puny and insignificant. The therapist coaches the patient to see their wants as real and important, as individualistic and not subject to popularity contests, and to pursue them with gusto and respect.

The very process of identifying meaning tends to engender change as the patient begins to recognize how their past experience and behavior are understandable attempts to resolve conflicting wants. The change in the patient is a shift from immediate experience to long-held (but perhaps unarticulated) values and needs. They feel less invalidated by their feelings because their feelings make sense in the newly and broadly focused context. Old behavior and old experience become understandable and fit within the new context. The insight is not about repressed memories or newly found (unconscious) urges but about making experience itself understandable through context (meaning).

Panic and meaning frequently go hand in hand, as seen in the following therapeutic dialogue.

Patient: My whole body became tense. I couldn't say a word to John. It was as if I were frozen in time. I thought I was going to have a panic attack.

DBTherapist: That's because you care so much about John, because your love for him is so meaningful to you.

Patient: I didn't think of that! I always think of my anxiety as a bad thing, as connected to my fear of failure. But you're right. My body was telling me how important John is to me. But why was I speechless?

DBTherapist: Did you expect John to give you those compliments?

Patient: Not on your life.

DBTherapist: So you were dumbfounded.

Patient: Yeah, I expect something bad from those I care about. So when something good, like compliments, comes along, I'm always surprised.

DBTherapist: So there is anxiety that this is a change. A change from what you expect.

Patient: And this time, for once, it was change the way I want it. I was getting what I have wanted for so long. I saw my body as my enemy, warning me that disaster was about to come again. But my body reacted exactly the same way when something good was happening.

DBTherapist: So your body reacts to change, not just to disaster.

This is meaning making as change, as the patient is able to increasingly recognize the map as opposed to the territory, to shift from focus on emotions to focus on solutions, to shift from focus on stressors to focus on satisfaction, and thus to shift from pain to focus on pain relief. It is "objectives effectiveness" (Linehan, 1993c) at its best.

Meaning Making as Acceptance

Meaning making can result in significant clinical change in patients or can result in "radical acceptance" (Linehan, 1993b, 1993c) of their situations as they are in the moment. The patient may find that they have been fighting urges and needs that need not be fought and that are entirely appropriate and even necessary aspects of being human. Without the need to deny or avoid these urges, the patient accepts their needs and desires and no longer struggles against them. The previous anticipatory anxiety, avoidance, and escape responses are no longer necessary. Instead of questioning the validity of the need, the patient can focus on the method or strategy to accomplish the need. This takes much less energy, is less emotionally invalidating, and results in less emotional conflict than prior to acceptance.

Meaning making is acceptance in that the patient learns the meaning of pain itself, that emotional pain defines and shapes meaning. This existential awareness prompts the individual to consider their emotions as useful and even essential aspects of their own humanity. Emotions become sources of guidance to be attended to rather than avoided. The patient recognizes the role of meaning in placing perspective on their experience. This brings to the forefront for the patient the universality of conflict and compromise and a normalization of suffering itself.

Acceptance of meaning and its role in providing perspective and valence will perhaps lead the patient to different conclusions than before (for example, that the trials of relationships are worth it, that the stressors of family and job are necessary evils that sustain larger purposes, and that frustration of goals is part and parcel of accomplishing the ultimate lifelong objectives the patient strives to achieve).

BEHAVIOR STRATEGIES INCREASE SOLUTION-FOCUSED COPING

DBT is dialectical; the dialectics are both theoretical foundations of treatment as well as practical treatment procedures themselves, since the dialectics shape the treatment focus and point to the transient issues to which both therapist and patient attend. DBT is also behavioral therapy that fosters desired changes in the patient. DBT is psychotherapy with a continuing flux of attention from the specific to the general, from emotion to cognition, from exposure to avoidance, from experience to ideas, from past to present, and from theoretical to practical. This latter emphasis on practicality is found in the behavioral strategies that prompt the patient to focus their thoughts on the effects of their behavior. Behavior strategies invite the patient to stop attending to their emotions and to emotion-focused coping and to analyze the potential consequences of their behavior in real-life situations. This results in more solution-focused coping, increases strategic behavior, and applies the DBT principle of skillful means, "doing what works" (Linehan, 1993c).

Dialectical issues in strategic behavior, taken from Marra (2004), are presented in table 7. Note that strategic behavior is not a unitary concept, in that the dialectics are not necessarily opposites. Strategic behavior is an attempt to apply wisdom (to increase the skillfulness of the problem-solving process by balancing our sense of knowing and doubting) to our everyday functioning. Strategic behavior skills involve use of behavior therapy principles to analyze prompts or antecedents (both external and internal), contingencies of reinforcement, and consequences of various potential actions or behaviors, and to compare the proposed effect (both short- and long-term) to our desired outcome. Performing such a self-analysis can be difficult, and the patient is reminded to attend to the sense of urgency or crisis that can make short-term goals seem inordinately important compared to longer-term (and typically more valued) goals. The behavior is wise in that the patient is prompted to compare the effects of their behavior to both short-term situational factors and meaningful objectives as seen from a distance.

Table 7: Dialectical Issues in Strategic Behavior		
Strategic focus	<————>	Wisdom focus
Attention to the moment	<————>	Attention to long-term objectives
Focus on the practical	<————>	Focus on values
Focus on self	<————>	Focus on others
Focus on techniques and procedures	<————>	Focus on ideas and ideals
Focus on knowledge and facts	<————>	Focus on doubts and feelings
Rational knowing	<————>	Intuitive knowing
"From the head"	<————>	"From the heart"
Confidence and pride	<————>	Humility and self-doubt
Behavioral focus	<————>	Emotional focus
Gets me what I want	<————>	Relinquishes what I want

The patient is also invited to attend to their own stimulus value, especially the dimension of emotional sensitivity and emotional disclosure. In acute mental disorders, patients typically either overreact emotionally (developing an urgent, expressive typology) or underreact emotionally (developing a guarded, flat affective typology). This emotional sensitivity and expressiveness may or may not have been present premorbidly and may or may not express underlying characterological features of the patient. Either way, the patient is instructed to take their current emotional transparency to others into account while generating their anticipations of others' reactions. The patient is instructed to attempt to see the situation from observing others' point of view and to compare their decision to express or withhold affect in any particular situation to their objectives. This can be emotionally validating for the patient, since it shifts the evaluative criteria away from whether their emotional intensity is right or wrong to whether the expression of the emotional intensity will help or hurt them in their attempt to obtain their interpersonal objectives.

The patient is invited to consider the powerful notion of mood-dependent behavior, in that their feelings can overly color their thought process in both specifying what their real goals are and determining the best methods to accomplish them. Having the patient attend to typical factors that increase emotional sensitivity over time (anxiety, alcohol or drug consumption, sleep deprivation, and emotionally provocative environments) and to purposefully moderate those variables helps to decrease emotional intensity.

The above issues, like many concepts in DBT, are complex. Patients need assistance breaking down complex situations into smaller steps and help in identifying relevant from irrelevant variables. The use of mnemonics, which help patients to remember key global variables in behavior or emotion analysis, is thus essential. Such mnemonics are provided in treatment manuals for borderline personality disorder in Linehan (1993c) and for depression and anxiety disorders in Marra (2004), and mnemonics appropriate for many acute disorders are provided in chapter 7. Use of behavior recording worksheets that similarly break down complex problem-solving processes into smaller and more manageable steps are also provided in such manuals for direct patient use. The therapist should be familiar with the intent and instructions of such forms prior to assisting patients in their use. Homework assignments between sessions thus prompt patients in the use of the behavior and coping skills, increasing the generalization of skills into the home environment and extending practice of new strategies beyond the hours of therapy.

The simple act of assigning worksheets to patients between sessions serves several functions. First, it emphasizes that verbal therapy alone will have less impact than repeated practice of the strategies discussed. Second, it helps the patient to understand that it is their behavior and coping process, not the therapist's, that results in most significant clinical gains. Third, it provides structure and prompting in new attentional strategies. Fourth, it provides repeated rote memorization of tools the patient can use, thus increasing the likelihood that they will use the new skills even when emotionally aroused. Fifth, it validates for the patient that these techniques and procedures are widely used therapeutic tools and not simply generated by the therapist to keep them busy. It increases hope that the tools can help them, increasing the probability that they will actually use them routinely. The overall effect is to increase solution-focused coping in the face of strong affect.

BALANCING ACCEPTANCE WITH CHANGE STRATEGIES

DBT encourages acceptance of emotions, conflicts, and situations as they are. DBT also encourages change of emotions, conflicts, and situations. Balancing acceptance with change strategies can be quite confusing to patients, who typically prefer to work only on changing their feelings or situations and who often actively dislike the notion of acceptance. The DBT therapist must thus provide the rationale, in-session practice, and repeated encouragement that acceptance can lead to change and that change can lead to acceptance.

Providing the patient with a phobia-based analogy can help. Most patients intuitively understand simple phobias, say of spiders. They understand that if they have a fear of spiders and stay away from spiders, that their fear is on hold and won't diminish with time. Show them a spider, and the fear (which has been in the background) immediately increases. The more successful the avoidance, the greater the fear. Add in one or two experiences of escape from spiders, and the fear becomes overwhelming. Add the presense of spiders in a safe environment, just close enough to see but not directly threatening, and the fear can slowly be reduced. Looking at the spiders is exposure, and the exposure results in acceptance of fear without external threat.

The DBT therapist is thus charged with balancing acceptance with change strategies in the psychotherapeutic process. While patients may wish to discuss their most immediate stressors during the entire therapy hour, it is the therapist's intervention (not the patient's) to nevertheless shift the focus of attention from the patient's immediate concerns to the DBT treatment plan, which demands periodic attention to mindfulness, meaning making, emotion regulation, dialectic analysis, distress tolerance, and strategic behavior. While the patient must ultimately identify their objectives in treatment, if the pathotopology involves high emotional arousal, slow return to emotional baseline, and hypervigilance for threat, then the treatment plan must account for episodic attention to each of the various elements of DBT. Otherwise the patient will be satisfied with your short-term attention to their emotions, but be dissatisfied with their long-term progress in treatment. The therapist who does not shift from one component of treatment to the other will accurately be perceived as understanding and validating but ultimately ineffective.

Chapter Summary

DBT involves balancing efforts to change with efforts toward acceptance. Frequently, change can't occur without acceptance. The DBT therapist provides a foundation of nurturance, acceptance, trust, and self-focus while slowly moving the patient toward emotional challenge, problem solving, and coaching toward behavioral action. The therapist is sensitive to issues of boundary violations, the terror of transparency, and the risks of dependence by acknowledging them openly as issues that can impede therapeutic progress while validating their weight and potency in the moment. Mindfulness provides the strategy for both acceptance and change. Meaning making provides the map for both acceptance and change. Strategic behavior skills provide the means for change.

CHAPTER 6

DBT: Not Just for Borderlines Anymore

Linehan (1993b) originally developed DBT for the treatment of borderline personality disorder. However, the theory of DBT is comprehensive and represents a global school of psychotherapy (see chapter 1), pathogenesis (chapter 2), and pathotopology (chapter 3). Given the topology of many acute mental disorders, which suggest the single factor of emotionality as critical in both genesis and treatment, DBT is applicable to a variety of classes of emotional disorders. In this chapter we will review the typical dialectics with the anxiety, mood, impulse-control, addictive, eating, and personality disorders. This review will show how DBT can be effectively used with most acute mental disorders, almost regardless of diagnosis.

The DBT therapist is keenly aware that many mental disorders become chronic or acute precisely because of comorbidity. There is not just one problem going on, there are many. Frequently, patients with intense emotional arousal, slow return to emotional baseline, and hypervigilance to threat cues develop chronic and unabating symptoms because they have characterological issues. Such issues may not reach the clinical severity to warrant an axis II diagnosis or may be so "mixed" between different personality disorders that almost any diagnosis would be equally valid. DBT thus does not simply attend to chief complaints or primary symptoms. It attends both to symptoms that cause immediate distress to patients and to identifying and targeting issues that are long-term and enduring maladaptive patterns to which the patient may have habituated but that are nevertheless evident. The therapist cannot adequately attend to most acute disorders by applying only one set of treatment targets. Many patients will present with a mixture of issues from the segregated diagnostic classifications listed below.

DIALECTICS WITH MOOD DISORDERS

Mood disorders involve central concerns with shame and feelings of emptiness, meaninglessness, boredom, despair, guilt, sin, hunger, and self-loathing. The depressed patient feels guilty and culpable, frequently with feelings of incompleteness. By punishing themselves (with judgmental thoughts that turn criticism against the self), they decrease perceived anxiety and increase perceived power—at least they can do *something* to change the feared hopelessness. Individuals with depression will at times idealize others then feel diminished in comparison to those they idealize.

The catastrophic thinking of some depressed patients is not without evidential merit, as studies have shown that even among depressed patients who receive treatment that alleviates their depression, a chronic course of depression predicted persistent social maladjustment, even among those who were depression free for six months (Agnosti, 1999).

Because the depressed person feels empty, their feelings themselves are defined as dangerous, since they bring hurt into focus. Many of the dialectics with mood disorders thus have to do with content themes of self-loathing, distrust of emotions, prediction of disaster, and abandonment fears. However, the most central dialectic is loss of energy versus desire for joy. The depressed person has desires but fears them, resulting in struggles with hope. When the depressed person is feeling less hope, they become increasingly passive.

In the common dialectics with mood disorders in table 8 (as with all disorders subsequently presented), the goal of the therapist is fivefold:

1. Openly identify the dialectic domains with the patient.

2. Identify the compromise formation currently formed by the patient (what they are achieving and what they are sacrificing by the current compromise).

3. Articulate the notion that no specific direction or "end" of the dialectic is always appropriate or reasonable, but that "place" along the dialectic is determined by contextual variables and goals or objectives held by the person.

4. Remind the patient to move between long-term and short-term objectives when evaluating contextual variables.

5. Help the patient identify if their analysis of contextual variables is solution focused (appropriate at times) or emotion focused (appropriate at times).

Dialectic domains thus remind the patient to shift their attentional focus between emotional goals and strategic behavioral goals, between attention to the environment and attention to self, between attention to body and attention to mind, between attention to short-term and long-term goals, and between experiential and epiphenomenal issues. Wisdom is obtained by sacrificing some issues in order to address other goals. Rigid adherence to some issues at the expense of other important goals (conscious or unconscious) defines psychological dysfunction.

DBT psychotherapy is thus about assisting the patient to shift from one arena of functioning to another, rather than invalidating their current sphere of attention as unimportant or wrong.

Table 8: Dialectics with Mood Disorders		
Pursuit of joy	←——→	Loss of energy
Want	←——→	Undeservingness
Hope	←——→	Hopelessness
Activity	←——→	Passivity
Efficacy	←——→	Impotence
Focus on self	←——→	Focus on others
Trust	←——→	Suspicion
Independence	←——→	Dependence
Problem solving	←——→	Behavioral paralysis

The above dialectics predict contradictory emotions (anger vs. desire; depression vs. hopefulness; despair vs. inspiration; deflation vs. powerfulness; resignation vs. initiative), oppositional thought patterns (desire to live vs. desire to die; feed me vs. ignore me; I'm worthless vs. don't dare mistreat me; I'm lonely vs. leave me alone; I need you vs. you're worthless), oppositional values (people are special to me vs. people are disgusting; things provide meaning to me vs. possessions are irrelevant; I seek spiritual peace vs. spirituality screws me up) and contradictory behavioral strategies (I can change this vs. trying is futile; I'll reward you vs. I'll punish you). These dynamics are more fully developed in Marra (2004).

The Goals of DBT

The goal in dialectical therapy with all diagnoses is to identify the polemics, verbalize them with the patient, and make the connections about how some behaviors and feelings are consistent with one end of the polemic, and others more consistent with the other end of the polemic. Helping the patient to shift their compromises to be more consistent with accomplishing important goals, balancing long-term and short-term objectives, and balancing acceptance with change strategies provides the overarching therapeutic treatment plan. The goal is to have the patient sustain attention to their feelings prior to trying to change those feelings, thus avoiding the emotional diminishing and escape strategies depressed patients use.

The severely depressed patient feels abnormal due to their extreme affect, and validation that such dysphoric mood is common and to be expected (given the patient's reduction in rewarding activities and their negativistic attitudes, prognostic failures, and self-absorption) helps them to decrease secondary emotional reactions. The patient's mood is accepted, but they are confronted about their strategy in dealing with their moods and their techniques to change their moods. DBT therapy embraces the cognitive behavioral targets of increasing positive daily experiences but adds the important component of mindfulness to pleasurable experiences when they occur. The predictive interpretation (Beck et al., 2004) that they will fail to attend to positive experiences because they fear that they will end or that they don't deserve them (Linehan, 1993b) is made. They are also trained to be unmindful of negative experiences (Linehan, 1993b), since the patient has already provided great valence to such experiences in the past. The goal is to increase solution-focused coping by increasing attention to contextual variables during training in strategic behavior skills. Increasing positive daily experiences is accomplished both in individual psychotherapy (through coaching, prompting, contracting, and support) and during training in emotion regulation skills and meaning-making skills. Decreased ruminative thinking and self-absorption is achieved through increasing absolute activity level, especially by prompting homework assignments to keep patients involved in new and different activities in spite of their lethargy and lack of initiation.

While many of the same treatment strategies used in cognitive treatments for depression (Beck et al., 1979) are utilized, the emphasis in DBT is to challenge patients to analyze their belief systems in dialectical ways rather than through logical analysis. Dialectical thinking requires the patient to examine their thoughts as products of underlying needs that are conflicting. Hopelessness is interpreted in light of a fear of failure as well as a great need for success. Loss of initiative is interpreted as a measure of how important their desire for achievement actually is for them. Passivity is interpreted as indication of how deeply the patient wishes to be efficacious, even when they're fearful of doomed efforts. In other words, the extremity of the feeling (especially when expressed negatively) indicates how powerfully the patient desires the opposing needs and wants.

Efforts are made to discriminate mood from identity. That the patient's behavior has become passive, dependent, hopeless, and negative does not mean that they have become passive, dependent, hopeless, and negative. Identity, or the true self, is composed of values and capabilities rather than behaviors and history. Installation of hope is thus a critical aspect of DBT treatment.

In the following dialogue, Terry is depressed. Notice the validation of depression, the emphasis on change, the installation of hope, and the confrontation of identity issues.

Patient: I just can't do anything. I don't have the energy. It's hard to even talk to you right now.

DBTherapist: And yet you *are* talking to me right now, which I greatly appreciate, given how deflated you're feeling. You feel no energy, yet you work hard to get through this thick mud of depression. So you must be feeling both things intensely—having no energy or initiative *and* the desire to have someone understand you and be with you in your pain. When it is really important to you, you do initiate and spend energy, even though it's hard to come by.

Patient: Yeah, but you don't know how hard it is. I do want you to help me, and I know that will only happen if I work hard here in therapy.

DBTherapist: Yes.

Patient: But this lack of energy, it just kills me.

DBTherapist: It does, especially because it takes so much energy to push through it.

Patient: And I can't always do it. I'm not always successful, no matter how important it is to me.

DBTherapist: You don't need to be perfect. It doesn't have to work 100 percent of the time. It only has to work sometimes. The times you are successful can create long-term improvements that may make it easier to be active the next time in spite of your depressed tiredness. Each time it works, you get just a little bit better.

Patient: You know, I didn't used to be this way.

DBTherapist: I know. It didn't take this effort and strain in the past.

Patient: I feel so different, so much less than what I used to be. I'm just not the same person anymore.

DBTherapist: You are depressed, but don't buy into the idea that that's who you are, your whole identity. You're Terry, and a lot more defines who Terry is beside your depression.

Patient: I guess I know what you're saying. I just want my energy back.

DBTherapist: Yes, and you'll get your energy back to the degree that you're able to increase joyful, playful, interesting, and stimulating experiences. In spite of your lack of energy, you do these things in order to eventually have the energy back.

Patient: I get overwhelmed just listening to you say that.

DBTherapist: It will be hard.

Patient: Why me? My brother doesn't have to do it. My mother doesn't have to do this. My friends don't have to do this.

DBTherapsit: It may not be fair. You didn't cause these problems, but unfortunately you are totally responsible for solving these problems.

Patient: I'm getting tired again listening to all of these demands.

DBTherapist: Are they demands or wants? You want your energy level back, and you're willing to do these effortful and hard things because you want it so badly. It's really hard, but I'm confident you can do it.

Patient: So ignore my tired feelings and do it anyway?

DBTherapist: Acknowledge the tired feelings, and commit yourself to increase your social and recreational events in the face of the tiredness.

Patient: (Tearful) I don't know if I can do it.

DBTherapist: I know you can do it, and you're feeling sad because you correctly understand that it will be hard, that you won't always be able to do it. You don't want to fail.

Patient: Who does?

DBTherapist: Yes, it's normal.

Patient: I'm empty.

DBTherapist: You're not empty. You just expressed sadness and even tears. You have great emotion inside, emotion you can draw on.

Patient: How can I draw upon depression to solve my problems?

DBTherapist: You draw upon the acknowledgment that your depression is so detestable that you're willing to do whatever it takes to get rid of it.

Patient: Use it as a reminder of why I'm doing these things I have no energy for?

DBTherapist: Yes.

Patient: I do hate this depression. It makes everything seem empty. I'm not hungry; I'm not interested in what people have to say. I just want to crawl into bed and stay there for days. Sleep—then I won't have to feel depressed.

DBTherapist: You want to avoid the feeling rather than deal with it.

Patient: Of course.

DBTherapist: It just prolongs the pain.

Patient: I know. Okay, I'll do the homework assignment to increase pleasurable events you asked me to do last week. Will you be mad at me if I don't do much?

DBTherapist: I won't be mad at you. I'll be disappointed that you will prolong your pain longer than you need to. I care about you, not your compliance with my requests.

Bipolar Disorder

A special case is noted for bipolar disorder, where emotions are especially prone to be prompted due to neurochemical influences rather than environmental ones.

Shifts from depressed to manic affect is particularly confusing to the patient and to those with whom they relate. Bipolar patients come to distrust their emotions, but because there is little they can do to control their feelings through simple psychological exertion, many bipolar patients distrust their emotions while they simultaneously surrender to them. They like the effect of the mania, feeling safer when irritable because they protect themselves more (or alternately enjoy the euphoria of positive affect that makes normal life affect pale in comparison). They surrender to the depression due to its immediacy and apparent lack of connection to specific thoughts or experiences.

Patients experiencing mania engage in behavior similar to that observed with anxious patients, in that there is substantial flight. While the anxious person flees from perceived threat, the manic patient flees from their experience of intensity. The frequent sexualization, intoxication, and hyperactivity of the manic patient can be viewed as mood-dependent behavior that serves to distract and fragment the otherwise observed emotional turbulence. While many bipolar patients look like they are seeking out arousal rather than avoiding it, the acting-out behavior serves to fragment and thus compartmentalize the arousal into more manageable and understandable urges.

While the bipolar patient is a stylized example of distrust of emotions, and the bipolar patient has even more reason to distrust their emotions due to the known genetic and biochemical genesis of the disorder, dialectic psychotherapy in conjunction with medications can be helpful. The move is from a "pathogen only" model of disease to a "host-pathogen interaction" model (Ray, 2004). With the bipolar patient, the therapist helps the patient to identify incongruence between their affect and their environment in the moment. The dialectic between focus on self versus focus on environment is particularly important work with the bipolar patient. Improving the bipolar's observational skills with mindfulness is especially important, and helping them to navigate the passivity versus activity dialectic is equally critical. Shifting from emotion-focused coping to solution-focused coping can help them improve their strategic behavior even in the face of uncontrollable affect.

Dialectic psychotherapy is thus applicable to bipolar disorder in spite of the known evidence that affect is at times beyond the control of the patient. In fact, DBT assumes that affect frequently is kindled neurologically with most acute emotional disorders (see chapter 3), and precisely this contributes to their high emotional arousal. DBT is designed to treat such conditions, as it helps the patient to make sense of their feelings, even those not under their conscious control, and to engage in coping responses based upon this knowledge.

DIALECTICS WITH ANXIETY DISORDERS

The central dialectic with anxiety is the desire for safety in the face of perceived threat. Inadequate synthesis of this dialectic (giving in to the desire for safety by validating the importance of the threat) results in loss of freedom as the patient places increasing restrictions on what they can and cannot do. Anxiety disorders have prominent content themes on threat, dependency, inadequacy, shame, and somatization. Emotional escape and avoidance are high-probability problems with all of the anxiety disorders. While self-focus increases (with attention to physiology and affect being prominent), anxious patients also have fear of being observed and humiliated in the public eye (other focus). This can lead to inconsistency in the dialectic of activity versus passivity. The anxious person decreases their trust in their own body, their own competence to control their body, and their competence to function in interpersonal environments. Anxious patients thus can be quite secretive, avoiding the perceived public humiliation that would be forthcoming if others could transparently observe their internal experience. They become ashamed of their dependency upon a few close friends or family members, and their sense of self-efficacy shrinks. They become observers rather than changers of their experience. Blame of self frequently replaces problem solving.

Fresco and his colleagues at Kent State University have noted that patients with generalized anxiety disorder have a marked inability to identify, describe, and accept emotional experience, with a corresponding inability to soothe themselves (Fresco, Wolfson, Crowther, and Docherty, 2002). Anxiety disorders, along with mood disorders, offer the greatest challenge for the patient who is fearful of their own affect, since their affect indeed can be overwhelming and threatening. Behavioral approaches to the treatment of major disorders have thus increasingly embraced the need for training in emotion regulation skills in these disorders (Samoilov and Goldfried, 2000).

Success with treatment of anxiety disorders is greater when there is no comorbid personality disorder. For example, socially phobic patients without personality disorders obtained clinically significant gains after only fifteen weeks of treatments, but those with a comorbid personality disorder were found without improvement (Turner, 1987). The same is true of agoraphobic patients, who find time-limited psychotherapy successful in 75 percent of the cases when there is no personality disorder but successful in only 25 percent of the cases when there is a comorbid personality disorder (Mavissakalian and Hamman, 1987). Patients with personality disorders are also significantly more likely to prematurely drop out of treatment (Persons, Burns, and Perloff, 1988). The DBT therapist is thus wise to adequately assess the presence of comorbid conditions prior to initiating treatment and include strategies that encompass personality issues when these influence the course and dynamics of the patient's presenting problem. Patients rarely present for treatment of a personality disorder per se and are more likely to have as chief complaints mood or anxiety symptoms (Beck et al., 2004).

Table 9: Dialectics with Anxiety Disorders

Desire for safety	←——→	Avoidance of threat
Want	←——→	Fear
Freedom	←——→	Restriction
React to broad input (from thoughts, emotions, environment)	←——→	React to restricted input (from body, from perceived threat)
Self-reliance	←——→	Dependence on others
Environment focus	←——→	Body focus
In the moment	←——→	Anticipating the future
Desire for reassurance	←——→	Secretiveness
Problem solving	←——→	Blame

With acute mental disorders, it is rare to see a purely anxious patient. As with mood disorders, once a disorder becomes chronic or lengthy, the probability of comorbid anxiety and depression increases. In a meta-analysis of studies for panic disorder, generalized anxiety disorder, and depression, it was found that "the majority of patients were excluded from participating in the average study," (Westen and Morrison, 2001, p. 880) due to the presence of comorbid conditions. Approximately two-thirds of the patients in studies reviewed for the meta-analysis were excluded due to comorbidity. This should not come as news, for others (Meichenbaum, 2003) have estimated that fewer than 20 percent of patients have only one clearly definable axis I diagnosis. These dialectics are thus presented as guideposts for therapists. Due to comorbidity and individual differences, the therapist is likely to find dialectic concerns of patients different from those here described. The reader is referred to Marra (2004) for a patient self-help treatment manual for comorbid mood and anxiety disorders.

DBT treatment of anxiety is based on validation: anxiety is a natural response to threat, and the anxious patient anticipates threat. This is normal, but the anxiety hurts, so designing methods to decrease the threat and the response to threat is reasonable. Vulnerability perception in the anxious patient is heightened, and the DBT therapist assesses skill deficits as well as cognitive schemas when formulating a treatment plan. Self-doubt can be either an indication of a skills deficit or of hypervigilance to threat. Both are targeted for intervention. With skills deficits, psychoeducation is the preferred treatment. With hypervigilance to threat, individual psychotherapy with the goal of increasing attention to safety cues is the preferred treatment.

While cognitive approaches to anxiety emphasize the Socratic method, an educational model, direction, and challenging evidence for beliefs (Beck, Emery, and

Greenberg, 1985), DBT invites the patient to first accept their feelings as real, under-standable, and valid. Exposure to anxiety precedes any cognitive reframing, as the patient is invited to first experientially challenge the notion that their anxiety is intolerable. Experiential avoidance and escape is explained to the patient, and valida-tion of their emotions precedes any attempt to modify the cause (either environmen-tal or intrapersonal) of the emotion. The DBT premise is that avoidance and escape of emotion per se is a more powerful predictor of symptom maintenance than cogni-tive processes.

Anxious patients tend to be self-absorbed with physiological and mental repre-sentations of their anxiety. The DBT therapist does not reinforce this perseverative focus on the body by asking the patient to engage in recording of anxiety experiences through graphs, diaries, or extensive reviews of daily or weekly experiences. This reinforces the self-absorption. Rather, the DBT therapist helps the patient to identify specific areas of physiological arousal within psychotherapy sessions. Mindfulness of anxiety precedes instruction in relaxation techniques (deep breathing, imagery of soothing experiences, progressive muscle relaxation, self-hypnosis, and positive self-talk) so that the patient first experientially confronts the intolerability of their anxiety. Acceptance precedes change strategies when using a DBT approach to anxi-ety disorders, and validation precedes the acceptance strategies.

The following in-session experiential acceptance exercise occurs only after tak-ing a complete history, including identification of threat and safety cues that precede and follow a panic attack. The patient must first feel understood and accepted. A trusting relationship has already been formed.

Patient: I feel like I'm going to die when I have a panic attack.

DBTherapist: Yes, it feels life threatening. Do you fear you're going to have a heart attack, a stroke, or pass out?

Patient: Sometimes all of them.

DBTherapist: That *must* feel life threatening.

Patient: It does.

DBTherapist: Can you make the panic attack come? Can you create it?

Patient: What?

DBTherapist: If you start paying attention to your heart rate, your breath-ing, and your anxiety level, can you start an anxiety attack on purpose?

Patient: I spend most of my time trying not to have one.

DBTherapist: Of course. But have you ever tried to have one on purpose?

Patient: No, because I don't want to have them. They're terrifying.

DBTherapist: Yes, they are so terrifying that you spend a great deal of energy—and anxiety—trying to avoid them. And this additional energy and anxiety of avoidance unintentionally powers them. Right now, and I'll help keep you safe by later helping you to relax, I want you to try to produce a panic attack.

Patient: I'm scared to do that.

DBTherapist: Of course you are. Just like you're scared to have one when you're not with me. That makes sense. We are going to increase your control over the panic by helping you to start and stop them purposefully. Does that make sense?

Patient: Kind of. But I don't want to have a panic attack.

DBTherapist: I know you don't. Who would? We're going to decrease the energy you are putting on top of the anxiety—the energy of avoidance and fear of the fear—and this will eventually reduce the chances you have attacks in the future.

Patient: That's what I want. But I don't want to have a panic attack.

DBTherapist: Has anything you've tried thus far stopped the attacks? Made them less frequent?

Patient: Only when I stay at home. But I have to work to support my family.

DBTherapist: Yes. And if you allow your world to shrink, if you obtain safety in your home, you give up a normal life. What I want you to do right now is pay attention to your heart rate. Is it beating fast or slow?

Patient: It's beating faster.

DBTherapist: Can you make it beat even a little bit faster right now by focusing on it?

Patient: It's beating faster.

DBTherapist: Just pay attention to your heart rate. Try to stay out of your head, your thoughts, and just pay attention to your heart rate and pressure. When you start thinking, gently bring your attention back to your heart.

Patient: I don't like this.

DBTherapist: I know. I wouldn't either. But are you willing to stick with me on this for just a few more seconds?

Patient: Okay. *(Closes eyes)*

DBTherapist: *(Almost whispering, speaking very slowly)* Pay attention to your heart. Hear the beats. Feel the blood flowing through your heart. Notice the rate and rhythm of your heart. Bring your mind back to your heart each time it wanders somewhere else. Hear the beats. Feel the blood flowing through your heart. Notice the rate and rhythm of your heart. Bring your mind back to your heart each time it wanders somewhere else. *(Pause)* What are you noticing?

Patient: It was beating fast, then faster, then your soothing voice made it slow down.

DBTherapist: So once you started really paying attention to it and felt safe, it started slowing down. First fast and anxious, then attention and acceptance, and the heart rate slowed down. No panic.

Patient: Not this time.

DBTherapist: Right, it may not always work. But the next time you fear having a panic attack, first accept that your bodily experience is there for a reason. First pay attention to what exactly is happening before you try to avoid or stop it.

Meaning-making skills help anxious patients put situational (contextual) variables into the backseat of consciousness while keeping sight of long-term and more powerful reinforcers. Mindfulness provides exposure, decreasing avoidance behaviors that perpetuate anxious responding. Emotion regulation skills assist the anxious patient to change environmental triggers to anxiety, while distress tolerance skills decrease escape behaviors that reinforce anxiety. Strategic behavior skills improve shifting of attention from self to environment, from anticipatory fear to planful behavior.

DIALECTICS IN EATING DISORDERS

Eating disorders involve central issues of identity, acceptability, indulgence or urge versus inhibition, self-control versus helplessness, and the fundamental acceptability of the individual to self and to society. The patient acts as if their hunger will destroy them as well as others. The conflict is between urge and self-control, with less attention focused on solution-focused coping (the behaviors that will help them to accomplish their goals). High emotional arousal results from their self-loathing rather than from food or eating food. Food is simply the focus of attention around which the underlying emotional dread and want dance.

Self-stimulation, or novelty seeking, is widely recognized as a genetically inherited need. It promotes survival of the species. However, stimulatory needs are rarely addressed in the professional literature as prompters of the urge to eat. Boredom eating, emotional eating, binge eating, and overeating are frequently reflections of novelty seeking or self-stimulation. In our modern society, people are frequently trapped in understimulating situations both at work and at home. We sit at a desk all day performing routine and repetitive tasks that are not personally rewarding or relevant. With the mechanization and mobilization of modern society, frequently people return from work (which is often routine and monotonous) to a stimulation-absent home environment. Many people turn to television for vicarious stimulation, but this is a weak alternative to direct sensory stimulation (involving tactual, olfactory, or taste sensations, or the kind of physical exertion required of our forefathers and anticipated by our bodies). Eating can replace the sensory deprivation experienced in modern society; eating and the satiety it provides can replace the emotional stimulation desired but not achieved.

The role of maladaptive emotion regulation in eating disorders has been well researched (Heatherton and Baumeister, 1991), and specific application of dialectical behavior therapy to the issue of eating disorders has been made (Safer, Telch, and Agras, 2001; Wiser and Telch, 1999). Eating disorders can be conceptualized as a way of avoiding affect by redirecting attention to less personally threatening stimuli (like food) and using binge or purge behaviors to modify affect through both positive and negative reinforcement. It has been proposed that bulimics are oversensitive to their environment and social demands (Heatherton and Baumeister, 1991), leading to anxiety and negative affect, and that binge and purge behaviors are used to enhance mood. Food is used to numb painful emotions (Arnow, Kennedy, and Agras, 1992). Individuals who present for treatment of eating disorders frequently have comorbid anxiety problems (Schwalberg, et al., 1992), and patients with both eating and anxiety disorders have been found to have higher maladaptive emotion regulation strategies (Fresco et al., 2002).

Table 10: Dialectics with Eating Disorders		
My body is disgusting.	←——→	My body can be improved.
I don't deserve nourishment.	←——→	Food is the only known nourishment.
People will love me for my appearance.	←——→	People don't love me.
I'm disgusting.	←——→	I need to hide my hideous self.
I have a secret.	←——→	I wish others would look hard enough to find my secret.
Food is my only consistent friend.	←——→	Food is my consistent enemy.
My needs are important.	←——→	My needs are revolting.
People would love me if my body was beautiful.	←——→	My self is not beautiful.
Hunger is my enemy.	←——→	Need fulfillment is urgent.
I can control my urges.	←——→	My urges are beyond control.
The sensual is in my mouth only.	←——→	The sensual can be found in each of my senses.
I'm empty.	←——→	I can be full.
My body is my self.	←——→	I'm more than my body.
I don't believe in me.	←——→	Only if others believe in me can I be adequate.
I'm lonely.	←——→	Food is my friend.
If I'm fat others will leave me alone.	←——→	If I'm thin others will want me.
Fullness will stop my emotional pain.	←——→	Emptiness will make me adequate.
I can satisfy my needs on my own (independence).	←——→	Others can bring satisfaction (dependence).
Want is dangerous (avoidance).	←——→	I can stop my want (escape).

The goals of the treatment of eating disorders using a DBT approach involve increasing the variety of emotional inputs available in the environment (training in emotion regulation skills), increasing the variety of need fulfillments in the environment (meaning-making skills), validating the worth of the individual regardless of met or unmet needs, increasing the frustration tolerance of the patient (distress tolerance skills), shifting contextual variables from short-term to long-term (strategic behavior skills), and most importantly, increasing sensory input (mindfulness skills) to substitute sensual activities for food satiety.

Both eating and substance-abuse disorders can be understood as anxiety relief (avoidance) strategies: "In order not to feel my emotional pain, I can eat (use drugs), and while doing so my pain is not so present."

The following dialogue with a patient with an overeating disorder (ED-NOS) demonstrates affect tolerance and acceptance.

Patient: I was doing great until Wednesday. I stuck to my program and ate healthy. I was so proud of myself. But then on Wednesday I ate half of the cheesecake that my mother brought home from work.

DBTherapist: Can you close your eyes and imagine yourself, where you were and what you looked like on Wednesday, prior to eating the cheesecake?

Patient: (*Eyes closed*) Yeah.

DBTherapist: See yourself before you go into the kitchen. Watch yourself like you were watching a movie, except you can also feel what is going on inside of you. What were you feeling? Be mindful, just as we practiced in the past, but this time be mindful of your memories. What were you feeling?

Patient: I felt bored. And disappointed. I came home, checked for messages, and John hadn't called me. No one else had come home yet. I felt bored, disappointed, alone.

DBTherapist: Okay, I want you to feel those feelings right now. Feel as bored, disappointed, and alone as you can. Can you do that?

Patient: Yes.

DBTherapist: Okay, keep your eyes closed. Now consider, if you had to, could you put up with feeling bored, alone, and disappointed for a long time?

Patient:	If I had to, yeah, I could put up with it.
DBTherapist:	Stick with those feelings: "I'm bored. I'm alone. I'm disappointed." *(Pause)* Okay, open your eyes. What bad thing happened by feeling bored, alone, and disappointed?
Patient:	Nothing. You're saying that I should have allowed myself to feel what I was feeling and not eat the cheesecake.
DBTherapist:	Right, just like we've talked about in past sessions. Eating has become a quick fix. You can transform what you're feeling, from frustration to satiety, so quickly and easily that you do it without even thinking. It's automatic.
Patient:	It just seems so urgent. I walk into the kitchen and see the cheesecake on the table.
DBTherapist:	And it looks so satisfying.
Patient:	It's like I go on automatic pilot. The food just jumps in my mouth.
DBTherapist:	Of course you want satisfaction. We all do. We all want to feel good and not to feel bad. What we are going to work on is having you recognize what you're feeling earlier in the sequence—first accepting your feelings before you try to change them.

DIALECTICS WITH SUBSTANCE ABUSE

Substance abuse is another area where there are known genetic and pathophysiological risk factors. Some individuals are more prone to addiction than others. Some individuals can experiment with alcohol, tobacco, and illicit drugs and never find cessation challenging. Many others are not so fortunate. The disease model of addiction predicts clearly that once addiction develops, it has a predictable (and frightfully irresistible) course. Substance-abuse issues easily fit within the dialectical model of treatment because what is being addressed are the affective urges that accompany the physiological craving. While DBT can not address the physiological craving (nor can it eliminate the kindling effect with other disorders), it can offer the same psychological coping skills to deal with the experience of high emotional arousal, slow return to emotional baseline, and hypervigilance to threat cues. The physiological response of craving and withdrawal are the threat cues, both experiential and anticipatory.

The central themes of addiction are self-control in the face of strong urges (Horvath, 1998), tolerability of affect, future satisfaction, and ability to artificially feel good. As with eating disorders, the addicted person becomes naturally focused on the strong physiological responses of the body. Again, emotion-focused rather than solution-focused coping becomes predominant, and it is difficult for the person to shift attention away from arousal-producing stimuli.

Table 11: Dialectics with Substance-Abuse Disorders		
I can control my body.	←——→	My body is beyond my control.
My impulses are my friend.	←——→	My impulses will devour me.
My feelings hurt.	←——→	I can stop this hurt.
I can take this.	←——→	This is intolerable.
There are lots of things that can bring satisfaction.	←——→	Only body euphoria can bring satisfaction.
I deserve pleasure.	←——→	The world will never give me what I really need.
I'm out of control.	←——→	Control is moment by moment.
I'll do this for others.	←——→	I'll do this for me.
I can do this on my own.	←——→	I need the support of others.
I'm okay.	←——→	I need to be punished.
My feelings are intolerable.	←——→	I can substitute pleasure for pain.
I'm empty.	←——→	I can be full.

DBT has not always been shown effective with substance abusers (Breslin, Zack, and McMain, 2002), and sensitivity to the unique features of addictive processes is therefore warranted. However, there is evidence that DBT can be a powerful source of change for substance abusers (Linehan et al., 2002). Experienced researchers in substance abuse (Marlatt, 2002) conclude that mindfulness can decrease relapse and that mindfulness as a method influences information processing (Breslin et al., 2002) and thus can be useful in the treatment of substance abuse.

DBT treatment includes assisting patients to recognize triggering events of substance use (strategic behavior skills); assisting the patient to shift contextual attention from internal to external (mindfulness skills); manipulating the environment to decrease triggering events (strategic behavior skills); validation of the patient's needs (but separating need fulfillment from the means to meet those needs); increasing other positive activities that may meet needs (Horvath, 1998), such as engaging in meaning-making skills; increasing distress tolerance skills to deal with cravings and withdrawal symptoms; and engaging in harm reduction strategies (Horvath, 1998) that balance acceptance with change.

In the following therapy session the therapist confronts drug use to avoid negative affect.

Patient: I know, I know—there are always good reasons to use.

DBTherapist: You've learned a lot from the 12-step program.

Patient: But I keep slipping.

DBTherapist: You listed several negative events that happened before you used again. I want you to go over them again with me, but this time focus on what you were feeling while they happened.

Patient: Obviously, I was feeling angry and annoyed that Joyce was picking on me.

DBTherapist: Tell me what is hard about feeling angry and annoyed at Joyce.

Patient: What do you mean, what's hard about it?

DBTherapist: You wanted to stop feeling angry and annoyed. You used drugs to help you not feel those feelings.

Patient: She can be such a bitch . . .

DBTherapist: Let's stick with the feelings. You wanted to stop feeling angry and annoyed.

Patient: I guess I've bought into all those fairy-tale stories of love and passion, where everything is supposed to have a happy ending.

DBTherapist: Stick with the feeling, "I can't stand being angry."

Patient: I can't stand being angry because it means that I've screwed up another marriage.

DBTherapist: Keep going. "I can't stand being angry."

Patient: I hate being angry. I got married to feel good, not to feel angry.

DBTherapist: I'm supposed to feel good, not bad.

Patient: Right.

DBTherapist: And drugs make you feel good, like you're supposed to.

Patient: Like I have a right to feel good.

DBTherapist: Of course you do. We all have the right to feel good. But it sounds like you're going beyond that. You're supposed to feel good, and not bad. You use drugs to avoid feelings that are unpleasant or unwanted.

Patient: But isn't the program supposed to help me resist the urges?

DBTherapist: Let's talk about the urges. Is the urge more than two things: the desire to feel good and the desire not to feel bad?

Patient: It's a lot more. There is this internal push, this craving, this force that sometimes is irresistible.

DBTherapist: So it's three things: the seemingly irresistible physical urge to decrease the physical craving, the desire to feel good, and the desire to not feel bad. Is that right?

Patient: Yeah.

DBTherapist: What if we could eliminate, or at least reduce, two of those three things? What if you could feel bad sometimes, like angry, and accept that as part of being human? What if you could know that the anger will eventually go away on its own, that nothing is forever? Something will eventually happen to make your emotions shift from anger to amusement, or from anger to regret, or from anger to peace. And what if you reminded yourself that lots of things make you feel good besides drugs, and you intentionally brought more of these into your life?

Patient: But I'd still have to deal with that physical craving.

DBTherapist: Yes, you would. Can you imagine that dealing with the craving alone would be easier than dealing with the craving *and* the demand that you always feel good and never bad?

Patient: Yeah, that would be easier.

DBTherapist: Let's work on tolerating the unwanted negative emotions first.

DIALECTICS WITH IMPULSE-CONTROL DISORDERS

Impulse-control disorders, like the other classifications, are a broad category intended to encompass dealing with urges that aren't substance based. An impulse occurs, and the person responds to it in spite of strong personal and social consequences against such expression. Anger, aggression or violence, gambling, indecent exposure, kleptomania, pyromania, and trichotillomania are examples. While *DSM-IV* (APA, 1994) classifies indecent exposure as a sexual disorder rather than an impulse-control disorder, exhibitionism and frotteurism can be viewed as impulse-control difficulties despite their sexual nature. *DSM-IV* categorizes the impulse-control problems as disorders "not elsewhere classified" (p. 609) to amplify the fact that many, if not most, mental disorders involve disorder of regulatory functions. Since essential affect-regulatory processes are not effectively operating, the impulse-control disorders are natural subjects of intervention for DBT.

The core thematic issues are overwhelming affect, a need to terminate the high affect as quickly and efficiently as possible, and a means (strategy) to do so. The pathological gambler finds that the risk and potential wins will ease their emotional suffering, the kleptomanic similarly finds the risk and escape derived from stealing behavior soothing, the frotteur finds the control and submission of their victim to be temporarily empowering, and the compulsive ritual of the trichotillomanic grants momentary peace from the preceding emotional tension. The behavior is thus always designed to decrease arousal, even if temporarily.

The specific content of conscious thought will thus vary, but the dialectics are similar. Below we examine the potential dialectics of intermittent explosive disorder, but the reader can easily see how these dynamics apply to the other impulse disorders.

Table 12: Dialectics with Intermittent Explosive Disorder

They made me do this.	←——→	I'm responsible for my own behavior.
I have a valid reason.	←——→	My feelings don't need justification.
I'm out of control.	←——→	I don't want to be in control.
They deserve my wrath.	←——→	My self-respect is more important than their consequences.
Feelings prompt immediate behavior.	←——→	My behavior is separate from my feelings.
Strike while the iron is hot.	←——→	I can be measured in my response.
Hurt me, and I'll hurt you.	←——→	I need to deal with my own hurt.
Winning is critical.	←——→	Getting what I really want is long-term.
Don't be a loser.	←——→	Winning is less important than happiness.
I'm not dependent on others.	←——→	I'm interdependent on others.
I won't feel vulnerable.	←——→	We are all vulnerable.
They did it to me first.	←——→	Justice is relative.
I won't hurt.	←——→	I'll hurt them first.
Emotions are primary.	←——→	Emotions are important but not all-important.

Note that dialectics are not always opposites. However, they are competing needs and aspirations. One essential characteristic of the impulse-control disorders is the perceived need of the individual to escape quickly from their dilemma. They have found a way to temporarily stop their arousal (no matter if that arousal is sexual, aggressive, social, or affective). DBT is designed to treat these emotional and escape behaviors by identifying dialectic conflict and thus bringing sacrifice and competition into focus. Exposure, acceptance, meaning making, distress tolerance skills (critically important in the impulse-control disorders), and behavioral technologies allow the patient to adapt better to their conflicting needs.

The goals of DBT treatment with impulse-control disorders are to increase long-term focus of attention (meaning-making skills); increase contextual attention to variables affecting the behavior (strategic behavior skills); increase specific attention to the *effect* of the behavior (strategic behavior skills); modify underlying affect prompting the behavior (emotion regulation skills); increase attention to internal (affective) rather than external (interpersonal) variables (mindfulness skills); and increase distress tolerance skills that can delay impulsive acting-out behaviors.

With the following impulse-control patient, the therapist distinguishes feelings from behavior, as well as prompts affect tolerance.

DBTherapist: Just before you threw the ashtray across the room, what were you feeling and thinking? I know you were angry, but can you describe it for me in more detail?

Patient: I was thinking, How dare she accuse me of having an affair with Wanda. She knows I can't stand Wanda. What does she think of me? That I'm some kind of animal who would sleep with someone I don't even like?

DBTherapist: So you wanted to demonstrate how outraged you were.

Patient: No. I wasn't trying to demonstrate anything. I was just mad.

DBTherapist: And how did your wife respond to your anger, after you threw the ashtray?

Patient: She started crying.

DBTherapist: And then how did you feel?

Patient: Like a heel. Like the animal she thinks I am.

DBTherapist: So demonstrating your anger with behavior made you feel worse and made your wife feel worse. Then things got even worse between the two of you.

Patient: Yeah, every time I get angry things get worse.

DBTherapist: Was it your anger that made things get worse or your behavior of throwing the ashtray?

Patient: My behavior.

DBTherapist: That's an important distinction. Sometimes when you act on your behavior things get worse. It's normal to get angry when we feel unjustly accused. It is not helpful to act out that anger, because you're practicing the anger by putting it into behavior. As before, lets look at the compromise formation you had to make. On the one hand, you were angry and outraged. On the other, you wanted your wife to understand your point of view about what was going on with Wanda. Right?

Patient: Sure. I wanted her to come to her senses. I wanted her to stop accusing me of stuff I know even she doesn't believe in her heart. Sometimes she says things just to make me angry.

DBTherapist: After things had settled down, did your wife say anything to suggest that she wanted you to be or become angry?

Patient: No. She talked about how insecure she is and how every man has cheated on her.

DBTherapist: So what she said was a reflection of her insecurity—it was about her and her feelings and not intended to make you mad.

Patient: Okay. Sometimes I just can't control myself.

DBTherapist: From this and some of the other situations you've described to me, it sounds as if you do things to *discharge* your anger. You hate feeling angry, so you expel your anger behaviorally, or least try to. It's like you're trying to act out of the feeling, rather than just accepting or tolerating it. What do you think?

Patient: Sometimes I just can't control myself.

DBTherapist: Let's perform a little experiment. We probably can't get you, here in the office, to feel as angry as you do at home. But let's try. I want you to imagine yourself in the living room with your wife, five minutes before you threw the ashtray. Close your eyes, like we've done in the past, and try to see it like a movie running in your head. This time, I want you to focus just on your feelings. Try to reconnect with the feelings of rage and dismay you felt. Remember your thoughts, "She must think I'm some kind of animal." "She's saying this stuff just to piss me off." "Who does she think I am?" Remember how your body felt. How did your muscles feel? Tight? Tense? Remember your forehead. Your eyes and eyebrows. Remember how fast your heart was beating. Feel the anger just like it felt before, or as much as possible. Can you reconnect with those angry feelings?

Patient: Yeah. They are not as strong as they were yesterday.

DBTherapist: But they are there?

Patient: Uh-huh.

DBTherapist: Stick with them for just a few more seconds. *(Pause)* Now, I noticed that you didn't throw anything here in the office today, in spite of feelings of anger. One reason might be that the angry feelings were not as intense, but I'd suggest an even more important reason: You gave yourself permission to feel angry. You were prepared to feel your feeling without acting on it.

DIALECTICS WITH PERSONALITY DISORDERS

I saved the personality disorders for last, both because they are the most complex with which to deal, and because personality disorders encompass a wide and variable set of dialectics. Although the literature on personality disorders is voluminous, only more recently have personality disorders been the subject of rigorous experimental inquiry (Gunderson et al., 2000). Personality disorders are defined as enduring patterns of inner experience that deviate markedly from the expectations of the individual's culture and include cognitive perceptual processes, unusual affectivity, impairment of interpersonal functioning, and impulse-control issues (APA, 1994). Unlike other broad diagnostic categories, such as mood disorders, where dialectic conflict (such as the desire to live versus the desire to die) refers to each specific diagnosis in the category, personality disorders offer no unity, other than the definitional criteria that the symptoms derive from deep characterological roots. Nevertheless, ample literature suggests that personality disorders exist in a diagnostically reliable manner (Grilo et al., 2001; Sanislow et al., 2002; Zanarini et al., 2000), are treatable (Grilo, McGlashan, and Skodol, 2000; Leichsenring and Leibing, 2003), and that the functional analysis (treatment plan) for personality disorder is no different from those of axis I disorders (Davidson, 2002). In fact, research indicates that in terms of intractability, personality disorders are less stable than anxiety disorders (Shea and Yen, 2003), suggesting that clinical change with personality disorders should be just as possible as with anxiety disorders. Since Dr. Linehan (1993b, 1993c) has ably and comprehensively described BPD, the reader is referred to her texts for the BPD dialectics.

Many private practitioners assume that they primarily treat axis I disorders and do not pay particular attention to personality disorders. The severity of axis I disorders increases with comorbid personality disorder (Tyrer et al., 1990), and many difficult-to-treat patients who are not responding to treatment may actually have a comorbid personality disorder that is not adequately diagnosed. For example, one study found that of patients who present to general practitioner physicians for treatment, fully one-third had a personality disorder (de Girolamo and Reich, 1993; Dowson and Grounds, 1995; Moran, 1999). This is true even though it is rarely reported as the reason for treatment, with primary personality disorder reported in only 4 percent of the cases (London Department of Health, 2000). The Collaborative Longitudinal Personality Disorders Study preliminary data suggests that mood disorders with an insidious onset and recurrence, chronicity, and progression in severity lead to a personality disorder diagnosis in young adults, especially avoidant, borderline, or dependent personality disorders (Skodol et al., 1999).

In spite of clinical lore that personality disorders are untreatable, or that such treatment rarely results in substantial clinical gain, a recent meta-analysis of both psychodynamically oriented and cognitive behavioral psychotherapies for personality disorders found that there is evidence that both methods are effective treatments (Leichsenring and Leibing, 2003). In this analysis, fourteen studies of psychodynamic therapy and eleven studies of cognitive behavioral therapy that met more rigorous experimental criteria were included in data analysis. Psychodynamic therapy yielded an overall effect size of 1.46, with effect sizes of 1.08 found for self-report measures and 1.79 for observer-rated measures. Cognitive behavioral studies of personality disorders found an overall effect size of 1.00, with effect sizes of 1.20 found for self-report measures and 0.87 for observer-rated measures. Clearly, personality disorders are effectively treatable with strategies often considered incompatible.

Personality disorders are thus complex and frequently occur comorbidly with other axis I disorders (McGlashan et al., 2000). Having a personality disorder during adolescence doubles the risk of having an anxiety or mood disorder, self-harm behavior, or substance-abuse disorder in adulthood (Johnson et al., 1999). Patients with borderline, antisocial, avoidant, and dependent personality disorder also have high rates of comorbid affective disorders (de Girolamo and Reich, 1993). Comorbidity of personality disorder with eating disorders, somatization disorders, schizophrenia, bipolar disorders, sexual disorders, obsessive-compulsive disorders, and dissociative disorders have also been found (Dowson and Grounds, 1995). Patients with mixed antisocial, borderline, narcissistic, and histrionic traits are likely to have mood, anxiety, substance, eating, and self-harm comorbidity (Higgit and Fonagy, 1992). In general, personality disorders are more likely to have functional impairments that are greater than those of simple axis I disorders (Skodol et al., 2002).

How does DBT treatment of personality disorders differ from cognitive or cognitive behavioral therapy (CBT) approaches? Essentially, cognitive psychology extends CBT for depression to the personality disorders: "The same techniques used in eliciting and evaluating automatic thoughts during depression or GAD (generalized anxiety disorder) are useful when dealing with personality problems" (Beck et al., 2004, p. 78). Cognitive therapy theory presupposes that dysfunctional feelings and conduct are due to schemas that produce consistently biased judgments and a concomitant tendency to make cognitive errors through attributional bias (Beck et al., 2004), while DBT invites the therapist to look for the wisdom or truth in how schemas are formed. The DBT therapist explores the schema and the underlying dialectic conflicts that must have produced it rather than performing "collaborative experiments" to prove their lack of utility (Beck et al., 2004). The DBT therapist does not work with dysfunctional interpretations so much as attempting to connect belief systems to underlying affect and need, thus assisting patients to reinterpret their belief systems based upon greater awareness of their feelings and needs. Rather than using "guided discovery" to dispel dysfunctional interpretations, as in CBT, DBT analyzes both the affective and cognitive inference process to determine how the schema was formed in the first place. This involves identifying deprivational emotional states in early development that could have produced fixation or perseveration and attentional constriction that could serve as protection from threatening internal or external cues. It also involves broadly examining the effects of negative reinforcement through emotional escape and avoidance strategies or inadequate psychological coping skills that could have been rewarded through the partial reinforcement effect. Rather than "labeling of inaccurate inferences or distortions, to make the patient aware of bias or unreasonableness of particular automatic patterns of thought" (Beck et al., 2004, p. 77), the dialectical therapist invites the patient to attend to the role of language in producing emotions. The patient changes language not because it is maladaptive or wrong, but because it produces emotions they wish to avoid.

Finally, DBT differs from CBT in treatment of personality disorders by adopting a nonpejorative interpretation of pathology. Even CBT therapists acknowledge the negativity in the description of many personality disorders: ". . . the therapist needs to be especially careful to be nonjudgmental. The very terms that we use to describe these disorders . . . carry a pejorative taint" (Beck et al., 2004, p. 110). It is difficult for the therapist to be nonjudgmental when using descriptors, for example, "devious, deceptive, disloyal, hostile, and malicious" (p. 119) in the paranoid personality disorder, or "needy, weak, helpless, and incompetent" (p. 39) in the dependent personality disorder. Instead, the DBT therapist sees behavior and strategy as operant behavior. The patient is attempting to avoid harm and seek pleasure, like most of us, but has difficulty successfully obtaining the desired outcome due to the pathogenesis and pathotopology of acute emotional disorders, as described in chapters 3 and 4 of this book. The DBT therapist assumes that inadequate compromises between competing and contradictory needs and desires form the core of psychopathology, and that helping patients to better navigate the accomplishment of their goals need never be pejorative.

There are, of course, many similarities between DBT and CBT. Both require a collaborative stance between patient and therapist, use modeling, coaching, imagery, and learning principles, analyze triggers and environmental prompts as sustainers of behavior, explore schemas, require behavioral change as well as emotional exploration, and plan for generalization of change into the daily life of the individual outside of the therapy consulting room. Both also acknowledge the critical importance of empathic responding (Sperry, 1999):

> [J]udicious use of empathic responding encourages sharing of past pain and anticipatory fears. When these patients feel that clinicians understand their hypersensitivity and will protect them, they become considerably more willing to trust and cooperate with treatment. After feeling safe and accepted, the atmosphere of the interview changes dramatically. When sufficient rapport has been established, they are more comfortable in describing their fears of being embarrassed and criticized, as well as their sensitivity to being misunderstood. They may experience these fears of being embarrassed as silly and express it. However, to the extent to which clinicians retreat from this empathic and accepting stance, these individuals are likely to feel ridiculed and withdraw again. (pp. 68-69)

How do personality disorders differ from other major diagnostic groups in terms of the DBT focus on underlying emotional arousal? While the urgency, impulsiveness, and affective avoidance involved in mood, anxiety, addiction, and eating disorders are intuitive, those of the personality disorders may be less evident to the casual observer. Greater attention will therefore be placed on the underlying affective conflicts with personality disorders in the discussion to follow.

Histrionic Personality Disorder

We begin with the most clearly similar diagnosis to our previous ones, histrionic personality disorder (HPD). The HPD patient is arousal seeking. They seek the attention, affection, and approval of others. Their attention and focus tend to be impressionistic, global, and imaginal. This personality style has been described as including a loss of reflective self-awareness (Horowitz et al., 1984). HPD patients are the people in the world who don't lose sight of the forest for the trees. In fact, at times they may even ignore the trees because they are so interested in the forest. The fact that they are frequently bruised by running into trees bothers them but doesn't stop them. They are on a mission—to entertain, mesmerize, and master the forest in order to prove their own sense of place within the forest. Deep feelings of sadness stemming from feelings of alienation from others are not clearly articulated, and their sense of loss is all but hidden from others. While the HPD patient does not necessarily feel empty (as in narcissistic personality disorder), like the individual with substance-abuse disorder, they crave immediate arousal and acceptability and doubt that such satisfaction can come from naturally occurring elements in the environment. They must create, design, and control the acceptance that otherwise will not be forthcoming.

The HPD patient thus is highly reactive to the environment and displays this immediately, but they don't quite understand how their impetuous behavior is driven by a need for intimacy. Their behavior is counterphobic in that they approach what they fear. Unlike the anxiety patient, who avoids what they fear, the HPD patient moves toward it like a bullet. This takes tremendous avoidance of affect (which seems paradoxical when describing the HPD patient, who is so affected, disclosive, and expressive). However, the HPD patient (unlike the patient with anxiety disorder) uses a temporarily effective defense against fear not used by those with anxiety disorders: they regress. The HPD patient seems to intentionally ignore their competencies, proven in previous situations, and to instead revert to earlier (and usually ineffectual) behavior strategies that may have worked when they were younger.

Unlike the obsessive-compulsive personality, the person with HPD has an incomplete split between affect and cognition. Their affective valence is so great that intellectual knowledge and wisdom are not adequately accessed. Previously learned knowledge, procedures, techniques, and strategies are not deployed. It's as if only the affect exists, and thoughts and ideas have been forgotten in service of primary attention to emotional needs and wants.

With HPD, the seeking of acceptability in a social world is primary. The main dialectic appears to be "I'm neglected, but others are powerful." This brings intense feelings of guilt, anger, and shame.

The DBT goal with HPD is thus to empower the cognitive aspects of functioning and to reduce the use of regression and arousal seeking as primary strategies in emotion-focused problem solving. Rather than employing traditional cognitive behavioral strategies (that would confront the irrationality of cognitive presumptions along each dialectic), the DBT therapist acknowledges the existential power, urgency, and identity-shattering effect of disapproval from others. As with all personality disorders, there is a method to the patient's madness. They attempt to operate on the environment in such a way that their strong needs get met. The arousal seeking, reactivity, and extroverted attempts to impress others in the environment are not manipulative or pejorative. This is operant behavior at its best. The role of the DBT therapist is to improve the focus and skills of the patient to better accomplish their objectives, rather than dispute the goal or objective (to obtain approval) itself.

Providing therapeutic focus can be challenging with an HPD patient, as shown in the dialogue below.

Patient: Then I told Kenny about my trip to Los Angeles and all of the interesting people I met there and how fascinating their stories were.

DBTherapist: (*Interrupting*) Did Kenny show interest in your stories?

Patient: He listened. There was this one woman who told me about her trip to the Amazon—

DBTherapist: (*Interrupting*) How did you feel when you were talking to Kenny?

Patient: I guess like I always do, like he was putting up with me.

DBTherapist: So it was not very satisfying sharing with Kenny your interesting stories about the people you met in LA?

Patient: No, that's why I like coming here to see you. You seem interested. Kenny hardly ever does.

DBTherapist: So this is another example of where you felt invisible with Kenny, in spite of the fact that you had something you felt was valuable to share.

Patient: Yes, it was. Let me tell you about this woman I met at the airport who went to the Amazon—

DBTherapist: Wait, I want to hear about her, but first I want to explore this repeating issue of invisibility you feel with Kenny. It's important, because you love Kenny so much and seek his attention so often. It's also important because if we could get a handle on this it would improve your life so much.

Patient: Kenny puts up with me, like so many of my family members. Kenny has an interesting life because his work provides so many fascinating opportunities. I don't have that because I stay at home to take care of the kids. If I had a job like Kenny's, then maybe people wouldn't ignore me so much.

DBTherapist: So you feel ignored and invisible, and what you try to do is find something equally interesting and noticeable to talk about with them. But it doesn't always work.

Patient: I guess not. Because Kenny doesn't value what I do as much as what he does.

DBTherapist: The goal is to be valued, in this case by Kenny. There is nothing wrong with being valued; we all want that. The need you have is to be valued. With Kenny, you evaluate if that need is being met by comparing how much attention he provides to you when you talk to him. And your strategy is to try to find interesting things to talk about, to increase your value to him. Do you think I have that right?

Patient: I guess so. Kenny's job allows him to travel, meet interesting people, be in the spotlight. I stay at home . . .

DBTherapist: What if it's not about how interesting your life is compared to your husband's life? What if it's more about what is going on specifically in the interaction in the moment between you and Kenny? You told me earlier that both you and Kenny decided early on in the marriage that you both thought it was important that the mom stay at home with the kids as they grow up. Right?

Patient: Yes. And he still tells me that he thinks it's important for the children that I be there with them. He felt he was secondary to his mother's and father's careers, and he doesn't want our children to feel that way.

DBTherapist: So his words tell you that he values what you do to contribute to the family, but you still feel ignored and invisible?

Patient: There is no way I'll ever be able to compete with the colorful life Kenny lives.

DBTherapist: As you were telling Kenny about your trip to LA, what was Kenny doing?

Patient: He was packing for his next business trip.

DBTherapist: Could it be the context, that Kenny was busy and preoccupied, rather than the content of what you were talking about, that made you feel invisible?

As the above psychotherapy dialogue suggests, the DBT therapist gently deals with issues of idealization of others, validates goals while questioning behavioral tactics the patient uses to accomplish their emotional goals, and helps to differentiate feelings from behavior. The DBT therapist is directive in sessions, frequently having to change the course of conversation desired by the patient, but this is tolerated by the patient if it is clear to the patient that this direction is clearly in the service of accomplishing the patient's previously identified objectives.

These recommendations are consistent with those made by more psychoanalytically oriented therapists, who suggest that the therapist should repeat and reflect the patient's verbalizations (assisting them to label emotions more clearly), ask for details, and sustain distance without being overly distant from the patient (Horowitz et al., 1984).

Table 13: Dialectics with Histrionic Personality Disorder		
I'm ignored.	◄——————►	Others are powerful.
I can be enchanting.	◄——————►	My feelings don't need justification.
I'm not out of control.	◄——————►	My feelings are real.
I'm not unreal.	◄——————►	My self-respect is more important than their consequences.
I feel.	◄——————►	My behavior is less relevant than my feelings.
My feelings are immediate.	◄——————►	Don't wait to respond to my feelings.
I hurt.	◄——————►	You can stop my hurt.
Attention is critical.	◄——————►	You can give me attention.
I'm nothing without your attention.	◄——————►	You're ignoring me.
I'm not dependent on others.	◄——————►	You're ignoring me.
I'm okay.	◄——————►	You're even better.
My needs could easily be met, if only you try.	◄——————►	You're not trying.
I'm not hurt.	◄——————►	Except that you hurt me, I'd be fine.
Emotions are primary.	◄——————►	You pay no attention to my emotions whatsoever.

Avoidant Personality Disorder

The patient with avoidant personality disorder (APD) is afraid of being hurt, rejected, or unsuccessful (Beck et al., 2004). They see themselves as socially inept and incompetent and want someone stronger and more skilled to protect them. To an extreme degree they are preoccupied with being criticized or rejected in social situations. They are thus painfully aware of what others might think or what they anticipate others (who are more socially adept) might think. Their fear of being shamed or ridiculed is high, and they intermittently view others as more powerful than themselves. At other times, the APD patient may ridicule the acceptability of others as a defense against want. If others are inadequate, then they don't have to take interpersonal risks.

Environmental triggers thus have to do with close relationships and situations that involve public contact. The demands of others are seen by the person with APD as perfectionistic and bringing rejection and humiliation. They tolerate aloneness as a compromise against perceived and anticipated rejection. An extreme sense of inadequacy and social emptiness pervades their sense of self, and their view of the world is that it is hostile and demeaning. They tend to be more than shy, with defenses against interpersonal transparency that are readily apparent. They are hypervigilant to criticism, desiring unusual guarantees of safety before they will engage in situations that are interpersonally unfamiliar. This is due to their sense of defectiveness and social inadequacy.

Because the APD patient fears negative social judgment from others, their level of transparency is low. Even when seeking treatment, they are likely to underestimate and underreport known personal, interpersonal, and behavioral fears, deficits, and behaviors. They are more likely to underestimate social inadequacy than those with any other personality disorder here described. When they report that they feel sad, they are likely to feel horrendously depressed. When they report that they are lonely, they are likely to have no friends whatsoever. When they report they are anxious, they are likely to experience terror that may be continuous even in their places of safety. The DBT therapist thus relies less on their immediate verbalizations and more on the assessment of behavioral activities: how often they have friends over on weekends, how often they go to movie theaters, how often they go to social gatherings, how often they date, and how many previous relationships they've had that involve intimacy and expectation of longevity.

The APD patient thus has core issues of safety vs. freedom; idealization of others vs. devaluation of self; dependency vs. independence; threat vs. safety; shame vs. safety; inadequacy vs. isolation; and transparency vs. humiliation. Avoidance is a core defense against anxiety, involving interpersonal situations, evaluative situations, public situations, and verbal and expressive situations. Their psychological defenses involve thoughts that defend against experienced affect, self-absorption, focus on short-term consequences, avoidance of affect, and transparency (or lack thereof).

Table 14: Dialectics with Avoidant Personality Disorder		
I'm fragile, and I'll get hurt if I get close to someone.	←——→	I'm extremely lonely.
People will see my deficiencies if I get close enough.	←——→	Better to be alone than to feel bad.
My anxiety will overwhelm me.	←——→	Better to be alone than to feel bad.
People's judgments of me can destroy me.	←——→	I destroy myself with my own judgments.
People notice me.	←——→	People ignore me.
It's shameful that I feel so deeply.	←——→	I must hide my sensitivity from others.
Social environments exhaust me.	←——→	Better to be alone than to feel bad.
I'm picky about who I let in.	←——→	No one ever meets my standards or expectations.
I deserve to be loved.	←——→	People hurt me so badly.
There is nothing wrong with me.	←——→	People tear me to shreds.
People expect too much from me.	←——→	I can protect myself from demands that prove my inadequacy.
I'm socially empty, I have nothing to say.	←——→	I'll be humiliated if I'm discovered.
Hope may cause me to leave my circle of safety.	←——→	Hope will increase my anxiety.
I'm incompetent.	←——→	I can be confident alone.
Others are powerful and influential.	←——→	I need someone to take care of me, but others can hurt me.
My needs are few, and I don't need much.	←——→	My needs are so strong they incapacitate me.

Sperry (1999) notes that APD treatment involves empathic responding, and consistent with the DBT approach of validation, the patient is encouraged to share their pain and anticipatory fears. Sperry notes that the more the clinician understands their hypersensitivity and communicates to the patient that they will help protect them, the more cooperative and transparent the patient will become in treatment. They will then more readily describe their fears of being embarrassed, humiliated, criticized, and rejected. The DBT therapist is extremely concerned with validation of affect and refrains from saying anything that could be seen as making the patient's concerns minimal or illogical. The DBT therapist does not confront their fears by challenging cognitive assumptions but rather empathically reflects back the underlying concerns and the compromises the patient has had to make in order to feel safe and free of intolerable ridicule from the social world.

Being nonjudgmental with the APD is thus especially important, as is directly communicating concern and understanding of the patient's anticipatory fears. Sperry (1999) notes that a "tentative bond" must be formed with the patient in the initial stages of treatment, and the DBT therapist should not request nor expect substantially different treatment from the patient than the patient has shown in all past relationships. The DBT therapist thus explicitly communicates to the patient that they understand and appreciate the need to remain safe from social criticism, and that such criticism would be catastrophic in the moment of its occurrence. The therapist requests the patient's cooperation in developing alternative sources of comfort while they expand their social support system in ways that indeed are threatening and scary.

Going slow in treatment, especially with homework assignments, is demonstrated below.

Patient: No, I didn't go to the movies like we talked about last session.

DBTherapist: Did you think about going?

Patient: Yeah, I thought about it.

DBTherapist: I'm glad you thought about it. From what you've told me, you usually don't even consider getting out on the weekends.

Patient: But I didn't go.

DBTherapist: You thought about it. That's the first step. When you thought about it, how did you feel?

Patient: I started feeling tense.

DBTherapist: I'm glad you recognized that. Just thinking about going out makes you tense. Just the anticipation of going out hurts.

Patient: Yeah, I'm such a wimp. I don't even know why I bother coming here.

DBTherapist: Brad, I'm pleased you're sticking with treatment. You've already made a lot of progress. You've disclosed to me huge feelings of shame that you've talked about with no one before, not even your mother. You've shown tremendous willingness in our sessions to feel the hurt that you protect yourself from normally.

Patient: Sure, but I can't do the homework. I can't force myself to get out of my apartment. What kind of progress is that?

DBTherapist: I think that's my fault, Brad, not yours. You're not ready yet to tolerate the anxiety. I picked something for homework that you're not yet prepared for.

Patient: That's okay.

DBTherapist: We talked last time about how your fear of being hurt and humiliated is greater than your pain of being alone. Do you remember that?

Patient: Yeah.

DBTherapist: Let's pick something that's not quite so threatening. What is something that you've actually done in the past, without support, but decided not to do again because you felt uncomfortable? What was doable but uncomfortable?

The capacity to tolerate feedback from others is slowly developed during treatment, as the patient is encouraged to take measured risks in relating to others (Sperry, 1999). The first such challenge is in the therapeutic relationship itself, and the patient is verbally complimented for their willingness to describe their fears of shame and humiliation. Verbal description of such fears in the therapy office is the first step the APD patient takes to expose themselves to social anxiety. This, per se, is therapeutic progress.

In later stages of treatment, exposing themselves to emotional arousal becomes the goal—just to experience the anticipatory anxiety of thinking about social interaction. The patient is encouraged to stay with and sustain their anxiety imaginally as they think about social interactions. They are encouraged to pay attention to their hypersensitivity and to identify all the threat cues that can be imagined as they anticipate social interactions. This is done prior to assignment of even minimal homework to expand their social support system.

An important dialectic in the middle portion of treatment is to have the patient become increasingly aware of their attention to negative outcomes and threat cues and their relative lack of attention to positive outcomes and safety cues. The APD patient is not told that their anticipation is wrong but instead is told that their emphasis is on one side of the dialectic (threat) to the sacrifice of the other end of the dialectic (safety).

The thought "If others really knew me, they would reject me" is, only in the last stage of treatment, reframed to "I already know me, and I am rejecting. My judgments of me are more powerfully critical than those others may have, and I project these negative feelings onto others."

DBT can be useful to the APD patient in a number of ways: exposure to anxiety (typically avoided) can be desensitizing and allow increased confidence in the ability to tolerate previously feared arousal; normalizing and validating expectations for approval can decrease shame and other secondary emotional responses; mindfulness can decrease self-absorption and increase the reality base of contextual cues (observing what is seen rather than what is expected); emotion regulation can decrease the arousal that powers hypervigilance for threat; meaning making can increase strategic focus such that the person responds to wants and needs rather than fears; strategic behavior focus can increase relevance of interpersonal cues; distress tolerance can improve perseverance in spite of fear; and dialectic thinking can help the APD patient identify dichotomous thinking that keeps their fear-avoidance cycle going.

Obsessive-Compulsive Personality Disorder

The patient with obsessive-compulsive personality disorder (OCP) has a sharp but narrowed focus of attention that makes them miss critical bits of information (Shapiro, 1965). The OCP patient seems both willful and without control of their own volition in that they seem penetratingly fixated on a goal or objective, but through pure rigidity have lost control of the method of achieving their aspirations. The fear of losing control in the OCP patient is so strong that affect itself becomes the enemy, as is the case in many acute mental disorders that are not personality disorders. Since the deliberateness of the OCP patient cannot effectively control their emotional pain, they begin to truncate their emotions, to squish them as much as possible. The result is that the OCP patient loses the ability to become spontaneous, whimsical, or playful (Beck et al., 2004). Their sense of deliberation and responsibility become overwhelming.

OCP has dynamics that are different from obsessive-compulsive disorder (OCD). While the OCD patient has direct anxiety-reducing rituals that involve associational learning (in that performance of the ritual reduces immediate arousal, but "stamps in" the phobic anticipatory response for the future), in OCP the role of dialectics is much stronger: the OCP patient has perfectly balanced rather than mixed feelings about situations (McWilliams, 1994). They withhold decision making because all of the forces, all of the pros and cons, are perceived to be in perfect balance, thus preventing any satisfactory synthesis. Perfectionism allows them to avoid failure at any cost (Horowitz et al., 1984).

While the HPD patient uses excessive experience in order to dig themselves out of conflict, the person with OCP restricts their attentional focus so narrowly that experience is lost. Minute technical details so completely flood their attention that actual experience of the world is lost (Shapiro, 1965), and new information is excluded from problem-solving awareness. New events are seen as distractions rather than as potentially generating new and different opportunities and challenges. The OCP patient is stuck in old conflicts, attends to past challenges rather than current conflicts, and exchanges experience for perceived control.

One core conflict for OCP is obedience or submission versus defiance. They are outraged at being controlled by the environment or by others, but they fear being punished if they fail to comply with social expectations. They thus feel isolated and abandoned and use drive or control as a defense against their own despair. This creates another, different dialectic: righteousness versus selfishness (McWilliams, 1994). The OCP patient fears being indulgent, fears that their initiative will result in abandonment by others, and thus they feel forced to reenact compromise formations until they get it perfectly. Sensing that their compromises are inadequate, they try again and again, using the same strategies. One reason that the OCP patient does not shift from a tried-and-failed strategy to an untried strategy is that they have separated affect from cognition (Horowitz et al., 1984). They do not use their feelings as sources of information about success, since they assume that their feelings must be irrelevant or others would have taken notice of their dialectical conflicts and provided soothing and comfort.

The dialectic analysis is particularly important for OCP patients, as demonstrated below.

Patient: I brought work home every night again. I remembered our discussion about taking some time for myself each evening, but my work requirements just were overwhelming.

DBTherapist: You felt you could control the anxiety of uncompleted work, of making a mistake by having things undone, by working harder and harder.

Patient: Yeah, I guess I did feel anxious. But I just focused on getting my work done.

DBTherapist:	What would have happened, just last week, if you hadn't completed all of your work?
Patient:	My clients would have been angry at me. They count on me to get the job done. That's why my business is so good. My clients know they can count on me to get the job done.
DBTherapist:	So people, in this case your clients, would have been angry at you if you did not get the job done promptly?
Patient:	Yes, that's why there are so many accountants out there who are screaming for business. When a new client comes in, they don't get the job done, and so they don't get the word-of-mouth referrals that I get.
DBTherapist:	Let's focus on the feelings. If you don't devote your life to work—more than others do—then your clients will abandon you. You are trading security for personal pleasure. Do you agree?
Patient:	How can I have pleasure if I'm worried about security?
DBTherapist:	Precisely. Your fear of lack of security, in this case economic security, is so strong that you compromise having a personal life of your own. You're making a choice between competing demands, security versus pleasure.
Patient:	And security is so important to me that I give up pleasure.
DBTherapist:	So the compromise you're making is to not have pain but to not have pleasure either.
Patient:	So my security is empty.

The OCP patient oscillates so rapidly between the dialectic poles of fear versus anger and guilt that nothing is ever really felt. Dominance versus submission is a frequent dialectic between the patient and therapist, and decision making is frequently avoided (Horowitz et al., 1984).

DBT with OCP is directed at the rigidity of attention, the judgmentalness to self and others, identifying the vulnerability to shame, identifying the substitution of behavior for affect, assisting in identifying the antecedents of shame, redefining (reframing) need as normal, refocusing attention to affect from exclusive attention to behavior, and normalizing strong affect.

Rigidity of attention is reduced through mindfulness practice, especially within sessions. Mindfulness allows the OCP patient to *do* nothing, which will create discomfort due to lack of practice. While these patients use their already focused and narrowed attention on internal experience (with the expectation that they are not to analyze or respond to this information), a new strategy can develop: observing and participating with experience rather than using effortful action to change experience. Mindfulness practice demands attending to and decreasing judgmentalness. Since the OCP person is used to dealing with past and strong conflicts, having them attend to their experience within sessions (when the environment is demanding ambiguous or affective responses rather than driven ones) decreases the importance of evaluative effort. There is less to judge. Practicing not judging experience is critical for the OCP patient.

Fear of self-indulgence is shown in the next therapeutic dialogue, a continuation of treatment with our previous accountant patient.

Patient: But I can't be always focusing on pleasure.

DBTherapist: How often do you focus on pleasure?

Patient: Hardly ever, I guess.

DBTherapist: So you're afraid of becoming self-indulgent, focusing on wants, so you intentionally avoid ever doing this.

The OCP patient uses thoughts to conceal feelings rather than express them. Since mindfulness can be a nonverbal experience, there is less reason to conceal. Experience itself is attended to rather than cognitions. This is quite uncomfortable for the OCP patient, so using psychosocial skills education between mindfulness practice can assist in having the OCP patient maintain treatment in the face of increasing emotional discomfort (frequently unverbalized).

While OCP patients may readily admit to feelings of inadequacy or shame, they engage in behavior that helps them to avoid the experience of inadequacy or shame. Therefore, simple verbal description from the OCP patient of such feelings, since they are not truly experienced during the verbalization, does not result in substantial clinical benefit. Rather, the DBT therapist elicits naming or identification of the feeling, the antecedents to the feeling, the thoughts that accompany the feeling, the bodily experience of the feeling, the behavior that follows the feeling, and the subsequent evaluation (jugmentalness or criticalness) by the patient. Following this cognitive chain analysis, the DBT therapist invites the patient to imaginally recreate the chain of events. Have the patient lie back in the chair, close their eyes, and breathe

Table 15: Dialectics with Obsessive Compulsive Personality Disorder

I must submit and comply with others or they will punish me.	<———>	Others have no right to define what is right for me. I'll defy them.
I'm outraged that others are trying to control me.	<———>	I'm afraid of being punished.
I can be in control.	<———>	I fear being out of control.
If I'm careful, I can avoid danger. I must use my drive.	<———>	It's no use; my drive is imperfect. I'm doomed
I need not feel.	<———>	My strategies can save me from my despair.
There is a right way and a wrong way of living life.	<———>	Don't be selfish.
I will not hurt.	<———>	I can atone for my sins.
The devil is in the details.	<———>	You can attend even more perfectly.
Your input is irrelevant. I must master this on my own.	<———>	You could save me from this. This is a test of my worthiness.
I'm dangerous and dirty.	<———>	The world is a dangerous and dirty place.
I'll be humiliated in public if I don't succeed.	<———>	You will punish me for these misdeeds.
My needs can be met with great effort and strain.	<———>	I'm unworthy of having my needs met.
The world is full of disorder than I can alleviate.	<———>	True order will point out my inadequacy.
What emotions?	<———>	I hurt desperately.

deeply; then the therapist recounts the chain analysis in a soft tone of voice, inviting the patient to re-experience it in their imagination. Since the patient is not using their intellect at the time to provide the words for the events, the words (cognitive expression) are less likely to be used as a method of defending against the feelings. They are more likely to experience their feelings (not avoid or escape them) during an imaginal practice session than they are during verbal therapy or in vivo. Since different attentional characteristics and processes are used imaginally, different outcomes are more likely.

Normalizing strong affect for the OCP patient can be difficult. Since the central fears are of failure, abandonment, and punishment, strong affect brings fear of self-indulgence (that they will act out their wants, then be punished by others). Moreover, since the person with OCP uses words (logic and cognition) to defend against affect, conversational therapy can go in circles. The DBT therapist thus uses analogy, metaphor, and storytelling interventions, hinting at normalization rather than directly stating it. Such interventions are aimed at the notions of being rather than doing, the universality of frailty, how most of us use defenses against great potential harm, and how conflict is a typical rather than extraordinary part of living. The DBT therapist is mindful of the OCP patient's focus on details, so metaphor, analogy, and storytelling are brief and to the point to avoid reinforcing the overly narrow and detailed attentional focus of the patient. Finally, the DBT therapist does not allow rapid shifting of conflicts, encouraging the OCP patient to stay with one experience long enough to allow exposure and counterconditioning.

Patient: And then I began the tedious process of—

DBTherapist: Let's go back to what you were feeling before you returned to work on your spreadsheet.

Patient: I was feeling bothered that my kids were distracting me from my work.

DBTherapist: Let's explore "bothered." What other words or labels can describe the experience of being bothered?

Patient: I guess it goes back to fear, fear that I'll fail to provide for my family.

DBTherapist: So the attention from members of your family that you're trying to protect become a nuisance.

Patient: Yeah, I guess I lose perspective because my anxiety is so high.

DBTherapist: What do you think would have happened if you allowed yourself to experience the anxiety when the kids interrupted your work rather than avoid the anxiety by returning to work?

Narcissistic Personality Disorder

The patient with narcissistic personality disorder (NPD) feels emotionally empty. The NPD patient seeks affirmation of self from the outside environment. They are extremely concerned with how they appear to others, and due to the split between self-concept and self as perceived by others, they have an exquisite sense of fraudulence. The underlying and certainly unarticulated affect is that they are empty, that they don't fit into society, and that they are loveless. The core issues for the NPD person are thus self-esteem and identity. The contents of affect are feelings of envy, inferiority, superiority, insufficiency, weakness, inadequacy, and shame.

The NPD patient is ideally suited for DBT treatment due to their high need for love (and frequently low output of love to others). The NPD patient's defenses against their own self-loathing make them unable to obtain that which they seek: the complete approval of others. The dialectic treatment is to bring their desire for approval from others into strategic focus and to help them more adequately meet their needs for approval. A primary therapeutic target is thus to decrease idealization and devaluation of others and to improve their interpersonal observational skills. Mindfulness of others, including their affect, needs, and behavior, helps the NPD patient to more adequately compare their own interpersonal output to interpersonal rewards provided by others. Helping the NPD patient to shift from short-term focus of interpersonal observation to long-term focus improves their strategic behavior.

In the following therapeutic encounter, the therapist directs the NPD patient to the balance between interpersonal giving and getting.

Patient: I'm concerned about my upcoming promotion and tenure evaluation. My department chair is so ignorant about my area of research and expertise. Actually, I think he's jealous of my accomplishments and will therefore thwart my advancement at the university.

DBTherapist: How long have you been working to have your chair recognize the work that you do?

Patient: He's so full of himself. He's only concerned with himself. I do everything within my power to avoid him.

DBTherapist: So you don't regularly interact with him?

Patient: No, I do everything I can to avoid him. The pompous bastard.

DBTherapist: Does he have substantial influence over your promotion and tenure decision?

Patient: As chair of the department, he holds all the cards. He gets to appoint the faculty members who serve on the committee that makes the recommendations.

DBTherapist: Okay, so he's a critical player in the decision. Yet you avoid him.

Patient: Yes—you would too. Every time I begin to describe my work, he starts talking about his own research. What's the use?

DBTherapist: You're both in the same department, the Department of Organizational and Leadership Behavior, right?

Patient: Of course, since he's my department chair, we're both in the same department.

DBTherapist: It sounds like you have not been careful in emotionally feeding your department chair's needs. He's more concerned, naturally, with his own area of research than yours. What if you spent more time between now and the Promotion and Tenure Committee meetings drawing the connections between your line of research and his?

Patient: You mean brownnose him?

DBTherapist: No, I mean connect the dots for him. Show him how your research is related in some way to things that he's interested in.

Patient: He's such an arrogant guy. He'd probably respond to that. But just the idea of playing into his needs makes me sick.

DBTherapist: You wouldn't be playing into his needs, you'd be trying to meet your own needs.

Patient: You mean manipulate him?

DBTherapist: Manipulation is when we try to get something deviously and surreptitiously from others. Here, you are being mindful of others' needs and interests and how they connect with your needs and interests and trying to achieve a balance. He gets his needs met, you get your needs met.

Mindfulness skills also help the NPD patient by decreasing judgmentalism. NPD patients are excruciatingly judgmental, as NPD is a disorder of comparison. They constantly compare themselves to others in order to reduce the sense of falseness and emptiness that they experience. They substitute pride for doubt, contempt for admiration, superiority for underlying feelings of inferiority. The constant evaluative (judgmental) focus helps to keep them in a cognitive frame of reference—a form of emotional avoidance and escape.

The NPD patient manipulates the meaning of actual events (Horowitz et al., 1984), which places greater strain on the patient to successfully use psychological coping strategies such as strategic behavior skills. While the DBT therapist attempts to deal with distortion through mindfulness and meaning-making skills, perhaps more with the NPD patient than any other, the DBT therapist has to allow natural changes (Linehan, 1993b) rather than attempt to corner the patient with rational logic as might be attempted with rational emotive therapy approaches.

Gratitude appears to be especially difficult for the NPD patient, as this serves to esteem others (which is perceived as a devaluation of self). DBT interventions in the early stage of treatment are thus to have patients be mindful of pleasant environmental (rather than interpersonal) events and to develop additional comfort and practice in the experience of gratitude that does not challenge their comparative interpersonal framework. Gradually and slowly, mindfulness is used to consider the self, coupled with viewing one's strengths and skills with gratitude. Finally, and only in the last stage of treatment, mindfulness toward others and the development of gratitude for their strengths and skills are encouraged.

NPD patients have a deep shame about asking for anything from others (McWilliams, 1994) and have the magical thinking that others should be able to read their minds about their needs and meet those needs without strain or effort. This sense of entitlement is a major therapy-interfering behavior and thus is a core target of DBT intervention. Rather than focus on assertiveness skills, the DBT therapist focuses on the dialectic conflict of shame versus acceptability. The therapist does not confront the cognition ("Others should easily meet my needs, since I'm deserving") but rather confronts the affect ("I hurt because others have ignored me"). Recognition of the hurt results in greater therapeutic gain, since it targets the reason for the defenses rather than the defenses themselves. Therapeutic focus on disappointment, thwarted need fulfillment, lack of affirmation from others, and finally the existential

Table 16: Dialectics with Narcissistic Personality Disorder

I'm empty.	←——→	You can fill me up.
I'm enchanting.	←——→	Why don't you have the intelligence to recognize that?
I'm in control.	←——→	I just don't let you see the control I have.
Image is all-important.	←——→	I'm a fraud.
I'm socially superior.	←——→	I don't fit in.
I don't need.	←——→	You should fill my needs effortlessly.
You should be better.	←——→	You can stop my hurt.
Attention is critical.	←——→	You can give me attention.
I'm nothing without your attention.	←——→	You're a fool for ignoring me.
You are perfect.	←——→	Why don't you love me?
I have all that it takes to succeed.	←——→	I will not ask you for what I desperately need.
My image is all that matters.	←——→	There is nothing inside to see.
I'm not hurt.	←——→	If you didn't hurt me, I'd be fine.
I'm ashamed.	←——→	You could have prevented my shame.
Self-disgust	←——→	Self-righteous
Idealization	←——→	Devaluation

emptiness of the NPD patient will decrease the sense of social fraudulence experienced by these patients.

NPD is a disorder of identity. DBT thus assists the patient to build an identity that relies less on social comparison (including image), and perfectionism. Skills training involves increasing the patient's ability to give affection to others without reciprocation, and building mastery and competence feelings through this activity. Coaching and prompting the patient to self-reinforce without comparison to others (decreasing idealization and devaluation of others) is a key therapeutic target. This can only be accomplished by validating the patient's deep needs for approval as acceptable and reasonable expectations of any human being. The DBT therapist challenges the methods of achieving the objective, not the objective or need itself.

Validation of the NPD patient needs to be more skillfully applied than with most DBT patients. The patient's underlying conception that they are false leads them to be critical of support and affirmation from others, even though this is ultimately what they deeply want and need. Direct compliments, such as "You were skillful in being able to discern that," are not as effective as coached self-compliments, such as "Did you give yourself credit when you did that?" Encouraging the patient to form their own appraisal ends the reliance on others for affirmation. Obviously this is a long-term therapeutic process accomplished over months, if not years, of therapy. Fortunately, the NPD patient infrequently presents with suicidal or parasuicidal behavior, and rather than dealing with constant environmental crisis, the DBT therapist is dealing with increasing loving behaviors to others, increasing long-term focus of attention, encouraging self-reinforcement, decreasing judgmentalism, and decreasing social comparison as (ineffective) methods to bolster a fragmented identity. NPD patients may regress in therapy due to their immature dependency (Horowitz et al., 1984), and balancing skill acquisition with psychotherapy is thus especially important. DBT with NPD is psychotherapy with identity and self-image targets. The behavioral focus on objectives (validating needs but challenging methods to meet those needs) over time assists the patient to revise their underlying schemas regarding self and others.

Schizoid Personality Disorder

The person with schizoid personality disorder (SPD) seeks safety through withdrawal. The core dialectic conflict is between integrity of self versus others. Others are perceived as a threat to their very existence, and the corollary dialectics of closeness versus distance, love versus fear, attachment versus engulfment, alienation versus aloneness, and compliance versus conformity (McWilliams, 1994) all inhere from this central dialectic of fear of obliteration by others.

Perhaps with no other disorder is the effect of an attachment disorder seen. The SPD patient has not learned how to tolerate their own affect. In fact, their affect was alternatively punished and rewarded without consistency. The SPD patient thus never learned the positive effect their emotions could have on others, but they became acutely aware of the inconsistency of effect of others' emotions on them. They feel alone but fear intimacy because this brings fears of engulfment. There is thus the predictable avoidance and escape of affect.

Distancing from others is used in order to prevent empathic responses that bring pain. Recent functional imaging studies have shown that the same neural pathways that define physical pain operate during empathic understanding of others' pain (Singer et al., 2004). The only major exception to this is that only the affective pathways and not the sensory pathways are activated. Intimacy with others involves empathy, and the history of the SPD patient predicts that intimacy and emotional pain are one and the same. They thus do not tolerate intimacy, abhor the empathic responses of others, and prefer situational intimacy over which they have rather complete control. Neuroimaging studies show that social exclusion fires the same neural net pathways as physical pain (Eisenberger, Lieberman, and Williams, 2003), and the SPD patient controls the experience of social exclusion by being the rejector rather than the rejected. The DBT therapist allows the patient to have such control over the intimacy of the psychotherapeutic relationship.

The control issues, lack of empathy, and lack of continuity between patient and therapist is shown below.

Patient: I'm in touch with my emotions only too well, so I don't know why you keep asking me to specify them.

DBTherapist: Because although you may be acutely aware of them, I can't tell from your nonverbal behavior. With many people, I can fairly accurately guess what they are feeling from what their face and body says, but you don't display your feelings in the same way. So I'm not trying to get you to feel something different from what you're feeling. I'm trying to determine from your own assessment what you're feeling.

Patient: Okay, if you find that necessary.

DBTherapist: (Pause) You were telling me why you find contact with others rather unnecessary.

Patient: I don't see the point. Most people are not interested in what I'm interested in, so I find them rather boring.

DBTherapist: So the reason you avoid others is not that they cause you anxiety or threaten you in some way, but that they don't interest you?

Patient:	Well, they also threaten and cause me anxiety, but mostly they do not interest me. If they don't interest me, then why should I spend time with them?
DBTherapist:	Do you feel lonely?
Patient:	No, I find all kinds of things to do on my own.
DBTherapist:	Remind me again why you chose to enter psychotherapy.
Patient:	Because my boss told me I was depressed, and because I'm receiving Social Security benefits and I should try to eliminate the disability so I can support myself rather than have the government supporting me.
DBTherapist:	So it's not personal pain that brought you into therapy, but the recommendations of others and your sense of responsibility that brings you in?
Patient:	I didn't say that. I said I thought it best that I resolve the issues that make me unemployable. My boss from my part-time job, whom I respect, told me she thought therapy would help.
DBTherapist:	What do you think makes you unemployable?
Patient:	Well, obviously my inability to relate to people. I applied for jobs for three years. Even menial jobs that paid minimum wage turned me down based on my interviews.
DBTherapist:	What do you think happened during the interviews that made them not employ you?
Patient:	Perhaps I'm too honest with people. When they ask me a question, I give them an honest answer. They don't like what I say.
DBTherapist:	Give me an example of an honest answer you might give them that may make them not employ you.
Patient:	Well, for example, they will ask how I get along with coworkers. I tell them that in general I keep to myself, since I find others to have rather superficial interests and to be rather unconscious of the ways they handle issues in the universe.

DBTherapist: Do they ask you what you mean by that?

Patient: Some do, some don't.

DBTherapist: For those who do, what do you tell them?

Patient: It depends.

DBTherapist: Okay, but you have a fairly good idea that some of your statements during the interview make them turn you down for employment, is that right?

Patient: Undoubtedly, since I've been turned down for perhaps a hundred jobs I've applied for over the last four years.

DBTherapist: So, on the one hand, you want to be employable. And that means that you have to have conventional answers to questions posed to you during employment interviews. And, on the other hand, you find yourself compelled to give honest answers to questions posed to you, and some of those answers are not very conventional and result in your unemployability. Is that right?

Patient: I guess that's right.

DBTherapist: So you either have to sacrifice your total honesty or your employability?

Patient: Are you suggesting that I lie in order to obtain a job?

DBTherapist: No, I'm suggesting that you can't have both. You can't both be totally honest and be employable.

Patient: (No response)

DBTherapist: Does that make you uncomfortable?

Patient: It makes me uncomfortable that I'd have to lie in order to get a job.

DBTherapist: Would you agree that your values and ways of understanding the world are somewhat different than most people's understanding?

Patient: Undoubtedly.

DBTherapist: If you were the employer rather than the employee applicant, what would be most important to you to assess in determining who to hire and who not to hire?

Patient: If they could do the job well or not. If I thought they could do the job required of them, I'd hire them. If I thought they could not do the job, I would not hire them. It would be a simple decision.

DBTherapist: So you would focus on job-related requirements, not their personal views of the universe. Right?

Patient: Right.

DBTherapist: But when the employer asks you questions, you feel compelled to answer them completely, including your views of the universe, rather than stick to your job-related capabilities.

Patient: I see your point. I give them too much information.

DBTherapist: And do you see the irony here? You're not interested in a personal relationship with your employer or many others in the world, but you give people so much information that you show them how different from them you are. Almost as if you were in a personal relationship with everybody.

Patient: (*No response*)

DBTherapist: What are your thoughts or feelings?

Patient: You didn't ask me a question.

DBTherapist: Can you see how giving "full disclosure" or lots of information about yourself is more consistent with having a personal and intimate relationship with people?

Patient: No.

DBTherapist: You might say hello to a stranger you sit next to on a bus—maybe not even that. Whereas you give lots of information to a person you want to have a relationship with.

Patient: (*No response*)

DBTherapist: What are your thoughts?

Patient: I don't have any at this moment.

DBTherapist: Is it uncomfortable for you to come here and talk to me? Like right now, is there any discomfort whatsoever in talking to me?

Patient: I'm always somewhat uncomfortable when I'm talking to someone. Now is no different than most of the time.

DBTherapist: I want you to monitor how you feel, especially in here when we are talking together. Because it's difficult for me to guess how you're feeling, I want you to tell me when any discomfort increases and even when it decreases.

Patient: I'm not sure how that could be helpful.

DBTherapist: Because one of my goals is to understand you, and also because one of my goals is to help you increase your comfort with others when you talk to them. I can't do that without the information.

Patient: (No response)

DBTherapist: Is that acceptable to you?

Patient: Yes.

One of the main methods the SPD patient uses for emotional avoidance and intimacy escape is unconventionality. They identify societal expectations and intentionally defy them. Such defiance is not antisocial in the sense of attempting to please themselves at the expense of others. Instead, the strategy (operant behavior) is to shock or disinterest others. They do not wish to be defined in terms of a predictable personality type, and thus attempts of the DBT therapist to interact with them in consistent ways will be initially rejected. The SPD patient will engage in approach when the therapist is distant and will engage in avoidance when the therapist attempts to approach. The schizoid tendency, unlike the BPD tendency, is not to breach boundaries but to keep them defined by the patient rather than the therapist. It is no different in their typical day-to-day interpersonal relationships.

While not oppositional, the SPD is not compliant either. Conformity, following rule-governed behavior defined by someone in close proximity, jeopardizes their operant strategy of keeping others at a distance. While they feel emotional deprivation, the offers of soothing and nourishment from others are seen as intrusions. Validation of affect and behavior is thus quite problematic with the SPD patient, since this is perceived as an attempt to bound them with rules of responding that could bring the feared (and needed) love they defend against. The most clearly defined and meaning-ful goal of the SPD patient is to keep safe from the engulfment they fear from you and everyone in their environment. Distance is the foundation of their safety, and thera-peutic strategies that threaten this distance will be resisted.

A major DBT goal with SPD is to normalize conflict. This is a dialectic in itself, since the therapist is normalizing unconventionality, making distancing behavior a natural precursor to closeness, making aloneness the expectable precursor of relation-ship, and indifference the beginning of meaningfulness. Schizoid personalities can respond well to direct dialectical interpretations, where opposites and paradoxes are made prominent. The SPD patient is attracted to the ambiguity of the dialectic, since it does not demand one certain response of all individuals to similar situations. It allows escape and avoidance from hyperarousal should closeness, engulfment, or threat to (defensive) identity become unmanageable. In fact, the person with SPD is invited to shift their position on the dialectics as frequently as their objectives desire. This freedom offers the SPD patient the opportunity to experiment with other modes of responding that their current coping techniques have prohibited.

As with the other disorders, mindfulness offers focus on affect. While the schiz-oid person is tempted to use rationality, especially in their pursuit of defiance of con-ventional authority and reasoning, mindfulness invites them to stop evaluating and analyzing situations and observe just their affect. One of the rules of mindfulness is that there is no objective or purpose in the observation (you are not trying to get them to relax, which can be seen as an attempt to weaken their defenses). Since there is no objective or striving toward a goal, the paradoxical result of successful mindfulness is that the SPD patient no longer needs to defend. Slowly they can drop their defenses because there is nothing to defend against. The DBT therapist invites them to notice their feelings. The only compliance requested is that they privately sustain their attention without evaluation or judgment. They need not come to any particular conclusion or react with any predictable course of action. They need not conform.

The greatest therapeutic challenge the DBT therapist meets with an SPD patient is with the behavior or strategic focus. When you invite them to examine the effect of their behavior on others, this request is seen as an intrusion. The attempt to have them use skillful means is abhorrent, since it involves recognition of how their objectives may depend on the feelings of others. The DBT principles of letting go of attachment and aversion are critical here. The goal is not to please others or to disap-point others. The goal is to accomplish our objectives while validating affect: the therapist acknowledges the reality base of the patient's sensitivity and the objective of maintaining identity integrity, while prompting change in method or strategy in accomplishing both.

Table 17: Dialectics with Schizoid Personality Disorder

I'm alone.	←——→	Don't invade my space.
Society will smother me if I let it.	←——→	Society punishes me for who I am.
Society wants me to feel a certain way, which I don't.	←——→	My feelings are real.
I can go it alone.	←——→	My self-respect is more important than their consequences.
I feel.	←——→	Society doesn't understand my feelings.
My principles are more important than my feelings.	←——→	Society rejects my principles, but I try not to care.
I don't need to hurt.	←——→	You can't stop my hurt.
Giving me attention is irrelevant.	←——→	Your attention can harm me.
I must be on my guard.	←——→	Please ignore me.
I'm not dependent on others.	←——→	Your care can hurt me.
I'm okay.	←——→	You're dangerous.
I try hard not to need anything from anyone else.	←——→	You're trying to make me need something from you.
I can handle my hurt.	←——→	Your empathy is an intrusion.
I am superior, therefore you can't hurt me.	←——→	You are inferior, therefore my fear is irrelevant.
My principles, even if unobtainable, are important.	←——→	The obtainable is unimportant.

Paranoid Personality Disorders

Anger and threat are the central contents of the emotional world of the person with paranoid personality disorder (PPD). Fear results from threat and anger results from continuous perceived threat. They feel overpowered and vulnerable. Their attentional style is rigid in that they look only for confirmation of their suspicions (Shapiro, 1965). Unlike the person with HPD, whose attention is global and who ignores details, the PPD patient examines the world quite attentively and with attention to detail. The failure is that the data is evaluated with great prejudice. Shapiro describes their attention as "rigidly intentional" (1965, p. 59) in that they are "searching for something." Danger in the environment, which they expected all along, is not as threatening as surprise. They do not want to be caught off guard, so they scan the environment carefully for threat and piece together data in order to support their underlying feelings. The obvious is less interesting to them than underlying meaning and intention (meaning-making activities thus invoke a special opportunity for change with PPD). The PPD patient is ready for counterattack and thus is extremely aroused emotionally in a rigid way. DBT treatment is therefore focused not at the contents or cognitions of the PPD patient, but at the rigidity of attention, the predetermination of conclusions, and the fixation of affect.

The dialectics are between anger vs. fear, anger vs. shame and humiliation, envy vs. love, impotency vs. the vindicated self, self vs. others, impotency vs. authority, attachment vs. betrayal, and failure of self vs. failure of others (McWilliams, 1994).

Although the PPD patient is capable of attachment and loyalty to others, their projection of internal threat (vulnerability) onto the external environment makes them difficult to deal with interpersonally. They will not access their substantial fear or sense of impotence, as this is seen as overwhelming and overpowering. The DBT goal of treatment is thus to increase the sense of safety, normalize the experience of fear, teach and coach shifting of attention from external to internal cues, reduce judgmentalism, reduce physiological arousal, reduce mood-dependent behavior, and establish clear boundaries between self and others. A primary treatment target is to make clear discrimination between thoughts and behavior, and between affect and behavior probabilities. Their thoughts of danger need not lead to behavior reactions, and their feelings need not result in defense against the environment. As with other personality disorders, this psychotherapeutic process is not brief.

In the following dialogue, watch how in DBT with paranoia the focus is on dialectics and affect rather than the veracity of cognitions.

Patient: My supervisor has been building this case to fire me. As I've told you, she is documenting my every movement within the company.

DBTherapist: You've well explained to me the evidence you have that both your supervisor and your coworkers are out to get you. No wonder you feel this significant sense of threat and danger. Now that you've given me the external dangers—the real and substantial threat of being fired from your job—I want to explore a different threat. The threat that comes from within you yourself.

Patient: What do you mean?

DBTherapist: Sometimes the environment, what is going on outside of us, can be the danger. But sometimes what is going on inside of us, our feelings and preparation, can be the downfall. I want to explore other ways that you can be prepared for the dangers that you are at risk for.

Patient: Okay. But I'm still not certain what you mean exactly.

DBTherapist: When you notice that your coworkers and supervisor are documenting your behavior, what do you notice is going on in your body? What are your muscles, your heart, your breathing, and your mind doing?

Patient: You mean, how does my body react to the danger?

DBTherapist: Exactly. How do you react to the danger?

Patient: I get tense and start thinking of ways that I can counter the arguments they're going to make against me.

DBTherapist: You begin planning your response?

Patient: Yes. For example, when Helen began taking notes when I was at the photocopier, I decided to keep a log of all the job-related photocopies I make so they can't accuse me of doing personal copies on the job.

DBTherapist: When you begin preparing like this for an attack, preparing to justify your work activities, what happens to your concentration?

Patient: I focus on my defense. I can have excellent concentration. As I've told you, I'm great at details. I notice all the small things that others tend to ignore. My concentration is fine.

DBTherapist: Your concentration is focused on the details of your defense, and I'm wondering if this impairs your attention to the details of your actual work.

Patient: It is difficult to focus on both getting my work done and preparing for their personnel actions.

DBTherapist: It is hard to focus on both your defense and your work?

Patient: But not impossible. I do the best I can.

DBTherapist: I'll bet your anger goes up every time Helen distracts you like that from your real work.

Patient: I try not to let my anger interfere.

DBTherapist: I'll bet that becomes increasingly difficult. First, you have to defend against their documentation. Second, you have to shift your attention to your actual work so they don't accuse you of being unproductive. Third, you have to control your anger so you don't look out of composure. That's a lot to have to handle!

Patient: It's been a struggle, and this has been going on for almost ten years. Helen has it in for me. She resented me from the minute I got to the company. She has kept me from being promoted and recognized for the contributions I make. She takes credit for everything I do.

DBTherapist: It must take major energy just to contain the anger you feel due to the injustice of it all.

Patient: Yes, sometimes I feel exhausted.

DBTherapist: On the one hand, you feel it unjust to let Helen win this battle of wits between the two of you. On the other hand, you're exhausted and feel increasingly less satisfaction in your work.

Patient: I'm not going to let Helen get the best of me.

DBTherapist: Nor should you. In a perfect world, certainly not the one you live in, you should be able to attend to your work content and not have to spend so much time defending against your supervisor. This tension inside, the effect of the anger, may be the greatest weakness you face.

Patient: That I'll get distracted by my feelings?

DBTherapist: No, the opposite. That you'll fail to take them into account.

Patient: What do you mean?

DBTherapist: You've spent years analyzing the intentions and strategies of Helen and others at work. I probably can't help you better analyze the threats that are coming from your environment. It sounds to me like you've already done a great job of doing that. As a psychologist, what I can do for you is help you better understand your internal vulnerabilities, like how the anger, frustration, and exhaustion might affect your ability to respond to external threats. I can also help you examine how your feelings affect your ability to effectively respond.

Patient: How can we do that?

DBTherapist: When we are under attack we become exceptionally attentive to what is going on outside of us, what is happening in the environment. We can become preoccupied with external danger, naturally. By becoming more attuned to what's going on inside of you, your feelings and thoughts, and shifting attention from outside to inside occasionally, you'll be better prepared to make your most strategic move in response to threats.

Patient: Okay.

DBTherapist: So you've focused a great deal on the situation per se, the environment. That naturally has decreased the amount of attention you pay to yourself, your feelings expressed in your heart and in your body. Let's practice attending to those sensations here in the safety of this environment.

Perhaps more important than with most other disorders is that the DBT therapist does not confront dysfunctional thoughts in the PPD patient. It is counterproductive to challenge the PPD patient's anticipation of danger and threat. They feel the threat, and for them in that moment that is sufficient evidence that a threat exists. To confront even the most projected and maladaptive conclusions of the PPD patient is simply to have them dismiss you as dishonest, untrustworthy, or stupid. With any of these conclusions, productive therapy is impossible and the therapist might as well refer the patient to a new therapist who has not been summarily dismissed. The PPD patient may not terminate therapy, but productive therapy has been terminated even if the sessions continue.

The DBT therapist works with the affect and invites the patient to shift attentional focus from internal to external cues, from antecedents in the environment to internal affect, from thoughts to affect. The patient should be the one to reevaluate their sense of threat, rather than the therapist providing reassurance that their feelings are wrong. While the DBT therapist is not submissive and does not agree with the patient's sense of threat and vulnerability, the therapist also declines to invite the patient to share a sense of safety before the patient is ready to adopt such safety cues. The therapist may redirect the patient to safety cues but invites the patient to form their own evaluations from such data.

Passive surrender is the most abhorrent experience for the PPD patient, and the DBT procedure of acceptance is thus highly resisted. Rather than straightforwardly explaining the benefits of acceptance, the DBT therapist works first with emotional pain tolerance and then (much later) with mindfulness as systematic desensitization. The stated goal is not to surrender and accept the pain but to make it more tolerable. As the rigidity of attentional focus on the environment is reduced and increased sensitivity to internal physiology is achieved, the patient becomes better at connecting thoughts to tension. While both the patient and the therapist may frame this as better preparing for the emotional battles by reducing baseline arousal, the result is that the patient achieves increased soothing and reduced hyperarousal.

Behaviorally oriented therapists are not accustomed to dealing with defensive mechanisms, such as projection, so prominent with PPD. Projection is when the patient takes an internal threat (such as vulnerability through aggression, abandonment, or homoerotic impulses) and attributes it to an external source ("He wishes to harm me" rather than "I'm afraid to be harmed"). Behavioral psychologists, particularly the academic ones, object to notions of psychological defense mechanisms because within Freudian theory they are so connected to dynamic psychology (the transformations and exchanges of energy within the personality), the central role of the unconscious, and the primitive role of sexuality in explaining pathology. However, Freud could be right in observing the psychological defensive mechanisms such as projection, identification with the aggressor, substitution, sublimation, and so forth, while being wrong about the reasons and import of these psychological coping mechanisms. Perhaps it is not the unconscious, exchanges of psychic energy, or the primacy of sexuality that causes these defensive maneuvers but simple reinforcement history (drive theory) and cognitive distortion based upon comparison of one's intense affect to what possibly could cause such intense affect (appraisal theory). The psychological defense mechanisms can easily be placed both within cognitive psychology and behavioral psychology, especially if the behavioral focus is on affect regulatory mechanisms, as exemplified in DBT.

Effective treatment of PPD must take into account projection of harm. The dialectic is between "the harm is within me" and "the harm is outside of me." As is

Table 18: Dialectics with Paranoid Personality Disorder

I'm angry that I'm being attacked.	◄——————►	I'm afraid they will really get me.
Society will hurt me if I let it.	◄——————►	Society punishes me for who I am.
Society pretends all is well and good.	◄——————►	My feelings of threat are real.
I may not be able to go it alone. Let me convince you of the threats.	◄——————►	You too may be the enemy since you refuse to listen to my warnings.
I want to feel the safety that others feel.	◄——————►	You may betray me if I trust in you.
Rules and principles are irrelevant when you're under attack.	◄——————►	Those social rules and principles may be part of the plan of attack against me.
I need to be safe.	◄——————►	There is no safety.
Your concern may be false.	◄——————►	Your attention can harm me.
I must be on my guard.	◄——————►	I want to be close to you.
I'm not dependent on others.	◄——————►	Your care can hurt me.
I'm okay.	◄——————►	You're dangerous.
I try hard not to need anything from anyone else.	◄——————►	You're trying to make me need something from you.
I'm capable.	◄——————►	I'm vulnerable.
The threat is from the outside.	◄——————►	The threat is from the inside.
I'm not vulnerable.	◄——————►	I'm ashamed and humiliated that I'm so vulnerable.

typical of all DBT treatment with any disorder, the DBT therapist agrees with both. In fact, the harm is both within them and outside of them. Their feelings are real and need to be explicitly validated rather than negated. The articulated goal with the patient is to help them to better discriminate the harms, to measure their responses based upon their objectives, and to protect themselves by not ignoring the threats that come from within. By recognizing and accepting both, projection is lowered and solution-focused coping can begin to progress.

CHAPTER 7

Psychological Coping Skills Replace Escape and Avoidance

While the previous chapter reviewed dialectics with various disorders and the typical conflicts in needs and wishes that vary by patient, this chapter will review psychological coping skills that are typically deficient in patients with acute mental disorders. Even when such patients have adequate psychological coping skills (the behaviors are within their repertoire), they frequently do not use them when in acute emotional pain. Many patients whom I have trained in the psychological coping skills presented below tell me, "I knew that. It only makes sense." However, when you follow their behavior during emotionally challenging situations they do not use the skills. Teaching the skills sets to patient populations from agricultural field-workers to Ph.D.'s has convinced me that intelligence, level of education, verbal articulateness, and specific diagnosis are all relatively irrelevant. Patients in acute emotional arousal need prompting and overlearning to make the skill sets habitual parts of their thinking process. Using mnemonics, which we'll explore later in this chapter, can help patients to actually use the skills already in their repertoire. In the allostatic load model, "It is important to note that it is not the coping skills that individuals have or do not have that are important. What counts are the coping skills that individuals believe they have or do not have" (Ray, 2004, p. 32). One main function of skills training is thus to teach new coping skills, but an equally important function is to remind patients to use existing coping skills that lie dormant. The DBT therapist thus teaches the obvious as well as prompts new skill development.

PSYCHOLOGICAL COPING SKILLS

This chapter will review the psychological coping skills of meaning-making, mindfulness, emotion regulation, distress tolerance, and strategic behavior. Very specific teaching points for each of these skills are included in the downloadable material (nhpubs.com/29064) that accompanies this book. In dealing with BPD, Linehan (1993b, 1993c) uses mindfulness, emotion regulation, distress tolerance, and interpersonal effectiveness skills. Meaning-making skills are added due to the overwhelming evidence of comorbidity in acute mental disorders (Clark and Watson, 1991; Garvey et al., 1991; Hudson and Pope, 1990; Westen and Morrison, 2001). It is unusual to find patients in acute stages of crisis who are not depressed or anxious, even if the presenting problem is an addiction, an eating disorder, or an impulse-control disorder. Meaning making serves to strengthen the resolve of patients to persevere even in the face of high arousal and provides additional direction to pursue emotion regulation skills. Interpersonal effectiveness skills are morphed into strategic behavior skills. While Linehan (1993b, 1993c) correctly identifies strained interpersonal factors in relationships, including the tendency to terminate relationships prematurely or hold on to toxic relationships too long, as central aspects of BPD (and interpersonal effectiveness skills are thus important in the treatment of this disorder), with many other disorders it is not relationships per se that are problematic. Rather, the problem lies in the more generalized issue of the patient being strategic or goal oriented in their behavior.

Readers familiar with Linehan's (1993c) skills modules will thus see similarities as well as differences from her original teaching manual. Dr. Linehan created the distress tolerance skills (1993c, pp. 96-103). No one prior to Dr. Linehan systematically taught skills in managing emotions that cannot be changed. More research and literature on mindfulness has occurred since Dr. Linehan's incorporation of mindfulness into DBT, and the reader will thus notice minor changes in mnemonics and recommendations to encompass problems with broader patient populations than BPD. Emotion regulation is a complex set of skills that require broad attentional focus of the patient to implement. This skills set was therefore reorganized into a single, broad mnemonic to activate the necessary shift in attention from internal to external, from solution-focused coping to emotion-focused coping, and to deploy the mindfulness required for successful implementation across a broad range of specific situations.

BALANCING PSYCHOTHERAPY WITH SKILLS TEACHING AND ACQUISITION

Think about your own training as a psychotherapist. You graduated from high school, went to college, selected a major, and decided to study psychology, marriage and family, social work, or premed. Once you graduated from college and entered graduate school or medical school, you effectively rejected teaching as a profession. Had you wanted to be a teacher, you would have enrolled in a school of education and obtained a teaching credential. Or, if you received your Ph.D. or MD, you would have immediately obtained a teaching position in a university or medical school. You didn't take that road. You wanted to treat patients. You wanted that one-on-one contact and individualized care, and you wanted to study human behavior at its most elemental levels. You chose psychotherapy rather than teaching. And your subsequent clerkships, internships, fellowships, supervision, and the eventual practice of your profession involved dealing with patients in psychotherapy, perhaps in individual psychotherapy, family psychotherapy, couples psychotherapy, or group psychotherapy (most often, during training, a combination of all of the above). You became comfortable in the free-floating arena of exploring the patient's thoughts, feelings, and history with little structure or few protocols, compared to teaching. What the patient brings to the table is more important than your personal agenda. Your objectives in treatment are brought into focus occasionally—you do have a plan. But the patient's experience in the moment is primary. In fact, veer too far from the patient's concerns and they will discontinue treatment altogether, leaving you with little opportunity to implement your treatment plan. So you stay very close to the patient and their experiences.

Teaching, including psychoeducation, is a different animal. You're probably not as comfortable with it. It is not consistent with your clerkships, internships, fellowships, and supervised professional practice. It is different. It has an agenda and protocols, and it's directive and more objective and relies more upon the preparation of the therapist than the patient. After your years of training in following the patient emotionally and behaviorally (having to undo much of your prior training that suggested that you lead rather than follow), it's most likely not as comfortable to be a trainer of specific skills. While once this may have been your element, it was forcefully trained out of you, on purpose, and by elder professionals who you respected.

The skills modules below are to be taught. You present the information to patients directly, and as with any good teaching, there should be discussion and application of the concepts to the patient's own situation and condition. However, the skills curricula below are not discussion starters in the sense that they are to help provoke emotional communication. The goal is not to have a lively and disclosive group psychotherapy session. The goal is to have the group understand the concepts, how they apply to their situation, and how to implement the treatment recommendations in their daily lives. Group discussion and self-disclosure are used to bring the material from the level of intellectual knowledge to specific strategies they can use to behave and feel differently than they have in the past. It is psychoeducation in the sense that the teaching is about their own psychology and psychological coping strategies.

Teaching the skills modules below is thus quite different than conducting psychotherapy or leading group psychotherapy. The skills modules are psychoeducation. Group participation is a necessary but insufficient condition for effectiveness; the concepts must be taught, understood, and applied by the group participants.

Throughout this chapter I will refer to group training. This is simply due to the fact that group psychoeducation has advantages of group interaction that can naturally provide emotional validation and normalization of experience. Group psychoeducation is also less expensive for the patient. However, I have successfully provided psychoeducation on an individual basis to patients who could not or would not attend a group. In more rural areas it may also be difficult to recruit sufficient numbers of patients to begin a group. Psychoeducation may thus be delivered either individually or within a group format.

Even if you do not intend to teach the following skill modules (perhaps because another professional is conducting the psychoeducational portion of treatment), as a DBT individual therapist, your familiarity with the skills (including the language, recommendations, and mnemonics outlined in this chapter) is essential to successful treatment. You will be able to prompt the use of the skills in challenging situations, clarify misunderstandings the patient may have developed about the intent or application of principles, and provide validation that the psychological coping skills are essential components of the treatment program to which they have committed.

In the dialogue below, Emily resists the psychosocial skills application while the DBT therapist perseveres.

Patient: This therapy approach is not working any better than all of the other therapy I've tried. I mean, you're nice and I like you, but I must be hopeless. I can't stand the constant struggle, the way nothing ever works out for me. The depression is just too much.

DBTherapist: You're feeling overwhelmed and hopeless again.

Patient: Yes, I am. John did it to me again this week, and the rejection is intolerable.

DBTherapist: I understand that you're feeling very frustrated with the lack of change. But I'm wondering, when you had that rejecting episode with John last week, did you attempt to employ the strategic behavior skills that you've been learning?

Patient: What do you mean?

DBTherapist: Did you go through the skills represented by the mnemonics OBJECTIVES or BEHAVIOR? Did you actually run through them, either in your head or on paper?

Patient: I understand all that stuff, but it's not helping!

DBTherapist: Emily, there is a tremendous difference between understanding something and using the information you understand. It is not a fair trial of the DBT approach unless you actually go through the steps. The steps are all in the mnemonics. When John begins his rejecting behavior, you go through the OBJECTIVES and BEHAVIOR steps, either in your mind as you are interacting with him or on paper between your encounters with him. *After* you've applied the steps, *then* you evaluate what differences, if any, they make in your relationship and in your feelings about yourself.

Patient: I don't think it's going to make any difference at all.

DBTherapist: I can understand how you feel that way, given that your relationship with John has been full of conflict and disappointment for so long. But let's try the steps together now. Let's start with OBJECTIVES. Last week, when John began being critical again, what exactly was happening outside, the "O" in OBJECTIVES?

Patient: I'd rather talk about my feelings with you. Not go through any steps.

DBTherapist: I'm very interested in your feelings, and I want to hear about them. But remember, one of the principles of DBT is that there has to be a balance between focusing on feelings and focusing on solutions to those feelings. We don't have to spend the entire session on strategic behavior, but let's run through the steps quickly, applying them specifically to what happened between you and John during this last week.

Patient: If I have to . . .

DBTherapist: Thanks for being flexible. Now, what was going on outside, the "O" in OBJECTIVES?

Even when conducting individual psychotherapy, therefore, the DBT therapist coaches the patient in the application of the skills modules to their individual problems and dynamics. All therapists participating in the DBT treatment program must therefore be quite familiar with the skills modules even if they are not directly involved in the psychoeducational component of the treatment.

This can be uncomfortable for some therapists who are trained to let the patient lead in treatment while they follow the emotional and psychological processes that evolve. While the DBT individual therapist, as in other psychotherapy approaches, also follows the patient's emotional and psychological processes, the DBT therapist occasionally prompts the patient to use the new psychological coping skills they are being taught. This is designed to decrease mood-dependent behavior and actually results in psychological change. The therapist must therefore be comfortable with leading in therapy as well as following. DBT is agenda based in that the role of the therapist is to prompt a new set of coping skills to old problems. Some patients, especially those with substantial characterological issues, will resist these attempts at change. The DBT therapist supportively validates that change is frustrating while prompting them to engage in the frustrating experiences anyway.

SELF-HELP MANUALS: THEIR ROLE AND EFFECTIVENESS

In some situations, the DBT therapist may rely more exclusively on self-help books or manuals (for example, Marra, 2004) rather than a structured psychoeducational skills training group that is attended concurrent to individual dialectical psychotherapy. Is this approach effective? First, it may be the only practical alternative. Many communities do not have professionals who are competent or interested in teaching the dialectical psychological coping skills here recommended. Or the skills group may not be currently offered, and the patient is in treatment now. Some patients may not be able to afford the payment of fees for the skills group but have adequate insurance coverage for psychotherapy. Individuals can have negative views that joining a group is stigmatizing to them and means that they are less adequate than others (Levy and Derby, 1992). Second, self-help books or self-guided learning can be effective.

A review by Beutler found that treatment manuals increase treatment effect (Beutler et al., 1994), and biblotherapy is essentially a self-guided treatment manual. He also concludes that it is the structure and consistency of psychotherapy rather than the techniques themselves that powerfully increase the effectiveness of treatment (Beutler and Howard, 2003). Certainly self-help treatment books, together with psychotherapy that guides and coaches the application of strategies, will increase the consistency and structure of the psychotherapy process. Biblotherapy is consistent with the goals of empirically supported treatments (Chambless and Ollendick, 2001; Chambless et al., 1996), and even quite brief bibliotherapy (six self-help booklets) has been found helpful (Evans et al., 1999). While only 5 to 15 percent of treatment outcome has been found related to "treatment packages" (Luborsky et al., 1999), self-help resources are empowering to patients (Perkins, 1995) as they can identify resources patients can pursue on their own, thus increasing their sense of self-efficacy and independence. Research has found that self-help procedures can be effective. For example, while few self-help books for depression have been experimentally tested, those that have been used in clinical trials have fared well, with an average effect size roughly equivalent to the average effect size obtained in psychotherapy (McKendree-Smith, Floyd, and Scogin, 2003).

A more recent meta-analysis of twenty-nine depression outcome studies of cognitive forms of bibliotherapy showed similar results. Gregory and his colleagues (Gregory et al., 2004) report seventeen studies with stronger research designs. The meta-analytic effect size of .77 is reported as more than moderate and almost large. The authors note that this is the seventh meta-analytic review of bibliotherapy, with all studies showing bibliotherapy to be effective. They note that some authors recommend therapist-monitored bibliotherapy, while at least two studies have shown that bibliotherapy without therapist contact is also effective.

In a study significant in that it examined real clinical outpatient practice, rather than laboratory- or university-based research institutes, Persons found outcomes comparable to those of the NIMH Treatment of Depression Collaborative Research Program despite the increased heterogeneity (7 percent bipolar, 18 percent panic disorder, 49 percent concurrent treatment) in the private practice setting compared to the Collaborative Research Program (Persons, Bostrom, and Bertagnolli, 1995).

Pennebaker asked students to write about either trivial or traumatic experiences and information for twenty minutes per day on four consecutive days. His research indicated that writing about feelings and trauma rather than trivia resulted in improved moods and greater physical health (Pennebaker, 1990; Pennebaker and Kiecolt-Glaser, 1988). Research into the clinical benefits of self-disclosure, including journaling effects without a present coach or therapist, is increasing (Kelly, 1999; Ray, 2004). Certainly self-help books that request writing about personal traumas and feelings can result in similar findings.

Since self-help books can guide the application of principles and procedures between psychotherapy sessions, and evidence indicates that this can assist in the treatment process, there is good reason to use them in the clinical process. Obviously, the preferable solution is to have mental-health professionals guide both the psychotherapy process and the psychoeducational process. But when this is not feasible, an adequate (and perhaps the only) alternative is guided bibliotherapy.

DEVELOPING A TEACHING STRATEGY

The amount of time you devote to any skills module below (no matter if delivered to an individual or to a group) will substantially depend on the clinical needs you have identified in your patient(s). Some patient populations have more frequent emotional avoidance and escape behaviors, demanding more time with mindfulness and distress tolerance, while others may have more behavioral deficits, such as impulsivity, demanding more time with strategic behavior skills. If you are dealing with a heterogeneous patient population and plan to run a group of patients through a structured, preset psychosocial skills development course, you might begin with mindfulness skills since these skills are necessary later for distress tolerance and emotion regulation skills. In this situation, I then move on to meaning-making skills and end with strategic behavior skills. Mindfulness practice sessions and the CARES skill set are interspersed throughout the course. The entire course can be accomplished in as little as seven two-hour sessions (for a very high-functioning group with lower emotional distress) to as much as twenty-one two-hour sessions.

How much time and energy you devote to each module will depend on your analysis of the needs of the group. In table 19, the function of each of the modules and the mnemonics are presented. Time for each module should thus have a direct relationship to the identified deficits in coping strategies evident in the patients to be treated.

Table 19: Function of DBT Skills Modules	
SPECIFIC PATHS *Meaning making*	■ Shift attention from self to environment ■ Shift attention from short- to long-term objectives ■ Increase reinforcer effectiveness ■ Increase pleasure; interrupt emotional pain ■ Perspective taking (act on values rather than immediate affect)
ONE MIND *Mindfulness*	■ Increase exposure to emotions (reduce avoidance and escape behaviors) ■ Shift attention from self to environment ■ Decrease attention to cognitions and rumination ■ Improve observational skills (increase contingent analysis) ■ Reduce attachment and aversion
EMOTIONS *Emotion regulation*	■ Shift attention from emotions to environment ■ Shift attention from self to environment ■ Discriminate short- from long-term contingencies ■ Move from emotion-focused coping to solution-focused coping

VISION *Distress tolerance*	■ Decrease emotional avoidance and escape behaviors ■ Shift from emotion-avoiding to emotion-coping strategy
DISTRACT *Distress tolerance*	■ Decrease attention to emotions ■ Decrease automatic avoidance of emotions and replace with strategic avoidance (not repression but based on acknowledgment of affect)
OBJECTIVES *Strategic behavior*	■ Move emotion-focused coping to solution-focused coping ■ Increase focus on specific contingencies ■ Balance short- and long-term perspectives
TRUST *Strategic behavior*	■ Decrease self-invalidation of affect ■ Acceptance of emotional sensitivity or insensitivity ■ Increase focus on audience (communication focus versus affect focus)
BEHAVIOR *Strategic behavior*	■ Move emotion-focused coping to solution-focused coping ■ Increase contextual evaluation (reduce rule-governed behavior) ■ Move from self-punishment to self-reward
CARES	■ Decrease high emotional arousal ■ Decrease mood-dependent behavior

Psychoeducational sessions have the following goals:

1. Provide information (such as teaching the biopsychosocial model)

2. Identify strategies (such as how to be mindful)

3. Practice mnemonic-based steps to implement strategies

4. Identify obstacles to change

5. Confront obstacles in order to overcome them

Patients should conclude their involvement in the group with an understanding of the strategies and how they apply to their life situation. They thus have the tools and the language to apply the strategies later. It is the role of individual DBT psychotherapy to then prompt, coach, shape, and cheerlead the practice of the principles over the subsequent weeks and months of therapy.

Having a common language between patient and therapist can be very powerful. Being able to say to a patient in individual psychotherapy who has experienced yet another failed interpersonal encounter, "Did you use the TRUST skills?" reminds the patient that it is not them but the processes used that determine failure or success.

TEACHING MINDFULNESS SKILLS

Mindfulness skills are among the most critical skills to teach in DBT and should be the last component a DBT therapist considers discretionary. Each patient experiencing the characteristic topography of high emotional arousal, slow return to emotional baseline following threat, and hypervigilance to threat cues (the very core psychopathology that DBT is designed to treat) will have difficulty shifting attention from internal to external and vice versa, shifting from observing rather than evaluating experience, and shifting from emotion-focused coping to solution-focused coping and vice versa. Mindfulness can increase the ability to shift attention, shift strategies, and decrease hypervigilance. It is thus an essential skill and yet the most ambiguous to teach. There is relatively little content or curricula available to assist you, and what content there is sounds simplistic and unimportant to most DBT patients, who are seeking immediate relief from the intensity of affect they experience. Patients often desire "unknown" or "insightful" strategies (the "aha" experience) rather than the straightforward instructions of mindfulness, which sound simple but are difficult for anyone to implement, even those without acute disorders.

The major teaching strategy with DBT is thus brief psychoeducation followed by prompting, reinforcement, shaping, modeling, and coaching of the desired behaviors. The DBT trainer helps the patient to adopt the mindfulness posture in spite of high arousal and even disbelief that the strategy will have a monumental effect upon them, which it can.

The DBT trainer/psychotherapist begins by explaining how the Western scientific tradition teaches people to observe briefly, categorize similarities and differences between the objects of their observation, and form generalizations. Placing the idiographic into the nomothetic, labeling the object of observation into a larger phenotype is the goal of scientific observation. The goal is to observe so that you can dismiss; once categorized, there is less interest in and attention to the object observed. Moreover, the Western tradition promotes multitasking and efficiency. Observe as little as you must, then go on to something else. Mindfulness is the reverse of this posture: mindfulness is about sustaining attention over time in spite of the tendency of the mind to wander; observing all of the idiographic elements of that which is observed, even those elements that seem unimportant or uninteresting; increasing the sensual aspects of observation (observing with as many senses as possible); and paying attention to experience rather than analytical thought.

These concepts can be explained to patients as the difference between "Doing Mind" and "Being Mind" (Segal et al., 2002). Doing Mind is intellectual: it analyzes and collects information, attends to fact, plans, and involves focused attention. Most of us are in Doing Mind most of the time. Being Mind, on the other hand, also observes and records information. But in Being Mind, we do not analyze. In Being Mind, we observe not for the purpose of analysis of our experience but to heighten experience itself. Being Mind is thus watchful and sensual (involving as many of the senses as possible). We observe but do not process the input. Instead, we observe and then observe more. In Being Mind we attempt as best we can to have our observations be free of our analytical thoughts so that observations can be vibrant and almost magical, as if that which we are observing is new and never before observed.

I frequently invite patients to think of the state of mindfulness as being like an alien from a distant planet. They are investigators sent from the mother ship to explore the uniqueness of the human experience. As an alien, they don't understand sensual knowing, emotional knowing, and intuitive knowing. So their job, as the advance party visiting Earth, is to try to understand this less rational way of experiencing the world. However, as a member of an exploratory team, their role is not to make total sense of the human experience. In fact, their role is simply to collect experience and to be able to describe it to their superiors with as much detail, vibrancy, specificity, and different points of reference as possible, so that their superiors will be able to later analyze their observations and make sense of them.

Observation vs. Analysis

Separating out observation from analysis is foreign to most people. Some patients will get caught up in abstractions about how analysis is necessary and essential and can't be turned off even if we wanted it to be. And, consistent with the DBT approach of validation, the trainer agrees that habits of the mind are indeed quite difficult to change. In fact, the mind will almost certainly wander into analysis. During mindfulness practice the patient will begin to think rather than experience. They are simply to notice this wandering of the mind, which is natural and expected, and bring the mind back as often as necessary into the experience and observation mode.

Another obstacle some patients have with the concept is that analysis of observation is a helpful and even an essential aspect of a good life. The therapist agrees and explains that mindfulness is another kind of knowing frequently ignored by most of us. So much emphasis is placed on analysis and Doing Mind that Being Mind is ignored. The goal is to develop a greater balance between the two kinds of mind, not to eliminate one in favor of the other. The goal is not to make each minute of every day mindful; in fact, this could be dangerous while trying to do something such as drive an automobile, operate machinery, or engage in activities that require substantial analytical skills. The goal is to sometimes choose to be mindful on purpose.

ONE MIND Mnemonic

Mindfulness is broken down into two major components by Linehan (1993b, 1993c): "what" skills of observing, describing, and participating, and "how" skills of taking a nonjudgmental stance, focusing on one thing in the moment, and using skillful means. I have developed a mnemonic to teach mindfulness: ONE MIND. The mnemonic prompts the following concepts: **O**ne thing in the moment; focus on the **N**ow; pay attention to the **E**nvironment; pay attention to the immediate **M**oment; **I**ncrease senses of touch, taste, hearing, and vision; take a **N**onjudgmental stance (not good or bad, right or wrong); and **D**escribe with words that are descriptive, not prescriptive or proscriptive.

For most people, not just patients, this welcoming of observation at the cost of analysis and processing (cognition) is quite difficult. Remind patients that many experiences that are now natural and fluid were not when they first began learning them: riding a bicycle without training wheels, touch-typing on a keyboard, snow skiing, playing the piano, or driving an automobile. Watching an infant first transitioning from crawling to walking on two feet without holding on to anything is a prime example. In the beginning, each movement is precarious, there is trial-and-error learning, much effort and strain is required, and there can be frustration and even anger. Over time, each of the behaviors becomes more habitual, automatic, and feels less foreign. The quality of participating with awareness, acknowledging the initial difficulties but sustaining attention in spite of frustration or boredom, is invited.

Escape and Avoidance

One of the benefits of mindfulness for patients experiencing acute mental disorders is eliminating automatic escape and avoidance strategies. Mindfulness is thus an excellent laboratory to experiment with sustaining attention to experience even when it's painful (not attempting to stop the experience) and to sustain attention to experience even when it is pleasant (without attempting to prolong the experience). Observation in mindfulness does not have a goal or objective (to increase pleasure or decrease pain).

In the therapeutic encounter below, notice that the DBT therapist does not promise the patient that they will immediately feel better by being mindful to their emotional pain. Nor does the therapist tell the patient that by being mindful in this moment they will feel relaxed or soothed. Instead, the carrot the DBT therapist holds out is that the patient will have additional freedom in their lives because they won't always be running away from something or running to something. Escape and avoidance behaviors take a lot of psychological energy, and in fact avoidance and escape may actually define the process of agony itself.

Patient: I feel so tight and anxious. I feel like I'm going to explode from the inside out.

DBTherapist: That must feel horrible. Lets practice mindfulness to this pain. Can you pay attention to the tightness, right now? Where do you feel it?

Patient: I feel it in my neck, in my shoulders, in my chest. Everywhere.

DBTherapist: Just focus on the muscles in your neck. Identify each and every muscle that's hurting you there. Identify the location. Then feel the individual muscle, if you can. Feel the tightness. Can you feel the individual muscles in your neck?

Patient: I don't think I can feel the individual muscles. Just all of them as a group.

DBTherapist: Focus on just one area of your neck. Feel the tension there.

Patient: It's tight, like someone was pulling on each end of the muscles and making them tight.

DBTherapist: Stick with that tightness, in that one location, for just a moment. Besides tightness, what else can you feel in that one location?

Patient: I'm beginning to think of what I have to do after our appointment is over.

DBTherapist: Your mind is wandering. That's okay. That's what minds do. They wander. Just gently bring your focus of attention back to that one area of your neck. Welcome attention to the tightness.

Patient: Okay, I'm back on my neck.

DBTherapist: What do you feel in your neck, that one area of your neck, besides tightness?

Patient: It feels warm and hard. And it makes my head feel heavy, like it just wants to rest rather than be tight.

DBTherapist: Attend to the warmth and hardness.

Patient: Okay, I can feel the heaviness.

DBTherapist: Good, focus on the heaviness. Can you describe in any other words what your neck feels like, especially in that one area you're focusing on?

Patient: No, but my chest and stomach don't feel as tight as before.

DBTherapist: Okay, notice that your mind wanders to other parts of your body. You notice that when you don't run from attention to your body, some areas of your body may relax a little. That's okay. Go back to your neck—pay attention to your neck. Can you describe any other sensations?

Patient: Just the heaviness, the warmth, the tightness.

DBTherapist: Okay, stick with that for just another half minute. *(Pause)*

Patient: Okay.

DBTherapist: That was great. You were able to pay attention and stick with it for a few minutes, even though it was uncomfortable. You didn't explode.

Patient: But I'm still tense.

DBTherapist: That's okay. In distress tolerance you've learned how to soothe your body in ways that may produce relaxation. But here we are trying to do something else, something just as important. We're learning to pay attention even to pain, to be mindful of pain, and not run from it. And that, too, is important. Eventually it will result in you having more freedom, because you won't be spending so much time running away from your experiences. You'll be able to notice your experience, experience it just for what it is, and then move on. But we have to notice what's happening before we can change what's happening. Most of us want to change unpleasant experience immediately, before we've even fully assessed what it is we are trying to change. Mindfulness is about observation, and some of the other parts of DBT are about change.

Patient: But will this mindfulness eventually help me feel less anxious?

DBTherapist: Maybe not. For a lot of people it does. But that isn't its purpose. The purpose of mindfulness is to attend better, notice more, and stick with experience rather than always trying to control our experiences.

The Power of Words

Description as an element of mindfulness deserves special attention. Cognitive psychology, preceded by the field of semantics, has long known that words can both define and obfuscate experience. Words are like maps. Language describes a territory but isn't the territory. The motto from semantics is highly relevant: "The map is not the territory." Patients with a history of emotional invalidation (so frequently seen in acute mental disorders) look to the outside world to tell them if their emotions, their observations, and their needs are accepted (right) or rejected (wrong) by others. They no longer trust their own observations, so they look to others to confirm or disconfirm their experience. Mindfulness can increase trust in one's own experience, particularly the more the practitioner of mindfulness is observing rather than analyzing experience. One large obstacle to increasing this trust is the use of language in describing experience.

Patients in emotional turmoil, seeking the external validation of their experience of threat and insecurity, may insist that they are "doing it wrong" when they practice mindfulness because the words they use are different from the words others use when describing their experience. So concerned that the "map" of their experience match the map that others provide, they engage in comparison and judgmentalism. Of course, this is not Being Mind but Doing Mind since it is analytical and judgmental rather than experiential. Encourage them to attend to their own experience, not what they perceive others perceive.

Nevertheless, the prescriptive and proscriptive functions of language should be explicitly addressed. In the **D**escribe component of ONE MIND, the patient is invited to use words to label their experience. Words can both define what we are seeing (describe) and serve to prescribe (to limit through anticipation and predefinition) our experience. If the patient is depressed and uses dark and destructive language, even internally, to explain their experience of the moment, they are invited to ask themselves if they are attending more to their emotions than to the object of the current experience. For example, if the patient is asked to attend to their breath and their words to describe their experience include such words as "horrible," "threatening," or "devilish," then they are not attending at all to their breathing but to the emotions that coexist with their breathing. Proscriptive language (language that limits or fails to take into account the full experience that is available) is similarly diagnostic. If the patient, during breathing mindfulness meditation, can only use words such as "in and out" and cannot label other aspects of their experience (for example, the up and down motion of their chest as they breathe, the temperature of the air as it enters and exits their nostrils, or the sensation of the air entering and leaving their lungs), then they are perseverating on one element and need to broaden their focus of attention. In both cases, the DBT therapist helps the patient to stay closer to the observational level and to refocus attention as necessary. As they observe during mindfulness, the patient is thus cued to pay attention to the functions of language in both describing and either heightening or limiting experience.

The function of mindfulness skills training is thus to offer opportunities for patients to learn to better observe their experience and their environment. The sole objective of mindfulness is to welcome experience rather than control it.

⌐ Using the Downloads

The downloadable materials (nhpubs.com/29064) included with this book contain sixty-six PowerPoint slides about mindfulness skills, which, depending on the size and homogeneity of your group receiving skills training, can take anywhere from one to three hours to present. The slides present the content and context of mindfulness teaching, described above, plus graphics of maps of the world in different orientations meant to represent the functions of language (how words both describe and shape our experience of our world). The leader of the skills group uses these slides to make patients increasingly aware of the function of their language in both describing and shaping experience. The major point in the map slides is to highlight the following issues: First, each description or "map" of experience is equally valid—they all describe the same territory. Second, some maps are welcoming of experience while others are foreboding of experience. And third, some are complex and detailed maps containing lots of color and sensuality, while others are plain and less exciting descriptions of the same territory. Mindfulness is designed to increase the level of identification and complexity of that which is being observed, but not necessarily to add more to the experience than exists.   ⌐

Practice

The role of practice in mindfulness is critical. Encourage patients to practice first within treatment settings and then later in vivo. Practice should occur daily. Recommend to patients that it is better to practice five minutes daily than forty-five minutes once per week. The more practice, the better. Patients can be invited to mindfully breath, mindfully walk, mindfully body scan, or mindfully wash the dishes. Later, as their comfort with mindfulness increases, they can mindfully attend to their emotions themselves. Most of the development of mindfulness skills is thus prompted and assessed from outside of the teaching or psychotherapy experience.

Understanding the concepts of mindfulness does little to promote greater emotional health; it is the practice of mindfulness on a routine basis that can create exceptional changes in perspective, arousal level, perceptions of comfort, and a greater ability to shift from one strategy to another.

TEACHING MEANING-MAKING SKILLS

Meaning itself is heightened in anxiety disorders (threats are extremely meaningful and portend disaster), shrinks in mood disorders (meaning is lost and effort is worthless), is distorted in personality disorders (meaning lies in protection from threat, rather than pursuit of rewards), found in impulsive actions that immediately dispel tension in impulse-control disorders, misdirected in eating disorders (meaning lies only in body image and food as nurturance), and solely physiologically focused in addictive disorders (where substances substitute for true meaning). Meaning is thus an important aspect of most acute mental disorders but one that is frequently only indirectly rather than strategically targeted in psychotherapy. DBT makes meaning making an explicit process in therapeutic change.

Meaning as Construction

Initially, the DBT trainer acknowledges that meaning is different for different people based upon their values, interests, and aspirations. However, the first point (and, at times, most difficult assumption for patients to accept) is that meaning is created. We make it up. It is not bestowed upon us by others, not even a higher power. We make meaning through decision, devotion, faith, and practice. This is true even of spiritual and religious beliefs. God does not command us to make him meaningful—he invites us to do so. The hard work, with all meaning, resides within the person, not outside.

Present meaning as a perspective, a way of looking at things, rather than as absolute values, which don't exist across people, cultures, and societies. Meaning, like love, is something you create yourself. You value and respect something, appreciating its rewards more than its costs, because you decide to do so. You take something seriously and value it highly because you have made a decision, conscious or unconscious, to do so. Meaning, like love, is something that can be multiplied, rather than divided: You can love many things, and love for one need not distract from love for another. Love and meaning can be renewed and generated. They are not in finite supply.

Review what many people find meaningful—religious beliefs, relationships, family, job, money, fame, possessions—and why. Review the notion that some things found exceptionally meaningful by one person may be seen as irrelevant by others. Review a major obstacle to creating meaning: the fear that it will be the "wrong" meaning. Fear is the most essential roadblock to developing meaning: fear that it won't work, that others will disapprove, that you'll regret it later, that you'll never find it, or that you don't deserve it.

Other obstacles to creating meaning include the assumption that our feelings are beyond our control, or that meaning is bestowed upon us supernaturally; both have assumptions of powerlessness. Moreover, failing to attend to experience that can be emotionally pivoting will decrease meaning in our lives.

The assumptions of meaning-making skills are thus that meaning is created rather than found; that it is activated in the relationship of self to the meaningful thing, not in the thing itself; that it must be practiced; and that meaning making is a long-term rather than short-term endeavor. The mnemonic for meaning making is SPECIFIC PATHS.

SPECIFIC PATHS Mnemonic

The first element in SPECIFIC PATHS is a **S**upreme concern. There need be nothing spiritual or religious about a supreme concern. It can be golf, our pet, or our house and home. The supreme concern is something that is valued highly, a choice among alternatives that matters to you. Patients may need considerable help identifying supreme concerns. There can be many supreme concerns, rather than only one. Probing questions about how they spent their time in the past, what they tend to miss when it's taken from them, what creates the strongest feelings in them, what they most admire or envy when others have it, what provides them with comfort, what threatens them, or what brings the greatest fulfillment are openings for the discovery of supreme concerns. Have patients identify what they believe others supremely value and why they agree with or reject such notions.

Practice is the "P" in SPECIFIC PATHS. Whatever is identified as a supreme concern will be unimportant unless the activity or process is practiced regularly. When practiced, it must be given **E**nergy and enthusiasm. The patient must practice the awe of the simple and routine in their supreme concerns. They must **C**oncentrate and focus, being mindful of the supreme concern rather than having it be automatic or thoughtless. The "**I**" in SPECIFIC PATHS regards the self (the me or I). The person is not just accomplishing a task or going through the motions, but they are attentive both to themselves and the task or activity they are performing. There is a constant shifting of attention from self to object, or self to other, and this allows experience to be noticed, highlighted, and absorbed. **F**aith is about trust, loyalty, and consistency. Faith is not about asking for proof or maintaining blind allegiance but about full engagement without reservation or analytical questioning. The patient engaged in analysis when they first selected their supreme concerns, but at that point analysis is over and—having made a choice—faith comes into play. They have already decided that what they are doing is **I**mportant, and they periodically remind themselves of this importance. At times this can take **C**ourage when doubts and judgmentalism come up.

It can also take **P**atience, a willingness to wait for results and to sustain effort over time because the outcome is so desired. **A**ttention is necessary in order to fully experience the supreme concern; one does it mindfully. The **T**ask is important, and the patient is to attend to the task, but a reminder is given that meaning is in the relationship to the supreme concern, not in the task itself. The patient attends to both, the task and their relationship to it, frequently shifting back and forth between the two. **H**umility is required. You need not be perfect or even particularly skillful in order for your supreme concern to create meaningfulness in your life. For example, gardening itself can be meaningful even if your garden pales in comparison to your neighbor's (who probably either has a lot more time to garden or pays others to do it for them). Humility reminds us that it is not so much a particular outcome we seek as the meaningfulness in the activity or process itself.

Finally, SPECIFIC PATHS remind us to be **S**ensitive to self. The meaningful activity is done for a specific feeling and value. When on SPECIFIC PATHS, the individual is watchful of their own responses, paying attention to themselves and allowing their experience to affect them.

SPECIFIC PATHS is thus a series of prompts to engage in a process that nurtures meaning: identifying supreme concerns; practicing with energy and concentration; focusing on the "I" that I do this for; applying faith; reminding myself of why this is important; applying courage, patience, and attention; paying attention to the task; having humility; and being sensitive to self.

As with mindfulness skills training, meaning-making skills training involves repeated prompts, coaching, modeling, and shaping behavior over the course of psychotherapy. The goal is to have the patient identify meaningful activities and pursue them seriously over time and not just have them complete some worksheets and go on to the next assignment. The skillful DBT therapist thus prompts patient practice of both mindfulness and meaning-making activities throughout the course of treatment. Both ONE MIND and SPECIFIC PATHS can provide strategies to integrate these new psychological coping skills into patients' daily routines. Observe how even in an individual psychotherapy session the skills are prompted.

Patient: I don't have energy to do anything. Everything takes such tremendous energy, and I have none.

DBTherapist: I understand that energy has been lacking these days. When was the last time you went through the SPECIFIC PATHS exercise?

Patient: I know I need more meaning in my life. But how can I pursue it when there is no passion, no energy to do anything?

DBTherapist: Yes, the "E" in SPECIFIC PATHS demands energy . . .

Patient:	I know what the letters stand for. I've tried to do it a hundred times. But it's not working for me.
DBTherapist:	When you engage in a supreme concern, do you do it with ONE MIND? Do you do it mindfully?
Patient:	Now you want me to do two skill sets at once?
DBTherapist:	Yes. You can't develop more meaning in your life if you don't do it mindfully.
Patient:	But when does the energy come? If I had the energy I'd gladly do all of these exercises in order to feel better.
DBTherapist:	The energy comes along with the meaning. As you create new meaning in your life, the energy will be more plentiful.

Using the Downloads

The downloadable materials (nhpubs.com/29064) included with this book contain fifty-two PowerPoint slides designed to assist in teaching the above concepts. These slides provide anywhere from one hour to three hours of psychoeducational program time, depending on the homogeneity and psychological sophistication of the group being taught. Therapists can also download worksheets on meaning-making skills to allow patients to practice SPECFIC PATHS meaning making in their daily lives.

The number of sessions devoted to training in either mindfulness skills or meaning-making skills will depend on the group dynamics, number of participants, diagnoses, and devotion of the participants to learning new skills. In mixed diagnostic groups having a separate psychoeducational instructor and individual psychotherapist, I suggest a minimum of three one-hour sessions for each module, including practice opportunities for each skill.

TEACHING EMOTION REGULATION SKILLS

Emotion regulation is "the processes by which individuals influence which emotions they have, when they have them, and how they experience and express these emotions" (Gross, 1995, p. 275). Deficits in emotion regulation are found in many forms of psychopathology (Gross and Munoz, 1995). The goals of emotion regulation skills are to help patients better understand their emotions, including providing a biopsychosocial theory that can decrease fear, guilt, and shame reactions many patients experience when they feel intensely; to help patients better observe and describe their emotions; to increase exposure to emotions as helpful sources of information, rather than being perceived as harmful; and to apply counterconditioning procedures that reduce the sense of urgency surrounding painful emotions. Patients should be prompted to increase positive emotional experiences in their lives (which tend to shrink during acute emotional illness), taught how to be mindful of positive emotions when they occur and how to be unmindful of negative emotional experiences when necessary, and taught how to use strategic rather than automatic avoidance and escape procedures when emotions become overwhelming. The overarching goal is thus to generate adaptive psychological coping strategies to emotions such that emotional intensity is not a controlling factor in patients' lives.

The DBT trainer acknowledges that emotional intensity, regardless of the specific emotion, be it anger, frustration, depression, anxiety, or shame, can be intolerable. In fact, the sense of urgency to escape such emotions can substantially decrease one's effectiveness in dealing with situations. Over time, experiences of being overwhelmed with emotions and the subsequent urgent attempts to escape them can make people distrust their emotions (Linehan, 1993b, 1993c). Moreover, with emotional intensity others in the environment will frequently punish the emotionally sensitive person with disapproval—comments such as "change your attitude," "just get over it," or "don't be so sensitive."

The Biopsychosocial Model

A biopsychosocial model of emotions is presented to patients. Emotions are seen as being prompted by the following factors:

- Genetic inheritance

- Physiological feedback systems

- Cognitive schemas, including interpretations, anticipations, and other rule-governed behaviors that may or may not be accurate

- Environmental triggers

- Previous learning history, including past experiences that may or may not be conscious

- Brain neurochemistry and neural networks, including kindling effects

- Feedback between each of the preceding factors that serves to either increase or decrease the current emotion

■   The aftereffects of the experience based upon both behavior/action responses and cognitive appraisals of the situation well after the outcome

Patients are introduced to the radical and powerful effects of beliefs, hopes, anticipations, and fears on both physical and emotional health (Ray, 2004). Patients are thus taught to attend to the broad categories of environmental, psychological, and biological factors that can all influence emotional experience.

Several conclusions are specifically drawn from the biopsychosocial model. First, emotions are patterned reactions to events from the past, present, and anticipation of the future. Feelings do not come out of nowhere, and therefore they can be controlled and modulated. Second, there are many points of intervention in changing emotions. There is hope that emotions can be changed in desired ways. Third, emotions are natural and required aspects of human functioning. They evolved in order to increase adaptiveness to crisis situations. Chronic high-intensity emotions tend to highly obscure the utility of emotions, but emotional responsiveness is a potentially useful source of information. Fourth, emotions are predictable. They are controlled by internal factors (cognitive, physiological, and affective systems) and external events (environmental and interpersonal). With sufficient and detailed attention to such factors, patients can identify triggers and change their triggers. There is hope of emotional change.

Primary and Secondary Emotional Reactions

One the prime concepts of emotion regulation is the notion of primary and secondary emotional reactions (Linehan, 1993b, 1993c). A primary emotion is a direct emotional reaction to an event; for example, feeling a sense of loss when a friend moves out of town, anger when a spouse ignores us, or despondency when we are fired from a job. A secondary emotion is a reaction to the primary emotion. Examples would be shame that one feels lonely, guilt that one is angry, or a person's anxiety that their depression will cause others to lose interest in them. These are feelings about feelings. When secondary emotional reactions occur, the individual is left having to deal with two intense emotions rather than only one. In fact, the number of secondary emotional reactions is unlimited, as the individual can start out with only one primary emotion (say, anger) then build multiple secondary emotional reactions on top of the first: feeling guilty that they experienced anger in the first place, depressed that their guilt is so powerful, anxious that their depression will never end, and rage that their anger, guilt, depression, and anxiety interfere so completely with their ability to enjoy life. Patients are informed that it is mostly the secondary emotional responses that provide the complexity, ambiguity, and intensity that they find intolerable. Most people could deal with primary emotions, even intense ones, if the secondary emotional responses were not piled on top of them. One problem is that differentiating primary from secondary emotional reactions is difficult, since the secondary emotional reactions overshadow the primary emotions.

Problem solving is difficult with secondary emotions because patients shift from solution-focused strategies to emotion-focused strategies. Emotional escape and avoidance behaviors (designed to reduce emotional intensity rather than solve issues that prompt such arousal) precede attempts to understand both the emotions themselves and the environmental or intrapsychic events that prompt them. An important goal is thus to teach the patient more specific strategies in observing and describing their emotions with attention to the following aspects (Linehan, 1993c):

- The event prompting the emotion

- Their interpretations of the event that prompted the emotion

- Their psychological experience, including thoughts, bodily reactions, and emotions

- Their behaviors expressing the emotion

- The aftereffects of the emotion on other types of functioning

The patient is thus invited to label their emotion and identify how it is expressed bodily, their thoughts about the emotion, its environmental precipitants, their resulting behavior, and the effect of their behavior. This is mindfulness to their current emotions.

Having invited patients to attend to the difference between primary and secondary emotions, primary emotions can still be difficult and intense. With primary emotions, patients are taught the following steps:

1. First notice their feelings.

2. Acknowledge the emotion.

3. Identify any judgmentalism they experience while having the emotion.

4. Dispute any judgmental thoughts they identify.

5. Sustain attention to the emotion (be mindful of it).

6. Self-soothe their ability to tolerate the primary emotion.

7. Stay with (tolerate) the primary emotion for just a while.

With secondary emotional reactions, patients are taught to first identify the emotion; second, differentiate primary from secondary emotional reactions; third, develop a plan to deal only with the primary emotion in the moment; and finally, develop a plan to deal with secondary emotions only later. Patients are thus encouraged not to attempt to deal with multiple emotions in an urgent and immediate way. Secondary emotions, by their nature, tend to be reoccurring. They are long-term tendencies (to be subject to guilt, anxiety, shame, or anger) and longer-term plans are needed to deal with such tendencies. Frequently, it's easier and more effective to deal with secondary emotional reactions when one is not feeling a sense of urgency. Helping patients to attend to long-term as well as short-term strategies is thus emphasized.

Emotionalism

Patients are encouraged to identify positive aspects of their emotions (how emotions help them, how they are useful aspects of the human experience) and to identify obstacles to changing emotions that hurt. Emotionalism is presented as a major obstacle to emotional self-regulation and is defined as the sense of urgency, impulsivity, and crisis that permeates intensity of affective experience. Long-term plans to reduce the sense of urgency (reducing emotional baseline) are critical, including adequate nutrition, eating regularly, obtaining adequate sleep, regularly exercising, treating any physical illnesses that may be present, abstaining from illicit drugs and alcohol, taking prescribed medications as directed, and increasing a sense of mastery by engaging in behavior that builds self-confidence and competence (Linehan, 1993c).

Increasing Positive Emotional Events

Substantial time should be devoted to increasing positive emotional experiences. Not only depressed patients reduce rewarding activities in their daily schedules; patients in the throes of emotionally overwhelming experience also tend to decrease activities that bring pleasure, amusement, relaxation, and joy. The short-term objective is to have patients increase small, daily, positive experiences, and over the long-term to make life changes so that pleasant experiences are prompted by the environment more often (Linehan, 1993c). Patients are taught how to be mindful of pleasure, even simple pleasures, and to attend to and be affected by such pleasures that occur in the environment. This can require modeling, coaching, and practice. Patients are cautioned not to attend to the transitory nature of such pleasure and, in fact, are reminded that all feelings end, which is the basis of hope and freedom. The DBT therapist should identify beliefs and perceived obstacles that prevent engagement in positive experiences and identify solutions to these objections and obstacles. A primary objection to increasing positive emotional experience is "I don't feel like it," or a variant "I used to feel like it, but it won't be the same." The DBT therapist acknowledges that, with acute emotional pain, the desire to engage in joyful activities decreases, but behavior change can result in emotion change. The patient is coached to engage in the positive experience in spite of their objections, and to attend to the following points:

- Pay attention to the activity mindfully.

- Be engaged in the activity in spite of their current feeling, paying more attention to the behavior and the environment than to their current feeling.

- Attend to the environment and not their thoughts—be in the now rather than thinking about when it will end, how long it will last, or if they deserve it.

- When the mind wanders (as it will), bring it back into the current moment.

- Don't judge the emotions or compare them to the past or the future, just notice the now.

Taking Opposite Action

The technique of taking opposite action (Linehan, 1993c) is explained as a strategy to create new feelings rather than deny present emotions. In taking opposite action the patient is invited to both acknowledge how they currently feel as well as to do the opposite to what they actually feel. An example would be to do something nice for a person one is angry with, to approach something one is afraid of, or to engage in a potentially rewarding activity even though one does not feel like it (Linehan, 1993c). Patients are cautioned to attend to their current feelings even as they take opposite action, to remind themselves that what they are doing is designed to change the feeling rather than deny its presence, and to give the strategy an adequate trial. This involves being mindful of both the action being taken and one's own current feeling, and predicting a positive and hopeful outcome.

While distress tolerance skills are more fully explored below, even during training in emotion regulation skills, the therapist encourages mindfulness of aversive or negative emotions. Patients are encouraged to sustain attention to unwanted feelings. This is done with guidance not to block, suppress, grow, or intensify the emotion, and to sustain such mindfulness for three to four minutes regardless of their desire to avoid such experience. Some patients are initially unable to do this due to the intolerability of their emotional pain. Patients are thus taught counterconditioning strategies. The patient is taught to go back and forth between being mindful of their pain for a just a moment, then shifting to a pleasant image or experience for just a moment, then shifting back to the unpleasant emotion, moving back and forth between the two (pleasant and unpleasant) until the painful emotion is tolerable. This increases the patient's sense of control over their emotions, provides exposure and thus extinction of the aversive emotion, and increases acceptance as a key tool in emotion regulation.

Rule-Governed Behavior

While DBT focuses more attention on affect than on cognition, the role of rule-governed behavior is nevertheless introduced. People have rules or belief systems about their emotions, and they tend to follow these rules or beliefs in spite of any contradictory information that may be available. Contingency-shaped behavior is under the control of consequences in the natural environment. It is often unconscious and intuitive. Rule-governed behavior, on the other hand, is under the control of verbal stimuli specifying relations between certain actions and consequences (Addis, 1997). Rule-governed behavior can be periodically helpful, but the literature suggests that rules can produce behavior that is insensitive to quickly changing environmental contingencies (Hayes, Zettle, and Rosenfarb, 1989). Patients are thus invited to identify the rules they have, which may be conscious or unconscious, and to question those assumptions or rules while they mindfully notice any emotional changes that may occur as a result.

Patients with intense emotions that have existed for long periods of time may begin to identify their emotions as essential aspects of their identity. In emotion regulation, patients are invited to separate their emotional states from their identity. They do this by applying the following strategies:

1. Identifying the emotion

2. Identifying the thoughts they have about how this reflects on their total personality or identity

3. Questioning how essential, permanent, consequential, or true the identity statements are

4. Practicing identity statements that are more consistent with what they want to be able to say about themselves (their identity)

5. Identifying the feelings they would have with greater practice of the desired identity elements

Note that in DBT, patients are not told that their feelings or thoughts are wrong or inappropriate. They are told that their feelings or thoughts prompt responses or results that they don't like, or that hurt, and this is sufficient reason to change them.

The general strategy is to help the patient move from emotion-focused coping to solution-focused coping, to move from problems to problem solving. Avoidance, escape, and giving up are presented as enemies of effective emotion regulation. An active rather than passive approach to modulating affect is presented: when afraid, approach what you're afraid of; when feeling guilt or shame, either make amends if the feeling is justified or move on to new situations that can prompt different feelings if the feeling is unjustified; when sad or depressed, get active; when angry, either change the situation that prompts the anger or distract yourself from the anger so you don't make the situation worse, assuming the situation can't be changed (Linehan, 1993c).

EMOTIONS Mnemonic

The mnemonic for emotion regulation is EMOTIONS. EMOTIONS can prompt patients to use the complex set of strategies described above. "E" prompts the patient to **E**xpose themselves to the emotions they are having. "M" prompts **M**indfulness of the current emotion. "O" prompts an **O**utline of a plan to deal only with primary emotion in the now. "T" prompts **T**aking opposite action. "I" prompts **I**ncreasing positive emotional experiences. "O" suggests attending to **O**utside precipitants. "N" prompts **N**oticing what's going on both inside and outside of oneself. "S" prompts that **S**econdary emotions are dealt with later in long-term planning.

⌂ *Using the Downloads*

The downloadable materials (nhpubs.com/29064) included with this book contain 124 PowerPoint slides about emotion regulation skills to present in psychoeducation with patients. While, again, the number of patients being seen within a group setting, group dynamics, patient diagnoses, and devotion to development of new skills will affect how long the emotion regulation module will take to teach, frequently six hours or more of instruction will be needed. The goal is not to simply cover the content but also to allow practice of the skills in relationship to patients' lives.

There is empirical support for the effectiveness of emotion regulation skills in a variety of contexts (Mennin, Heimberg, Turk, and Fresco, 2002).   ⌂

TEACHING DISTRESS TOLERANCE SKILLS

Distress tolerance skills are perhaps the most easily digested by patients in acute emotional pain since they are consistent with their own goals, namely to decrease the pain of the moment. Linehan (1993b, 1993c) was the first to specifically delineate and systematize skills to tolerate emotional distress. She created the mnemonics ACCEPTS and IMPROVE to integrate the various strategies important in tolerating distress. The general strategies are to increase mindfulness to emotional distress, thus decreasing the agony associated with emotional pain, and to increase psychological coping skills in dealing with chronic or lingering emotional pain. The skill sets are mindfulness, self-soothing, distraction, improving the moment (respite), and acceptance (Linehan 1993b, 1993c). The downloads contain the specific curriculum for teaching these skills.

Mindfulness to emotional discomfort is the least tolerated of the skill sets. It invites patients to accept the pain of the moment in order to reduce both secondary emotional reactions and avoidance strategies that increase urgency and prolong pain. The ONE MIND mnemonic from mindfulness skills training is directly applied to emotional discomfort. The tendencies to rehearse or practice emotional pain (which increase it) are dialectically presented as opposite to the tendencies to avoid or escape emotional pain. Neither strategy, as an extreme on the dialectic continuum, is helpful. Mindfulness to emotional discomfort is thus presented as a compromise between prolonging pain through avoidance or escape and denial of emotional pain that does little to influence it.

The role of avoidance and escape conditioning in increasing emotional suffering should be explicitly reviewed using examples of such disorders as PTSD, pathological grieving, phobias, and chronic physical pain (Linehan, 1993c).

ACCEPT Mnemonic

ACCEPT invites patients to engage in the **A**cceptance process so that they can distract from their current emotional state; to **C**oncentrate on their current emotional pain rather than avoid it; to **C**reate a sense of acceptance through tolerance and giving up of willfulness; to focus on aspects of the **E**nvironment (what they can either *do* or observe) that make them feel positive and hopeful; to use **P**rayer or meditation to build strength from higher sources of power; and to specifically attend to the **T**ime dimension (that all experiences end or change over time, and acceptance of emotional pain in just this moment (rather than use of struggle) can decrease agony. The dialectic notion of opposites is explicitly stated for patients, that the mnemonic ACCEPT paradoxically is about distraction and distancing from current emotions. Both acceptance and change are promoted in distress tolerance, as in all DBT therapeutic interventions.

Soothing Oneself

Self-soothing is a skill set many of us use routinely. If we were effectively soothed as children, we intuitively remember how to use soothing as a strategy to induce comfort. If a patient experiences high emotional arousal or has a history of lack of attachment, loss, trauma, or emotional invalidation, it's likely they were never effectively soothed, have long forgotten how to self-soothe, or developed the schema that they did not deserve soothing. All of these can decrease self-soothing behaviors. Whatever the cause, patients are reminded that all suffering humans deserve soothing, and that self-soothing is the most effective and strategic method since it is potentially always available. Soothing can occur with any of the senses (vision, hearing, smell, taste, touch) or cognitively by providing comforting, nurturing, gentle, and kind thoughts and acknowledgments. The VISION mnemonic, included in the downloadable materials, prompts the use of self-soothing.

In addition to feelings of undeservingness, patients frequently object that they should not have to soothe themselves, that they deserve the same soothing from others that they perceive everyone else in the world receives (Linehan, 1993c). These objections are directly confronted.

VISION Mnemonic

The VISION mnemonic reminds the patient to replace current emotional pain with at least momentary joyful emotions. The patient is encouraged to change their appraisal of situations by giving great attention to new experiences that may bring new and different feelings. **V**ision invites the patient to see things differently than before, to look at different things so that different experiences are generated, and to remind the patient to *look* or observe rather than always think and be in a cognitive mode. **I**magery reminds the patient that looking can be imaginal (you don't have to actually be there to envision a pleasant experience). The patient is invited to use their imagination. **S**oothing invites relaxation through both body comfort (through progressive relaxation, deep breathing, taking a warm bath, soothing music, etc.) and through accepting reality with the body (being mindful of bodily tension and accepting such tension without struggle). Soothing should involve as many of the senses as possible. **I**nspiration reminds the patient that a great deal of the power of any technique has to do with belief and expectation. What can the patient do to inspire hope, increase commitment, and bring additional confidence? **O**ne thing at a time reminds the patient that no technique is successful if they simply go through the motions without attending to what they are doing and why. Do one thing, pay attention to it, and bring your attention back to that one thing each time your mind wanders. **N**otice even the small changes that occur with each intervention made. Don't expect immediate and powerful changes with simple and time-limited techniques. Each intervention, when noticed, can be additive and eventually reduce baseline arousal.

DISTRACT Mnemonic

Distress tolerance is the process of self-soothing, acceptance, and distraction. The DISTRACT mnemonic cues the patient in the distraction process. **D**o something else besides paying attention to emotional pain. Engage in any activity that can either improve mood, allow concentration to different processes, or improve self-worth. **I**mages remind the patient again that attention can be placed inwardly (through memory, visualization, fantasy, and imagination) and that they don't actually have to be in a pleasant place in order to react to pleasant stimuli (those stimuli can be self-generated). **S**ense reminds the patient to move from a cognitive process to an experiential process. Use of senses to distract can be powerful (for example, taking a bubble bath, having a massage, putting on skin lotion, wearing a new perfume, etc.). When the patient is overly ruminative and simply can't shift their focus of attention from the cognitive realm, sometimes simply **T**hink of something else. Generate thoughts totally different from the ones that are currently causing emotional pain. **R**emember times that were better, where the person felt stronger and more capable. **A**ccept that pain is a part of life, but also **C**reate new meanings by engaging in meaning-making skills (SPECIFIC PATHS). Finally, **T**ake opposite action (Linehan, 1993c) to what is being felt in the current moment in the attempt to generate different feelings.

Using the Downloads

The downloadable materials (nhpubs.com/29064) that accompany this book include sixty-two PowerPoint slides for training in distress tolerance skills. This program may comprise up to three hours of patient psychoeducation, again depending on the group psychological mindedness and homogeneity. As with training in the other skills sets, the number of sessions depends on the dynamics of the group being trained.

TEACHING STRATEGIC BEHAVIOR SKILLS

Teaching strategic behavior skills involves the most prompting and content compared to the other modules. The overarching goal in this module is help patients shift from emotion-focused to solution-focused coping, to shift from short- to long-term goals and problem solving, and to increase the use of skillful means (mindful use of problem-solving strategies that incorporate both knowledge of feelings and knowledge of rational objectives). These goals are obtained by breaking down both objectives and strategies to obtain them in small, manageable steps. Strategic behavior is presented to patients as using "wisdom" in problem solving.

Using the Downloads

The downloads that accompany this book include a PowerPoint slide show that contains visual aids for the therapist to teach strategic behavior skills to their clients. The file contains 127 slides. Depending on the size of the group you are teaching, their psychological mindedness, and their heterogeneity, teaching this module or skill set can take anywhere from three to six hours of group time.

Wisdom

Wisdom is defined as an understanding of what is true, right, or lasting. Wisdom involves the use of good judgment. Wisdom seeks balance between knowing and doubting and goes beyond fact-finding to include the person's values. Wisdom involves a keen sense of timing as well as recognition of one's perseverance in making small steps toward long-term objectives. Wisdom is juxtaposed with intelligence (the ability to think logically, conceptualize and abstract from reality, do fact-finding, analyze triggers to wanted and unwanted behavior, etc.). While intelligence can be wrong (one's ideas or theories may sound good, but be wrong; accepted facts may be untrue), wisdom invites balance by placing emphasis on both knowing and doubting, balancing values and facts, and balancing what is "right" with what is "practical," and appreciates that timing and perseverance frequently have more value than pure skill alone.

Wisdom has been defined as the interplay of intellectual, affective, and motivational aspects of human functioning that involves good intentions (Baltes and Staudinger, 2000). Baltes and Staudinger introduce the notion of the "fundamental pragmatics of life" to help explore the broad nature of wisdom, which they define as "knowledge and judgment about the essence of the human condition and the ways and means of planning, managing, and understanding a good life" (p. 124). They list multiple factors involved in the human condition, including knowledge about the conditions and variability of life development; knowledge of life's obligations and life goals; the spiritual incomprehensibilities of life; understanding contextually intertwined variables (including life's finitude, cultural conditioning, and incompleteness); and knowledge about oneself and the limits of one's own knowledge and the translation of knowledge into overt behavior. Interestingly, they list dialectical thinking as one important facet of the wisdom-related domain of expertise.

Combining wisdom and intelligence involves analysis of prompts, both external and internal, that keep wanted feelings or behavior going or sustain unwanted feelings or behavior. The combination of wisdom and intelligence involves attending to meaning, being mindful, and keeping objectives in mind, including plans, methods, and techniques to accomplish objectives. Wisdom and intelligence thus define how we obtain meaning and purpose in life.

Dialectics of Strategic Behavior

Strategic behavior offers typical dialectic conflicts that patients are asked to attend to, acknowledge, and navigate as they perform situational analysis of what needs to be done to improve their lives. At times they are asked to be practical, and at other times to be more motivated by their values and beliefs. At times they are asked to focus on themselves, and at other times to focus on others. At times they are asked to attend to the moment, and at other times to attend to their long-term objectives.

Table 20: Dialectics of Strategic Behavior		
Strategic focus	◄———►	Wisdom focus
Attention to the moment	◄———►	Attention to long-term objectives
Focus on practical	◄———►	Focus on values
Focus on self	◄———►	Focus on others
Focus on techniques and procedures	◄———►	Focus on ideas and ideals
Focus on knowledge and facts	◄———►	Focus on doubts and feelings
Rational knowing	◄———►	Intuitive knowing
"From the head"	◄———►	"From the heart"
Confidence and pride	◄———►	Humility and self-doubt
Behavioral focus	◄———►	Emotional focus
Gets me what I want	◄———►	Relinquishes what I want

Strategic behavior thus involves central compromises among potentially con-flicting aspirations and emotions. Strategic behavior depends on judgment, which is circumstantial and unwavering. Strategic behavior moves beyond the circumstantial toward meaningfulness itself.

One obstacle to accomplishing successful strategic behavior is the sense of urgency that strong affect brings. This sense of urgency leads to impulsive behavior, distortion of judgment, and erratic problem solving. Urgency leads to short-term solutions at the cost of long-term objectives. Patients are invited to ask themselves how their sense of urgency may cloud or even totally repress their longer-term, typically more meaningful, goals in life. They are invited to look at the effect of mood-dependent behavior (to constantly be mindful of their current mood and the effect it may have on their current assessments and strategies), and to lower their short-term expectations in service of their long-term wants and needs.

Assisting the patient to break down both their long-term and short-term goals is the essential skill involved in this module. What is the environmental prompt for their current action tendency? What is their mood at this moment? What is their short-term goal or objective? What is their long-term goal or objective? What behavior or action will accomplish their goals? Finally, they are invited to compare the results of their anticipated plans to their objectives. Will expressing their mood in this moment accomplish anything of import? Will it interfere with their accomplishment of their short- or long-term goal? Mood-dependent behavior is not strategic or wise.

OBJECTIVES Mnemonic

The mnemonics for strategic behavior skills is OBJECTIVES. "O" is for **O**utside. What is going on outside of you that prompts you to do this or that? What is happening in the environment? Is the outside requesting some sort of action from you? "B" is for **B**eliefs. What do you believe or think about what is going on outside of you? What are your thoughts, anticipations, and interpretations about the event to which you are about to react? "J" is for **J**udicial. Wisdom involves a judicial stance toward the world, where the judge evaluates the adaptiveness and correctness of potential courses of action. This judgment function is different from judgmentalism since it helps you to navigate the maps that you yourself design. The judicial court is thus kind and self-serving rather than punishing and aversive. "E" is for **E**motions. What are you feeling? Be mindful of emotions and give them voice and power over your decision making. Place feelings into the equation of what your response should be, but not in a mood-dependent fashion. "C" is for **C**onsequences. What will happen if you express your emotion? What reactions of others or of the environment will occur? Do you accept and want these reactions? Patients are reminded that their feelings can be valid, even if the consequences of their actions are negative. Again, a dialectic between effect and accuracy of emotion is presented. "T" is for **T**ime. Patients are invited to evaluate the timeliness of their reactions in the moment. They are reminded that timing can be among the most powerful variables in deciding whether to express or suppress their immediate feelings in the moment. Is their assessment of timing based on their current moods? On their long-term goals? On their judicial self? "I" is for **I**ntrospection. Look into your self, your goals, and your assessment of what is meaningful, and respond to what is ultimately valuable and important rather than what is most impending and urgent. "V" is for **V**alues. Does this have sustaining interest and meaning, or is it just a distraction from something that's provoking anxiety? Life is presented as a series of compromises, and the wise individual seeks balance rather than perfection in living their values. "E" is for **E**ndings and **E**xposure. At some point, analysis is over and the patient must act to obtain their goals; they must expose themselves to risk by making a choice. Finally, "S" is for **S**hort- and long-term goals. Patients are requested to be mindful of how often they serve each end of the continuum, and if they are pursuing one end more than the other, to shift toward the less-practiced end more often.

The OBJECTIVES mnemonic requests the patient to examine their feelings, compare their feelings to their objectives, and to act in ways that are self-enhancing in both the short- and long-term frames of reference.

Emotional Sensitivity

The high emotional arousal found in patients who are candidates for DBT treatment causes frequent shame, guilt, and embarrassment regarding their emotionality and emotional sensitivity. Many patients distrust their emotions and feel shamed that they emote so easily. They feel that they are "different" because they cry so easily, get excited so quickly, or feel dejection so rapidly. Such individuals subsequently protect themselves from emotionally provocative events, inadvertently also shielding themselves from emotional events that could change the negative affect they currently experience. Some individuals look to others to tell them how they *should* be feeling. Either process (shielding from emotional experiences, an avoidance strategy, or giving greater credence to others' opinions about how they should be feeling) is invalidating. The dialectic conflict is thus between emotional receptivity versus emotional blunting—to express or repress experience.

The psychoeducation necessary is to reinforce the notion that emotional sensitivity is an inborn difference, no different than how tall a person is, the color of their eyes, or other aspects of their physical appearance. Some of us are born reserved and less responsive, and others of us are born expressive and responsive. There is no right or wrong to such genetic manifestations. Like most things in life, there are advantages and disadvantages to each. The expressive person tends to be more spontaneous, requires less effort to put themselves forward in social situations, and is more in touch with their feelings. The less expressive person tends to be more cautious and thus less vulnerable to environmental events, but they are also harder to get to know and less comfortable in social settings. Patients are taught that rather than judging themselves for the way they were born, they should use this information about themselves to increase their adaptiveness in responding. The mnemonic to accomplish this utility is TRUST.

TRUST Mnemonic

Using the TRUST mnemonic, the patient is cued toward positive, sustaining thoughts and behaviors. They are reminded to **T**rust that the feeling they're having is acceptable, to **R**edirect their attention to their objectives and goals, and to **U**se their understanding of their personality to make rational choices. They **S**ense their face, muscles, voice, and posture, and **T**ame the expression of their emotion to fit their objectives. The TRUST mnemonic requests that the patient use information about their emotional responsiveness to gauge their behavior in interpersonal situations, frequently (but not always) becoming more expressive for the emotionally reserved individual and less expressive for the emotionally sensitive person. Assisting patients to understand how the TRUST mnemonic will work differently with the two different personality types is essential, as is validating that for both types the feelings themselves are always valid, but the behavior may have to be modulated to take the feeling and the expressiveness style into account. Rather than being apologetic about their level of emotional responsiveness, the patient is invited to use the information in a problem-solving process.

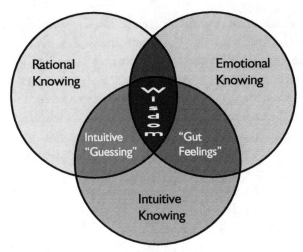

Figure 2: Wisdom attends to all forms of knowing available

The therapist validates that it is acceptable to be expressive, even effusive, in interpersonal encounters, and that it is equally acceptable to be unexpressive. The criterion for success with expressiveness is situational rather than static. In work situations the reserved style may be optimal, while in party situations the effusive style may work best. TRUST helps the patient to break down situational factors and compare them to their baseline expressiveness tendencies toward accomplishing specific objectives or goals.

Emotionalism

Patients are taught to differentiate emotional sensitivity (the threshold at which one becomes expressive of affect) from emotionalism, which is defined as getting urgently caught up in one's emotions. Running fast from anxiety, frantically trying to escape depression, or engaging in impulsive behaviors to stop any strong feeling are all characteristic of emotionalism.

In the above figure (presented to patients during training), wisdom is defined as the intersection between rational knowing, emotional knowing, and intuitive knowing. Wisdom is exceptionally difficult to obtain under the influence of emotionalism. In fact, engaging in any strategic behavior is difficult coupled with emotionalism. The mnemonic to prevent emotionalism is CARES. CARES is presented as a preventive strategy to be used continuously, rather than waiting until emotionalism occurs.

CARES Mnemonic

CARES represents **C**alm, **C**oached practice. Patients are encouraged to choose someone to do something soothing with (go for a walk, jog, meditate, pray, sunbathe, do yoga, practice mindfulness, etc.). It is coached in the sense that it is planned and done with someone else (the patient has a date and a plan). Patients are encouraged to plan something calming every day, even if just for a few minutes each day. "A" is for **A**rousal. Patients are asked to monitor their body, thoughts, and feelings on a continuing basis rather than waiting for arousal to become overwhelming. "A" is also for **A**bstinence. Patients are taught to abstain from alcohol and illicit drugs, to abstain from entering known provocative environments, and to be compliant with prescribed medications. "R" is for **R**elaxation. Relaxation should occur each day, every day: stretch, get in the hot tub, listen to great music, walk the dog, enjoy your shower mindfully, plan recreational activities, engage in progressive relaxation, use pleasant imagery, do deep breathing. "E" is for **E**motions and **E**nvironment. The patient is asked to shift attention to both the environment and their emotions. They are taught the role of expectations and anticipations in shaping their view of events. Not becoming a prisoner of the environment (feeling free to take a "time out" from stressful events, occasionally refusing activities that are stressful, or modifying the environment when possible) can increase the ability to modulate emotional arousal. "S" is for **S**leep. Patients in crisis can frequently see sleep either as a discretionary ele-ment in their life that they can do without, compared to the interpersonal and intrapsychic demands that press upon them, or as a convenient method of escape from life's demands. Patients are taught that too much sleep is just as bad as too little sleep. They are instructed to listen to their body carefully about the amount of sleep they truly need and to compare their assessment to how much sleep they required prior to the development of acute emotional pain.

Behavior Focus

Patients are reminded that it is difficult to be strategic when emotionality is high, as the attentional focus typically becomes narrowly attuned to the emotions themselves. Wisdom requires a broad focus of attention on feelings and the situation, as well as on behavior. The mnemonic to guide this shifting of attention from narrow to broad, and from internal to external, is BEHAVIOR.

BEHAVIOR Mnemonic

The "B" in BEHAVIOR stands for **B**ehavior. Could you be doing something that is causing this to happen? What do you do immediately before the undesired event occurs? How do you influence other people's behavior? "E" is for **E**nvironment. What in the environment is prompting this to occur? What are the demand charac-teristics of this environment? "H" is for **H**ealing versus **H**urting. Are you doing some-thing to heal yourself that is really hurting you? Are you avoiding or escaping? Are you seeing what you want to see rather than what is really happening? "A" is for

Antecedents. Rather than focusing on the powerful feelings of the moment, what came before? The intensity of current emotions can skew perspective. "V" is for **V**alues. What motivates or is important to you? Needs and a sense of deprivation or want can be powerful motivators of behavior. What is it that you're getting out of this situation? If you stay in it, despite your pain, there must be something, on balance, that you're getting out of it. "I" is for **I**nterval. We tend to pay attention only to things that occur regularly and steadily, but events that occur only occasionally can be powerful sustainers of behavior. What powerful but infrequent events may be sustaining these crises? "O" is for **O**utcome. What effect do these events have on you? What is the outcome, the effect? What bad thing is avoided by keeping this going? "R" is for **R**einforcement. What is the payoff? What increases the probability of this behavior? What sustains you in this process? What keeps the cycle going?

BEHAVIOR thus prompts attention to internal factors, external factors, current factors, past factors, future factors, and reinforcing dynamics between all factors. Attention to emotions, attention to environment, and strategic focus on behavior, and shifting between each domain of attention are prompted by the BEHAVIOR mnemonic.

At times, the DBT therapist may walk the patient through the mnemonic with a difficult situation, as below.

DBTherapist: Lets go through the BEHAVIOR skill set to understand better what's going on in this situation.

Patient: Okay.

DBTherapist: What behavior were you engaging in with your friend? I mean, what was going on just before she told you that you were too demanding to have as a friend?

Patient: I was just telling her about what went on between my boss and me, how she was being critical of my performance at work.

DBTherapist: Okay, and what was going on in the environment? In other words, what was going on between you and Alice just before and during your conversation with Alice?

Patient: Alice is not very attentive; she never is. She always seems to be in a rush. She was acting just like she always does, not interested. I thought she would appreciate me telling her about Mary Ann because she knows her too.

DBTherapist: So your behavior is trying to make better friends with Alice by telling Alice about a mutually known person. But Alice, like usual, appears uninterested. You try to pick a topic that will be more interesting to Alice, but the environment—her reaction to you—is telling you that it's not working.

Patient: Yeah, I really understood that once she told me that I was too demanding to have as a friend.

DBTherapist: Let's wait. Before Alice tells you that you're too demanding, let's go to "H" for healing or hurting. By trying so hard to be friends with Alice, in spite of the fact that she repeatedly shows low interest, are you healing yourself or hurting yourself?

Patient: Well, I think both. It's healing to have friends, but it hurts when they reject me.

DBTherapist: Good. So if it "works"—if Alice shows interest—then you'll conclude that it's healing. If it doesn't work, then you'll conclude that it is hurting. Is that right?

Patient: I guess so.

DBTherapist: "A" is for antecedents, what came before. Now, you said that Alice always looks disinterested, right?

Patient: Yeah, she's always in a rush.

DBTherapist: So, if you swing in the healing direction of wanting closer friends, you'll choose to take the risk of trying again to build a stronger bond with Alice. But if you swing in the direction of hurting, you won't take yet another risk of rejection because Alice has not given much indication that she is as interested in a closer bond. Now, "V" stands for values. I'm thinking that you value friendship more than Alice seems to. So you're more willing to take interpersonal risks than maybe she is. Is that right?

Patient: Yes, I want friends more than she seems to. I guess it's her independence that attracts me to her. I wish I could be as independent as she is.

DBTherapist: That would certainly make you safer—you'd expose yourself to less risk than now. But is that really your value, to be safe but have fewer friends?

Patient: No. I need more friends. I'm a friendly and social person. I like having others around me.

DBTherapist: The "I" is for interval. Incidents like this are always about timing. Was this the right time to try to strike up a conversation with Alice?

Patient: It's never the right time. She always seems busy and not interested in what I have to say.

DBTherapist: So if Alice is ever going to be friendlier toward you, maybe the interval thing needs adjusting. Try less frequently. And try only when Alice doesn't seem busy. That may not occur very often, so you'll have to be patient.

Patient: You don't think I should just give up on Alice altogether?

DBTherapist: That depends on your values and if the behavior is really healing or hurting you. It's all about balancing those needs and desires.

Patient: Okay, we already know the outcome. It didn't work. She not only brushed me off, she kind of insulted me. So I definitely didn't get any reinforcement.

DBTherapist: Well, we know it didn't work, but you were seeking reinforcement. What you were after, your potential reward, was a better friendship with Alice. And friendships are important to you, maybe sometimes so important to you that you don't pay attention to other variables that will predict if you'll meet your needs or not, like Alice looking disinterested and being in a rush even before you started to talk to her.

Strategic behavior skills thus involve four separate mnemonics: OBJECTIVES, TRUST, BEHAVIOR, and CARES. These four mnemonics teach patients a practical problem-solving approach that validates the role of emotions in their life while simultaneously inviting them to balance knowing and doubt, which is especially important in the treatment of personality disorders. Central concepts are environmental analysis (looking for prompts, triggers, and sustainers of behaviors), decreasing the sense of urgency, increasing attention to timing of behavior, balancing short- and long-term objectives, decreasing mood-dependent behavior, and shifting attention from internal to external variables (and vice versa).

⌐ *Using the Downloads*

The downloadable material (nhpubs.com/29064) included with this book contains 126 PowerPoint slides to teach strategic behavior skills. This skills module can take anywhere up to six hours of patient education, depending on group dynamics. When combined with meaning-making, mindfulness, emotion regulation, and distress tolerance skills, strategic behavior skills can substantially assist patients in reducing emotional pain. In review, meaning-making skills restore perspective and reinforce effectiveness. Mindfulness skills increase powers of observation, help focus and sustain attention, increase attention to the moment of experience, and decrease avoidance and escape behavior from affect. Emotion regulation skills allow understanding emotions from a biopsychosocial model, and intervening in various points in the model to change affect, becoming mindful of pleasant experiences, discriminating primary from secondary emotional reactions, increasing positive experiences, and taking opposite action. Distress tolerance skills involve nonreinforced exposure to affect through mindfulness, self-soothing, distracting, and acceptance.

When patients complain that this DBT approach does not work for them, have them attend to the level of emotionalism that permeates their life and their level of practice of the principles on a day-by-day and experience-by-experience basis, and assist them with being more judicial with their objectives, rather than trying to do too much or too little.

The downloads included with this book thus contain more than four hundred PowerPoint slides to assist in teaching the modules (mindfulness skills, emotion regulation skills, distress tolerance skills, meaning-making skills, and strategic behavior skills). Depending on the acuity of the patient population you are serving, the psychoeducational component of DBT treatment can take anywhere from seven to twenty-one hours of patient contact.   ⌐

CHAPTER 8

Conducting DBT in Private Practice

In the preceeding chapter we reviewed the psychological skills aspects of DBT. In this chapter we'll examine the mechanics from a mostly practical perspective of conducting DBT in a private practice setting. I emphasize private practice because most therapists work in solo and group practices, and even in group practices most therapists simply share overhead and office space. Most private therapists do not regularly share treatment responsibilities, instead using shared space for a sense of collegiality—at least they can occasionally run into one another during breaks or after work. This is not consistent with Linehan's (1993b, 1993c) treatment manual on BPD, in which she correctly identifies the need for a treatment team and consultation from other professionals in the treatment of BPD. BPD involves special challenges for a therapist, including high suicidality, high parasuicidal behavior, splitting, and boundary issues that make treatment quite difficult (but not impossible) in a traditional private practice setting.

However, DBT is appropriate for many disorders and most do not involve the intensity of acting out and splitting that the BPD engages in. Therefore, DBT can be used with different and less intensive interventions than are the case for BPD. This chapter will outline the use of DBT with mood, anxiety, impulse-control, addictive, eating, and personality disorders other than BPD in the realities of a private practice setting.

DBT WITHOUT A TREATMENT TEAM

Therapists who work within hospital, residential, and clinic settings enjoy the benefit of a treatment team where cases are staffed, alternative interpretations of data are offered, therapist support and confrontation can be typical aspects of case conferences, and multiple therapists from the multidisciplinary treatment team (psychologists, psychiatrists, family counselors, social workers, psychiatric technicians, psychiatric nurses, and even administrative staff) deal with the same patients. Each person brings their own unique training, specialty, and perspective to bear on the patient's dilemmas and symptoms. There are many advantages to such a system of care. For example, the collaborative working relationship between the psychiatrist and therapist can identify the drug-seeking behavior of patients early, social workers bring new information about the living conditions and systems that the patient is attempting to navigate, the family therapist provides the broader perspective of the patient's interactions with other family members, nurses bring to the table important health information about the patient, and other staff can identify how the patient reacts outside the controlled environment of a psychotherapy office.

A multidisciplinary perspective on the patient is invaluable. Even having the observation of two different therapists from the same discipline can be helpful in both identifying patient dynamics and supporting one another and gaining protection from the effects of burnout. Unfortunately, most private practitioners don't have the luxury or benefit of this support.

Moreover, DBT bifurcates treatment into two major, complementary treatment modes: skills training and psychotherapy. Patients who are appropriate candidates for DBT treatment are in acute distress, and they therefore demand the kind of individual attention and intervention that psychotherapy offers. The DBT patient typically does not want their therapist to shift into the teaching mode for skills acquisition, and having one professional conduct the group skills training and another professional conduct the individual psychotherapy is thus an ideal solution. In this ideal construction, the DBT patient understands that psychotherapy will occur in the individual format and that teaching occurs in the group format. Most DBT patients can handle and even appreciate this separation of tasks. However, most communities currently do not have enough professionals trained in the DBT model to have the recommended separation of psychoeducational specialist and psychotherapy specialist. Ideally, each community would have one therapist who sees patients in a group setting, conducting formal teaching sessions in skills acquisition (to teach mindfulness, distress tolerance, meaning-making, strategic behavior, and emotion regulation skills) and another, different professional who conducts individual DBT psychotherapy. The two professionals, of course, would consult one another about their shared patients.

DBT has increasingly been accepted into the public mental-health-care systems, but because DBT has traditionally been conceptualized as a treatment for BPD patients, who typically end up in public mental-health systems due to their repeated suicidal and parasuicidal behaviors, DBT psychotherapy has not penetrated the private mental-health-care systems as thoroughly. While some private therapists have adopted the skills portions of DBT, fewer still have mastered the dialectical analysis required of DBT individual psychotherapy. Our current expansion of DBT to other diagnostic groups, more frequently seen in private practice, can shift the emphasis of DBT acceptance into both the public and private mental-health-care systems. It is my hope that this book and my book on treatment of comorbid depression and anxiety (Marra, 2004) will change that. Perhaps in your community, in the future, the more convenient bifurcation of treatment into psychoeducational and psychotherapeutic by two different private practice professionals will be possible. For now, if two collaborative professionals are unavailable, the following recommendations may help.

Conducting Both Psychosocial Skills Training and Psychotherapy

If the same professional is conducting both psychotherapy and psychosocial skills teaching, the therapist must be aware of the following tendencies in acute patients. They will resist shifting from one of the following modes to the other:

- From talking to listening modes of interaction

- From acceptance modes to learning modes

- From patient role to student mode

- From individual therapy to group mode (assuming the skills training occurs in a group format)

Behaviors typical of such resistance include not keeping scheduled psychoeducation sessions (appearing for psychotherapy only), interrupting teaching presentations and attempting to refocus on their daily emotional and interpersonal experiences, coming in late to psychoeducational sessions, and engaging other participants in one-on-one interactions rather than respecting the group process. These are treated as therapy-interfering behaviors and can be decreased by the following strategic behaviors by the therapist:

- Use one room for therapy and a different room for psychoeducation.

- Have the psychoeducation room set up like a classroom or conference room, rather than a living room or office.

- At the outset, the therapist/trainer verbally draws a distinction between group psychotherapy (exploring feelings and situations in an interpersonal group context) and psychoeducation (learning about feelings and how to handle situations).

■ Use handouts, visual aids (PowerPoint presentations, whiteboards, easels, projectors, etc.), and desks to encourage patients to write and take notes.

■ The therapist should stand during the presentation (denoting their teaching function), while patients are in the classroom setting.

■ An agenda (curriculum or treatment manual with patient handouts) sets the occasion for the psychoeducational session.

■ The therapist begins each session by reviewing the agenda for the session first, then beginning with a review of participants' experiences in completing the homework assignments from the previous session.

■ The therapist/trainer calls upon participants by name to share their homework experiences, again emphasizing the learning and classroomlike demand characteristics of the session, rather than asking the group a question and waiting for someone in the group to respond.

■ The therapist/trainer constantly redirects the group discussion back to the agenda and the curriculum without needing to be apologetic for so doing. Just like in mindfulness, where it is explained that minds naturally wander, in group interpersonal contexts discussions wander and it is the therapist's responsibility to bring the focus to the group.

■ When complex individual issues begin to take up too much group time, the therapist acceptingly redirects the group discussion by stating, "That's very interesting. Let's deal with that individually in our next psychotherapy session. Now let's move to . . ."

■ While, just as in individual therapy, sharing feelings and relevant experiences about topics explored in psychoeducational sessions is encouraged and fostered, in psychoeducation, content must be covered in a paced and reasonable fashion, and the agenda should thus be planned with a fixed (rather than open-ended) number of sessions for each module.

■ It is best to have a small number of patients (six to eight) begin and progress through the entire curriculum together, rather than adding new patients along the way. If this is not possible, have new patients enter at the beginning of a new module rather than midway through a particular module.

If the therapist does not have an additional conference or group room to use, then the furniture in the consulting room needs to be rearranged so that chairs all face the easel or screen. The therapist stands at the easel or screen, and each chair has a clipboard or set of handouts and paper and pencil. If the therapist/trainer does not shift the environment of the consulting room, patients will assume that the same behavior expected during psychotherapy is expected (accepted) during psychoeducation. The result is that the therapist/trainer will never be given an adequate opportunity to actually engage in psychoeducation, and all sessions will be psychotherapy sessions. Since DBT assumes that patients with acute mental disorders fail to use available psychological coping mechanisms, or have inadequate coping skills available to them, then engaging only in psychotherapy and not psychoeducation is incomplete and inadequate treatment for the patient's condition.

The Consultant or Consultation Group

Private practice can be a very lonely experience for the therapist, even though their day is filled with seeing patients hour after scheduled hour. First, our confidentiality requirements are so appropriately strict that, unlike many other professions, we are not allowed to "decompress" when we come home by discussing our patients and the challenges we face. Second, on those occasions when we do get to discuss treatment with a managed-care organization or insurance company, the purpose really is not to promote treatment but to justify treatment. We are on edge and defending what we are doing and how. This is not very satisfying. In fact, it is stressful. Third, while we may have been well trained and may be competent in both psycho-diagnostics and psychotherapy, every busy therapist sees patients who do not easily fit into preconceived molds. A competent therapist will continue to see some, if not all, of their patients as mysterious, curious, baffling, and confusing—if you don't, you're probably burnt out on private practice and need a sabbatical.

While private practitioners do not enjoy the benefits of a multidisciplinary treatment team, they can still have consultants or a consultation group. This can make some therapists feel very vulnerable. The purpose of having a consultant in psychotherapy is to be able to check out diagnoses, treatment plans, and specific interventions with another professional who may offer a fresh perspective, confront your interpretation of behavioral data, or warn you of boundary violations you are unwittingly slipping into. The vulnerability is not just that you have to present your case and your approach, but that you intentionally mention things that you're not sure of, mistakes you're certain you've made, and resistances you have not been able to overcome. Of course this is scary for the therapist—if it isn't, then, again, maybe you need a sabbatical from private practice. We should not ask of our patients anything we would not ask of ourselves, and we ask our patients to expose themselves to their fears rather than avoid or escape them. Consultation with another professional, especially when we ourselves have been out of training for years, can be very challenging.

Pick someone to consult with whom you respect, who you think is competent, and who has experience with the population of patients you are treating. Have a formal consultation agreement that both you and the consultant are engaging in professional consultation and that the same confidentiality agreements apply as in psychotherapy. Pay your consultant, even if the session costs are only one dollar, and even if you are consulting to each other (pay each other a dollar a session). This reminds both of you that this is not professional chatter and banter, but services regulated by law that demand confidentiality and maintaining high standards of care for the other.

More ideally, rather than working with a single consultant, you would establish or join a consultation group. A group of therapists in private practice pay each other for the privilege to serve each other to improve their skills, knowledge, and approach when dealing with difficult patients. Again, there should a formal, written agreement for services that includes fees and confidentiality. In group consultation there should be specific requirements regarding what happens in the group when one therapist begins to recognize the identity of a specific patient who is being described. If the patient is a friend or acquaintance of another therapist in the group, then the therapist who knows the patient socially should excuse themselves from the group while that patient is being discussed.

How often should consultation with other professionals take place? In hospital settings, reports can occur each change of shift; in residential treatment settings or clinics, such meetings can occur daily or weekly. In private practice, especially in rural areas, only monthly consultation may be practical. The point is not the regularity of meetings but the commitment of the therapist to open themselves up to the input of others on difficult cases. This may occur sporadically or routinely. If the therapist is treating patients with high suicidality or parasuicidality (such as patients with acute mood disorders, bipolar disorder, or BPD), then such consultation should occur at least monthly. If the therapist is newly trained or inexperienced with the population they now find themselves treating, then the consultation should occur at least weekly. You don't have a treatment team, so you need to use an abundance of caution. Your caution should increase with the severity of the patient's symptoms and the degree that those symptoms place the patient's safety in jeopardy. This is demanded not just by current standards of practice, but by our ethics codes.

Do Your Consultants Need to Be DBT Therapists?

Ideally, the professionals with whom you consult are DBT-trained therapists. However, as mentioned above, many private practice communities don't have one therapist well trained in DBT, let alone a group of such therapists who can provide support and education for one another. It is therefore impractical for the DBT therapist to accept only other DBT therapists with whom to consult. In this case, the DBT therapist minimally provides consultants with references from the professional literature (Dimidjian and Linehan, 2003; Koerner and Linehan, 2000; Linehan, 1987,

1993a, 1993b, 1993c; Linehan et al., 1999; Marra, 2004; Rizvi and Linehan, 2001; Shearin and Linehan, 1994) and begins the consultation process by formally presenting DBT theory and practice to the consultants prior to presenting a case for consultation.

As already noted, therapy outcome studies demonstrate that differing psychotherapy schools produce similar successful outcomes (Messer and Warren, 1995), and therapist effects can overshadow specific techniques, strategy, or psychological orientation (Luborsky et al., 1986). If your consultation group has professionals who are more interested in understanding the patient with whom you are dealing than they are in proving that their theories are better than yours, then you're probably in safe hands. If, on the other hand, you find that your consultants are more interested in you trying strategies derived from their theoretical orientation (without necessarily redefining the problems that you've presented), then you should be skeptical. Are your consultants trying to understand the patient, their symptom pattern, their diagnosis, and their treatment needs? Do they provide you with a fresh perspective on what may be going on? Do they challenge you to look at how your behavior (your interventions) may be causing the very resistance you seek to reduce? If so, then belay your suspicions. Theory is important because it helps therapists to see what is not stated overtly, to look for underlying needs and urges about which the patient may not be aware, to look for causes of the behavior or feelings the patient wishes to decrease that may be delayed or intermittent, and to map out a plan of treatment that targets both immediate symptoms (known to the patient) and causes of symptoms (perhaps unknown to the patient).

Good therapy, regardless of orientation, involves understanding the patient's perspective, even if the therapist does not approve of or agree with that perspective; moving beyond the patient's perspective; and offering hope and strategy in changing the patient's experience and/or environment in ways that change their perspective and experience in desired ways. Good therapy also offers sustainability of change across time without the therapist's prompting or continued interventions. If your consultants accept this definition of good therapy, then they need not fully embrace the DBT model of treatment in order to be adequate coaches to your professional conduct.

DBT Training

Obviously, consultation alone is not adequate training or preparation for conducting DBT. There are training resources available to help you or your consultants learn more about the practical application of DBT. Dr. Linehan has a training organization, Behavioral Technology Transfer Group, that provides extensive one-, two-, three-, or four-week workshops for treatment teams. The group's training content and patient population vary by workshop. They can be contacted at www.behavioral tech.com. The group also sells tapes, CDs, videos, workbooks, behavior recording forms, and books. Alternatively, you can contact the nonprofit Center for Dialectical Behavioral Therapy, with which I am associated, at www.depressedandanxious.com.

How else can an interested therapist or treatment team be adequately trained to apply DBT? At Monterey Psychiatric Health Facility we used a self- and team-teaching model. Training began with a twenty-hour workshop that included rapid PowerPoint presentation of each of the skills modules (Linehan, 1993c). Each week, small groups of treatment professionals were assigned to read and present to another small group of professionals one chapter from Linehan's original work (Linehan, 1993b). Similarly, each week small groups variously read and presented one of the skills modules (Linehan, 1993c) to another group of professionals. Then each member of the treatment team was required to present each of the skills modules using the PowerPoint slides and therapist treatment manual that was written to accompany the slides. They would first present the modules to other professionals who were also studying the material, before they led any patient groups using the materials.

The self- and team-teaching method was time-intensive and extensive—the training period lasted approximately two months. However, the results were that the entire treatment team was enthusiastic about the approach, used the same language to describe patient problems, used consistent approaches with patient problems, and adequately learned to balance acceptance with change strategies and psychotherapy with skills acquisition. You don't necessarily need a guru, but you do need education, practice, feedback, and coaching from competent professional partners.

It is my hope that this book will significantly reduce the training time required for preparation to deploy DBT treatment in private practice settings.

DIALECTICAL INDIVIDUAL PSYCHOTHERAPY

In the previous chapter we explored psychosocial skills teaching, while in this section we more fully explore individual psychotherapy from a DBT perspective. While good therapy from any theoretical orientation shares essential similarities, in the remainder of this book we will examine what makes DBT unique from other perspectives.

The First Session

The first session of DBT has the same essential characteristics as any good therapy: take an adequate history and set patient expectations for what is to come in subsequent sessions. Ask the patient to come in fifteen minutes early for the first meeting, so they have plenty of time to complete your history, biographical, confidentiality, HIPAA, fees contract, and insurance forms prior to beginning the interview. As with any good psychotherapy, the initial meeting with the patient involves taking a comprehensive history, including questions like "Where did you grow up? Did your mother and father stay married during your childhood? If not, how old were you when they separated? Do you have brothers and sisters? Where were you chronologically, compared to your siblings? What was your relationship with your mother like? What was your relationship with your father like? Did you and your siblings get along? Was your childhood happy and satisfying? Why or why not? Were there traumas or especially challenging events as you grew up? Did any physical, sexual, or emotional abuse occur when you were a child? Did you have any extensive or painful medical problems when a child? How would you compare your childhood to your friends' childhoods? Did people in your family discuss feelings openly?" Your history questionnaire can briefly capture a good deal of this information, which you then review with the patient.

Other important questions include "Did you consider yourself an independent adolescent? Did the family promote your sense of competence as a developing adult? Is there an alcohol or drug history? When did you begin to date? When did you first marry? How long have you been in that relationship? Have there been periods of separation or divorce? How would you characterize the relationship? Have you ever been depressed? Suicidal? Hospitalized? Do you have any current medical problems? When was your last physical checkup? Do you take any medications?"

Continue with "When did your symptoms first begin? Have you sought previous help for them? When do they occur (frequency, intensity, prompted by what environment)? What do you typically do when they occur? Does it help? How is your sleep? Your appetite? Your sex drive? Your sex frequency? Can you concentrate well? How is your work/school performance?" Obviously, your specific review of symptoms will be directed by the nature, course, and type of symptoms that the patient describes. Your questions should provide specific information to make a general diagnosis, including your assessment of the patient's current mental status: presence, even if not verbally disclosed, of anxiety, depression, ability to form sustained and satisfying interpersonal relationships, avoidance and escape of affect, underlying thought-process integrity, delusional or hallucinatory material, suicidal potential, homicidal potential, gross learning or educational deficits, and general ability to adapt to their current environmental demands.

Once you have a general overview of the patient's life history, go back to the description of symptoms. Begin to probe into the attitude and judgments the patient is making about their symptoms. Are they shamed because they have them? Do they hide them from others? What have the symptoms prevented them from having or doing? What is the cost to them, psychologically, of having these symptoms? Identify the competing and contradictory needs the patient is attempting to satisfy. Some of these sacrifices or compromises may be unsatisfactory to the patient, while others may be totally acceptable. While there will not be time to identify all or even most of the patient's dialectical conflicts, you should be able to identify some of the core struggles the patient is experiencing that prompted them to enter treatment at this moment in time.

I have found that patients really appreciate a thorough history, especially if they feel that the purpose of your questions is to understand them as fully as possible.

Allow ten minutes at the conclusion of the initial intake interview to do the following: tell them your initial diagnostic impressions (not just the name but the main symptoms that define the disorder), your general treatment plan to help them with their diagnosis, and a very brief description of DBT and how it fits into the treatment plan. Ask them if there are any other goals they wish to accomplish while in therapy. Provide them with a brief written summary of DBT (you can adopt or alter the one called "What Is Dialectical Behavior Therapy?" available in the downloads at (nhpubs.com/29064) to read prior to the next session, and explain that you will be happy to answer their questions about the reading and treatment approach at the beginning of the next session. The last few minutes should be allocated to the patient: "I've asked you a lot of questions, and I know it can be tedious to review all the things we did today, so I appreciate your tolerance in sticking with me through this. Do you have any questions of me before we end?"

Throughout the process of taking the first history, the therapist provides validation: "That must have felt good," "That must have really hurt," "I can understand why you say that," "How horrible!" Confrontation does not belong in the first intake interview. If the patient asks questions or seeks information, brief responses that address the question should be given rather than putting them off by telling them that you'll get to that later in the treatment process. For example, if the patient asks, "How do I end these horrible panic attacks?" the therapist responds "I have a very specific protocol or step-by-step process that can help you reduce those horrible things. I can even give you some handouts on them, but first let's return to . . ."

In the first session, the therapist adopts a very accepting stance toward the patient. Of course they feel the way they feel and want the bad feelings terminated immediately (and without much effort) who wouldn't? Of course they want everyone to love them—so would you. You understand why they feel like dying—they want their pain to stop. The therapist need not approve of the patient's thoughts, only accept that they have these thoughts and feelings.

While I always take notes in the first session as the patient makes their disclosures, I also make certain that I give plenty of eye contact as well. Abbreviate your notes, as in taking a Rorschach, rather than trying to get every word and detail exactly. Nonverbally show interest, warmth, and reaction to the feelings they disclose. If all of the information being provided is thoughts and judgments rather than feelings, show interest in these as well. Acceptance of the patient's perspective as important is the second most important objective in the intake interview, with an adequate history and diagnostic formulation being the most important.

Finally, ask them if they read the treatment agreement before they signed it. If they didn't, ask them to read it prior to coming to the next session. If they did, ask if they have any questions about your cancellation fee policy, fees, or the limits of confidentiality.

The Second Session

Tell the patient you're glad to see them again. If they had not read the treatment agreement before they signed it last time, ask them if they have now read it. If they haven't, go through each provision with them. Review the major symptoms they have and the treatment you now plan to provide to decrease those symptoms. Ask them if they read the DBT description you gave them and any other disorder-specific handouts you may have provided them with at the first session. If they haven't, briefly review the DBT treatment goal of forming better compromises to life's difficult conflicts. Use their own conflicts, identified in the first session, as the example of a dialectic conflict. Review the skills modules training sessions you would like them to attend and ask if they are willing to attend these as well as psychotherapy. If the patient is not willing initially to attend the psychological coping skills sessions, accept this decision but tell the patient that you would like to be able to revisit the decision should it become clear in the course of treatment that they're missing important skills in completing the homework assignments you will be giving them. I often find that patients initially unwilling to commit to the skills groups will do so once a good working psychotherapeutic relationship is established. I also use prompts throughout therapy, such as "If you were attending the mindfulness skills group, you would have learned how to . . ." These prompts show the patient the importance of the skills groups in more rapidly solving their problems. Very few patients will, over the course of treatment, consistently refuse to attend the skills modules when they see how important the skills are to the issues they raise in individual psychotherapy. So I don't push them in the beginning stage of treatment to commit to both, but I do engage in consistent welcoming to attend both throughout treatment.

Then ask the patient how their symptoms were between the first and current session. Rather than allowing the patient to give a blow-by-blow report of everything that happened during the week (recitations like that easily can fill hours of therapy time), the goal is to get an overview. During this overview, and throughout the entire course of DBT therapy, the therapist begins to ask questions designed to meet the following goals:

- Identify dialectic conflict

- Identify emotional escape and avoidance behaviors

- Identify environmental prompts for the symptoms

- Identify physiological prompts for the exacerbation of symptoms

- Identify internal thoughts and judgments about the symptoms

- Identify mood-dependent behavior in response to symptoms

■   Identify when the patient is capable of using strategic behavior and
when they are using emotion-focused coping

The above goals are broad, so table 21 attempts to provide examples of how
they would be exemplified in treatment.

Table 21: Examples of DBT Interventions	
DBT Psychotherapy Target	**Examples of Psychotherapy Target**
Identify dialectic conflict	"What I'm hearing is that you are struggling with initiative on the one hand and a sense of hopelessness on the other. Sometimes, depending on your mood in the moment, you can do the things you see as important, but when your mood gets low you give up and do nothing. This inconsistency decreases your faith in yourself."
Identify emotional escape and avoidance behaviors	"What I'm observing is that each time someone tries to get close to you, you withdraw both emotionally and in your behavior. This makes others feel that you are uninterested in having close relationships, but the truth is that you desire closeness but fear it greatly."
Identify environmental prompts for the symptoms	"It feels like your anxiety comes out of nowhere, but I've noticed so far that it appears you get anxious each time you feel exposed. When people can see you, not just your body but your self, you feel terror."
Identify physiological prompts for the exacerbation of symptoms	"It appears that each time you think of threat—these suspicions you have about how others want to harm you—your muscles get tight, especially in your forehead and around your eyes. You become quiet, because you don't want to give them any more information about you that they could use against you, but you notice your body is suspicious of danger, too."
Identify internal thoughts and judgments about the symptoms	"I've noticed that whenever you begin to feel disappointment in yourself, a whole silent but well-rehearsed dialogue begins in your head that goes something like this: 'I've always known I'm incompetent, that my efforts are meaningless, that I'm doomed to failure, and that I might as well give up.'"

Identify mood-dependent behavior in response to symptoms	"Whenever you feel emptiness inside, this vague sense of boredom and uselessness you've described, it's followed by an urgent desire to use drugs. When you're preoccupied with work or engaged in tasks, you resist or don't even experience the need to use drugs. When you have free time, and you begin to think and feel about yourself, it seems like that's when the urgency to break your abstinence happens."
Identify when the patient is capable of using strategic behavior and when they are using emotion-focused coping	"You've told me at work you're considered a top performer, and even when your coworkers are nasty you're able to put it aside and focus on your mission. But at home, when your wife becomes nasty, you meet fire with fire. What do you think allows you self-control at work, even in the face of obstacles, but not at home?"

The second session should introduce the patient to dialectical thinking through examples from the patient's own descriptions. Reframe what the patient has said so the dialectics are clear. For example, the patient tells you that their spouse nagged them all week about drinking an entire bottle of scotch, and this just made them want to drink more to show their spouse how they couldn't be controlled. They felt guilty for drinking but also angry that their spouse was trying to make them feel guilty. They don't feel that they're an alcoholic (they don't typically drink that much), but they admit that their behavior is typically extreme. When they drink, they drink too much. When they go shopping, they spend too much. When they argue, they yell and throw a tantrum. The DBT therapist might respond, "I hear you saying that you're struggling with extremes. You're fighting being indulgent on the one hand and feeling deserving on the other. When you indulge, you feel guilty. When you resist indulgence, you feel deprived and controlled. You have not found a happy medium yet."

By the end of the second session, the DBT therapist should have a strategic homework assignment for the patient to complete between the second and third sessions. The homework assignment should be targeted at one of the dialectics identified in the first two sessions. For example, if the patient is experiencing an anxiety disorder and has unsuccessfully compromised along the safety versus freedom dialectic, the DBT therapist might assign the patient to attend very carefully to all the ways they have made themselves safe over the course of the week until the next session. Not just to notice the big stuff, like turning down a social date, but also to notice the small stuff, like sitting in the back of the classroom, avoiding eye contact with other students, changing the station on the television when romantic commercials appear, getting upset when they see a couple walking hand in hand, etc. The point of such an exercise is to help the patient see how extremely they have sacrificed freedom in their lives prior to asking them to take risks to sacrifice safety in later stages of treatment.

Within the first two sessions, the therapist has openly acknowledged to the patient that commitment to psychotherapy will be hard. If change were easy, they would not need therapy to begin with. They are strong because they've made a commitment to do something difficult and challenging.

The Initial Stages of Treatment

In the initial stages of treatment, the DBT therapist may find that some patients, particularly those with personality disorders, seem to ignore the dialectic analysis verbalized by the therapist and simply continue in their specific description of their feelings, experiences, and events as if the therapist had said nothing. This is a critical observation and points both to the patient's attentional strategy (to be self-absorbed and defend against input from the environment) and to the major interventions the DBT therapist will later use to help them (teaching them mindfulness and strategic behavior skills). The DBT therapist is not put off by this attempt by the patient to differentially reinforce the therapist to simply approve of and understand their perspective. In fact, it confirms why the patient needs DBT treatment in the first place: they have experienced so much invalidation of affect in the past that they are desperate for validation. The therapist provides the validation sought directly ("Yes, your reaction makes sense") and summarizes and reflects upon the patient's point of view ("When you blew your top with your husband, it reflected the years of mistreatment you have suffered in the marriage"). When the patient describes clearly maladaptive behaviors, the DBT therapist first identifies how those behaviors were attempted solutions to problems, then comments upon the effects of the behaviors. For example, the therapist might say "You got drunk last week because you could not tolerate the anxiety and hopelessness you've been feeling. You just could no longer take those feelings that have gone on so long. But then later you felt guilty and worthless and now have two sets of problems to deal with: the hopelessness *and* the guilt."

DBT theory departs from standard cognitive behavioral therapy by placing increased emphasis on providing opportunities for emotional expression within the psychotherapy sessions. This is not simple venting of affect, and the therapist does not simply congratulate themselves for providing a context within which the patient can unbashfully feel. The purpose of exploring affect is, over time, to teach the patient to better observe their own emotional process, increasing the identification and labeling skills the patient deploys, and to learn to shift strategies (attending to internal versus external cues, attending to emotional versus cognitive cues, attending to short-term versus long-term goals and aspirations, and shifting from escape and avoidance strategies to acceptance strategies). This requires quite active direction, refocusing, and involvement of the DBT therapist, who does not simply sit and listen to the patient's affect but actively coaches, models, and shapes the shifts desired.

Table 22: DBT Examples of Shifting Strategies	
Method of attending to emotional stimuli	Able to observe and describe (label) feeling states rather than simply react to emotional push without first observing the emotional process: "I felt a sense of crisis, that my world would fall apart unless I did something immediately to change it. You've called it urgency, I call it danger."
Attending to external cues	Pays attention to what is going on in the environment (events), what is going on in others (interpersonal dynamics), and is able to identify antecedents and consequences: "We both wanted to have a good time, so we went to the club. She wanted to dance, and I wanted to have a beer. A guy came up and asked her to dance, then I blew my top. She looked interested in him."
Attending to internal cues	Pays attention to what is going on in their thoughts, body, and feelings: "I thought to myself that she really didn't want to have a good time with me, she was just using me. I felt shame, like I always do, but my body was wanting to punch both of them in the mouth."
Attending to cognitive cues	Able to identify assumptions, rules, and imperatives they have formed: "I guess my rule is that when I have a date, all of my date's attention should be focused on me only."
Attending to emotional cues	Able to identify affect in the moment: "I was so worked up, I'm not sure what I was feeling, but I guess it was inadequacy." The therapist invites the patient to attend to feelings in the moment, so that in the future they are not guessing what their feelings might have been but know, because they access their emotions more immediately, such as "I'm angry now."
Attending to short-term objectives	Able to identify what they want (what their goal is) in this particular moment or situation: "I wanted to have a good time, to feel some joy and amusement for once in my life."
Attending to long-term objectives	Able to identify what they want (what their goal is) beyond the current situation or event: "I want someone to love me. I want to feel valued."

Using escape and avoidance strategies intentionally rather than automatically	Able to identify reasonable tolerance levels for discomfort and take strategic action: "I knew that my anxiety was rising quickly. I remembered what you told me about escape. I waited thirty seconds or so, paid attention to my breathing, took a deep breath, then left the room. I didn't feel like I was running away."
Increasingly using acceptance and exposure to painful affect	Willing to embrace that emotional pain and suffering are a part of life and that exposure in small doses to such pain makes them stronger: "It was so hard, but I paid attention to my despair like you've been asking me to do. I closed my eyes and just watched the ugly feeling for ten minutes. Then I called my friend on the phone and we went shopping. You were right—having the feeling didn't necessarily spoil my whole day."
Shifting these strategies frequently	Able to identify which strategy in the moment is more likely to result in the outcomes they desire: "I wanted to avoid, but I knew that would make my anxiety grow. So I bit the bullet and stayed, even though my anxiety was telling me to flee." Or, alternatively, "I want to think of myself as strong, that I could still hang out with my old drinking buddies and not drink. But then I asked myself why I should place myself in temptation's way, so I left."

Like any good therapy, the goals of the initial stage of treatment are to establish a positive therapeutic relationship (also note the role of transference later in this chapter). The working relationship must be founded on warmth, positive regard, acceptance, nurturance, focused attention from the therapist, flexibility (balancing following the patient's needs while pursuing the therapeutic treatment plan), and keeping the patient's reasons for entering therapy in mind.

Within each session, regardless of the stage of treatment, the DBT therapist balances acceptance with change strategies. Linehan (1993b) develops the dialectics of acceptance versus change, nurturing versus demanding initiative, being flexible versus being persistent, and focusing on capabilities versus focusing on deficits. While the DBT therapist validates the patient's needs and wants, they also attempt to control and influence the therapy session in pursuit of the treatment plan. The shifting back and forth within each session of focusing on affect versus objectives, on details versus generalities, on intrapsychic events versus external behavioral and interpersonal events, and on reason versus experience differentiates DBT from other forms of therapy. The shifting from analysis to synthesis occurs in all good therapy, but it is done strategically and consciously in DBT and more frequently—within sessions, not just between sessions. One goal of this constant shifting of perspective is to model for the patient the rapid changes in perspective needed for successful adaptation to the complex demands of modern living.

The Role of Judgement

The dialectic opposite to validation can be defined as judgmentalism. Patients in acute emotional distress frequently increase their judgmental functions. Everything is evaluated in terms of good and bad, wanted and unwanted, moral and immoral, right and wrong, to be sought and to be avoided. Judgmentalism perpetuates avoidance and escape of affect because it defines an immediate direction toward change without necessarily first experiencing that which is being judged. Judgmentalism is thus a form of distancing; it invokes rationalization over experience. While it temporarily provides a sense of safety (something has been categorized and thus need not be further processed), it increases the probability of impulsiveness and decreases the probability of actual experience. The DBT therapist thus identifies the prevalence of judgmental stances when verbalized by the patient. A typical patient will point out that judgmental perspectives are common, normal, and even unavoidable. You validate the patient that they are correct, but point out that like most extremes on a dialectic, judgementalism sacrifices the processes on the other end of the polemic: acceptance, experience, and sustaining observation over time. Confronting judgmentalism should thus begin in the early stage of treatment. This must be done quite gently with patients with personality disorders, who often base their entire experience on strongly held judgments about the world. Shaping behavior over time rather than direct confrontation of central judgments is thus the rule rather the exception when dealing with personality disorders.

The Special Role of Validation in DBT

It is important to note that in DBT, validation of the patient's perspective is not simply an attempt to improve the therapeutic working relationship. It's not used simply as a way to seduce patients to engage in change strategies, and it's not done simply to make the patient feel good. (However, validation may indeed increase each of the above functions.) Validation is recognition that the patient's perspective is not wrong, however many maladaptive consequences it may have. For example, a child who has obsessive-compulsive disorder informs you that the ritual of saying good-bye protects them from bad things happening. You note that this is not simple politeness on the child's part, because there is a driven quality to the behavior of saying good-bye, that anxiety increases dramatically when the behavior is somehow prevented, and that a lack of reply from others once the behavior is engaged in also increases the intensity of anxiety. When the ritual is performed well (the patient says good-bye and the other acknowledges the behavior), anxiety decreases. Telling the patient that they are simply prolonging their distress by engaging in the behavior is not validating. It tells the patient that they are wrong, when clearly, on an experiential level, they know that they are right. After all, each time they engage in the ritual their anxiety indeed does decrease. The bad thing they are avoiding is their own anxiety, not really something catastrophic happening in the future, although they might fear this, too. Validation would be to tell the child that of course they are fearful of stopping the behavior because they know it will make them feel bad. You understand that they want to avoid anxiety—you would too. You then begin to help them with the behavioral processes of exposure and response prevention in spite of your validation of their perspective and their resistance. You continue to validate that they are right even as you pursue the treatment plan of decreasing obsessive-compulsive behavior. The more you validate their perspective and insist on adherence to the treatment procedures (having compassionately explained why you want them to expose themselves to the very things they are trying so hard to avoid), the greater your (and their) probability of success. Validation is thus understanding the world from the patient's perspective. They are not wrong—they are exactly right.

Validation is especially important when dealing with suicidal feelings and can be particularly difficult when the depression is experienced both as internal dejection and external hostility. An example of how this might play out in therapy follows.

Patient: My life sucks, and that's why I feel like killing myself all the time.

DBTherapist: From what you've said about your life, I can understand why you feel like killing yourself. You try hard, but you're not getting what you want.

Patient: Yeah, but it's a lot more than that. Even when I'm alone, I'm so depressed that life doesn't seem worth the effort.

DBTherapist: You hurt, and you want the hurt to stop.

Patient: Why do you agree with me all the time? Isn't it your job to talk me out of my feelings of wanting to kill myself?

DBTherapist: No, Kyle, my job is to help you change your feelings over time so that life is very much worth living.

Patient: Well, it's not worth it now. Life sucks.

DBTherapist: Can you remember a time when life felt different, when you didn't feel bad as much as now?

Patient: No. I can't. I've always felt rotten.

DBTherapist: So you've always wanted to kill yourself?

Patient: No, those feelings just started about six months ago. That's why my mom insisted that I start coming to you.

DBTherapist: So, even though your life sucked for all of these twenty-three years, only in the last half year have you felt suicidal?

Patient: Yeah, since my girlfriend broke up with me.

DBTherapist: So even though life sucked, your relationship with your girlfriend made life worth living or at least tolerable.

Patient: Yeah, she was my only reason for living.

DBTherapist: So back then, before the breakup, you both wanted to die, because life sucked, and wanted to live, because your girlfriend brought joy.

Patient: Yeah, but now I just have the shit and no one to love.

DBTherapist: You're in pain now, but it wasn't as intense with your girlfriend.

Patient: And now I don't have a girlfriend, so the rest doesn't matter.

DBTherapist: It does matter, because your feelings changed. They were different, back then.

Patient: But that was then, and this is now.

DBTherapist: I understand you're mostly concerned with immediate feelings, but your feelings from the past may point to how to change your feelings in the future.

Patient: What's wrong with me? I can't keep a girlfriend. Shit, my mother and father have been together for twenty-five years, and I can't keep a girlfriend for longer than a year! Nobody understands how I feel. No one has had these crappy feelings. I can't take it any more.

DBTherapist: I understand you want your pain to end.

Patient: Can't you do anything but agree with me?

DBTherapist: You'd prefer I argue with you?

Patient:	No, I . . . *(Cries)*
DBTherapist:	Maybe you're supposed to feel this pain. I mean, losing someone you love is supposed to hurt.
Patient:	*(Silent, obviously uncomfortable that the hostility defense is not working as well)*
DBTherapist:	It's okay to hurt.
Patient:	I don't like it.
DBTherapist:	I know.

Validation is thus good therapy because it means that the therapist is able to see the world through the eyes of the patient, as well as through their own eyes. Validation is verbalizing your understanding of the patient's worldview or schema. The DBT therapist uses validation as way both to check out if they have adequately understood the meaning construction of the patient (how events are evaluated in terms of importance or potential influence over their goals and needs) and to communicate this understanding to the patient. This increases intimacy between the patient and the therapist and thus increases therapeutic safety. Patients are better able to shift their focus from one end of a dialectic conflict to the other when they know that someone is watching them, understanding their inner terror, and can provide a safety net if they falter. The patient wants the same opportunity for success that you, as the therapist, do.

There are many ways to validate in DBT psychotherapy (Linehan, 1993b). The first and easiest is simply to acknowledge that you understand why the patient feels or thinks the way they do. You reflect back to the patient what they have said in a respectful and agreeable tone of voice. You verbalize the meaning that a patient attaches to an event or process, even if the patient has not explicitly stated such meaningfulness. You articulate the assumptions that the patient is making that must have occurred for them to get from point A to point B, without challenging those assumptions. You identify the dialectic conflict, which implicitly recognizes the needs the patient is attempting to accomplish.

Linehan (1993b) refers to "cheerleading strategies" that include communicating that the patient is doing their best, expressing faith that the patient will make it, focusing on the patient's capabilities and strengths, modulating external criticism from others, providing reassurance, and acknowledging both the emotion the patient is experiencing and an understanding that this emotion is normal given what they are dealing with. Validation must occur within each session, across each stage of treatment.

The Middle Stages of Treatment

The very process of dividing treatment into stages is somewhat confusing in DBT, since within-session shift of focus is so critical to success. The stages of treatment are therefore somewhat artificial, but perhaps a necessary construction in terms of making practical sense of DBT for therapists less familiar with DBT on an experiential level.

Identifying Ineffective Behavioral Strategies

Exploring with the patient ineffective behavioral strategies is critical to any form of good therapy. In DBT this is accomplished through both validation and confrontation (an inherent dialectic!). This is the core of dialectic analysis, validating that the patient has good reasons to be where they are on the dialectic pole (meeting needs in some way) and to sacrifice other important needs at the opposite end of the dialectic pole (the reason the behavior is ineffective). Confrontation is not criticism. It is pointing out to the patient what is lost—what compromises they are making about which they may not be aware. Once the patient is aware of the sacrifice (frequently due to fear), the DBT therapist expresses support and belief that they eventually will be able to tolerate the fear and thereby sacrifice less in the future. The therapist validates the patient's disappointment in themselves (Linehan, 1993b), again directly confronting the sacrifice that powers the maladaptiveness of the strategy currently used. Validation can thus be both support and confrontation, and confrontation can thus be validation.

Problem-Solving Strategies and Behavior Focus

Frequently, the primary strategy used by patients in acute emotional pain is emotional escape and avoidance. However, this is not always the case, and the competent DBT therapist also has expertise in behavior therapy skills. While all therapists have had basic training in learning theories and behavior therapy, many therapists have not had such education since their undergraduate psychology coursework, which may have been a long time ago. We will thus briefly review some basic concepts of operant and respondent procedures for behavior change to refresh memory.

Self-recording brings attention and focus to an unwanted behavior in a new or different way. Linehan (1993c) includes an Emotion Diary, Crisis Survival Strategy worksheet prompts, and a variety of other behavior prompting worksheets. Marra (2004) uses a DBT Log, DBT Practice Sheet, and other skill-specific worksheets that prompt patients to handle situations differently than they have in the past. Self-recording sheets can bring focus to individual psychotherapy sessions by dealing with high-frequency problems rather than what the patient happens to bring to the table from memory. The DBT therapist uses modeling, behavior rehearsals, and practice to assist the patient to modify behavior. Helping the patient to design self-reinforcement schedules and modify the environment in order to obtain goals is exceptionally important.

Interventions that restrict, reduce, or eliminate behavior include extinction, which removes contingencies maintaining a behavior; satiation, which removes a sense of urgency, need, or deprivation that drives behavior; response cost, which involves removal of a reinforcer contingent on some behavior; time out, which weakens behavior by imposing a period of time during which reinforcers are not available; restraint and confinement (not easily accomplished in real-life situations), which are designed to obscure contingencies of reinforcement and delay impulsive acting out; and reinforcement of omission, also called omission training or differential reinforcement of other behaviors. In omission training, reinforcement is made contingent upon the absence or omission of behavior, while in differential reinforcement of other behaviors, the rewards are targeted to behaviors incompatible with the behavior that is desired to be decreased. All these are considered "operant" procedures because typically the patient is operating upon their environment (trying to achieve a purpose or obtain a reward).

In respondent procedures, the patient is simply responding to events that occur. With classical conditioning, the anxiety the patient experiences is due to repeated exposure or association to anxiety-provoking situations. The DBT therapist provides anxiety relief conditioning, where "safety" occurs only after self-soothing, and graduated extinction, where the anxiety-producing stimulus is attenuated to a level the individual can tolerate without undue anxiety. Desensitization or counterconditioning can be systematic imaginal, in vivo, or modeling (vicarious) desensitization. Desensitization always involves teaching relaxation skills, constructing a hierarchy of anxiety arousal situations, and pairing the hierarchy items with relaxation.

Most behavior therapy interventions in private practice involve self-control procedures where the patient and therapist together analyze the situation (observe) in terms of unwanted behavior (frequency, topography, urgency); covariants of unwanted behavior (both wanted, unwanted, and neutral); wanted behavior (frequency, topography, urgency); and antecedents and consequences (sustainers of unwanted behavior and barriers to achieving wanted behaviors) that constitute a sequence analysis. The therapist and patient locate and withhold the reinforcers maintaining the unwanted behavior, always starting with the possible and building in initial successes for the patient. Decreasing discriminative stimuli for unwanted behavior and increasing discriminative stimuli for wanted behavior is important for any behavior management plan. This is especially important for addictive, impulse-control, and eating disorders. Selecting appropriate consequences that are easy to manage, using commitment strategies (including contracting, cheerleading, and contingent reinforcement), and evaluating the successfulness of each attempt to modify behavior are all important.

Exposure-Based Interventions

Exposure-based interventions are essential rather than discretionary aspects of DBT. DBT is designed to treat patients with high emotional arousal, slow return to emotional baseline, and hypervigilance to threat cues. Exposure-based interventions can alter this generalized psychological pathology. While almost everyone understands positive reinforcement, DBT therapists may be surprised at how many of their patients do not understand escape conditioning. Escape conditioning is based on negative reinforcement—the strengthening of behavior by the removal of a punisher. The punisher being removed is frequently anxiety or depression, and avoidance or escape is rewarded by the removal of the aversive state. Each time the patient successfully avoids or escapes their feelings, they unwittingly negatively reinforce the behavior of avoidance and escape. The emotion phobia increases rather than decreases. This is explicitly explained to the patient, and the DBT therapist obtains the permission of the patient to engage in exposure procedures prior to using them (Linehan, 1993b).

The first step in exposure is to have the patient be able to identify their anxiety and depression. This is not an obvious process for many patients, especially those with externalizing personality disorders such as paranoid, schizoid, and obsessive-compulsive types. Patients are so adept at keeping their attention focused on thoughts or the external environment rather than their bodily or affective response to situations that they are totally or substantially unaware of any affect. Mindfulness skills are used to redirect attention to the body and the emotions, and the patient is asked to describe what they experience when they engage in mindfulness. Avoidance and escape often have become so automatic that the most difficult therapeutic task is not having them be mindful of their body and affect. Rather, the biggest challenge is to have them sustain their mindfulness long enough to effectively redirect attention from their habitual focus on the external environment or the cognitive thoughts about which they ruminate. A graduated procedure is recommended, where first the patient refines their mindfulness skills on innocuous external objects, and only after weeks of practice of these new skills are patients invited to be mindful of themselves and their emotions.

The DBT therapist begins with guided mindfulness, verbally coaching the patient to attend to their breathing, their muscles, their skin temperature, their heart rate, and so forth. The verbal prompts of the therapist are continuous in initial practice sessions and gradually fade, with periods of silence in each session so that patients can internally guide their own observation. When patients are able to sustain attention to their own body and emotions, even if only for three minutes, then the DBT therapist initiates mindfulness with verbal prompts. Allow the patient to sustain their mindfulness as long as possible during the session and then to report (identify and label the affect) to the therapist what they noticed.

The following dialogue demonstrates the mindfulness approach in DBT.

Patient: I'm aware that my muscles are tight, my body is rigid and uncomfortable, and I feel stiff. There is a heaviness on my chest, and breathing is difficult. That heaviness is increasing the more I pay attention to it.

DBTherapist: Stick with the heaviness in your chest for just a few moments if you can. *(Pause)* Try not to think about the heaviness, only observe it as carefully and thoroughly as you can. Welcome the sensory observation even though the heaviness itself is unwanted. Can you do that? Can you pay attention to the discomfort without trying to change it or analyze it?

Patient: It's hard, because I keep thinking about how I don't like it and how I know that's not part of ONE MIND.

DBTherapist: It's good that you notice the thoughts. Gently redirect your attention to the heaviness, leaving the thoughts behind. *(Pause)* Can you do that?

Patient: Yes.

DBTherapist: Describe, put into words, what you're noticing.

Patient: I'm noticing the tightness. It's right in the middle of my chest. It's between my lungs, and it feels as if the tightness is restricting my lungs, making it hard to breathe. I can feel my pulse, I can hear it. The heaviness has a center. First it felt like it was lying on top of my skin, but now it feels deeper, like an energy rather than a pressure. *(Pause)* It's getting lighter, slowly, like it's disappearing. I'm watching it, but it's going away. I'm more aware of my breath now and less of the heaviness as it fades.

DBTherapist: That's great! You were able to pay attention to the discomfort without fighting with it, without struggling with it. And by taking away the struggle, it went away on its own. It may not always be like that. Sometimes the discomfort is not simply a product of resistance. But sometimes it totally is about such avoidance struggles.

Eventually, the goal is to have the patient expose themselves to painful emotions long enough to elicit unwanted emotions and then sustain attention to the unwanted affect until it's reduced without avoidance or escape.

The DBT therapist avoids the use of flooding. The goal is not to have the patient feel a loss of control and be overwhelmed by their feelings. This would increase their avoidance and escape strategies, not to mention decrease their assessment of the therapist as providing safety. Instead, the DBT therapist collaborates with the patient in designing affect-arousing events and exposure intensity, which increases their sense of self-control (Linehan, 1993b).

The DBT therapist is quite sensitive to the patient's level of tolerance. Some patients can tolerate very little affect in initial stages of exposure, while others can tolerate quite a bit. The DBT therapist validates that the patient knows their own tolerance levels better than anyone else. The objective is to expose them to some, then increasingly more, affect over time. The exposure procedures must be completed on the patient's schedule, not the therapist's. Exposure therapy is successful only when the patient is able to terminate the affective experience voluntarily rather than automatically (Linehan, 1993b). Even if the steps are small, voluntary termination of affect decreases escape and avoidance tendencies.

The End Stage of Treatment

The DBT therapist knows they have reached the end stage of treatment when the patient can readily tolerate affect without escape and avoidance strategies, when the patient has developed skills to reduce their baseline emotional arousal level, and when threat cues and safety cues are given equal weight. Acute mental disorders, as outlined in chapters 2 and 3, have both biological and psychological precipitants that make full recovery difficult. Just as the disease model of addiction predicts that even clean and sober patients are "in recovery" rather than cured, the same is true for many acute emotional disorders. The DBT therapist does not offer hope that emotional challenges will be totally resolved and that the patient will live a carefree life devoid of emotional sensitivity. Instead, the DBT therapist holds out the carrot that their life will involve more freedom and that they will have more skill in making choices that are conscious and not based upon the kind of pressure and urgency that make them feel emotionally crippled. They can feel a lot better and possess the skills to handle the inevitable challenges that life holds for all of us.

The later stage of DBT involves generalization of skills. More emphasis is placed on the patient's practice outside the consultation room of those skills generated during psychosocial skills training and individual psychotherapy. The patient is invited to push the envelope of what they have tried before with an eye to situations where they are likely to have success experiences. In the later stages of treatment, the DBT therapist becomes more insistent rather than permissive about using the self-recording diaries and worksheets, and more focus is placed on practice of skills in the everyday environment. Dependence on the therapist is explored, and attending to environmental rewards (which occur outside the consulting room) to sustain behaviors over time is essential.

Dialectic issues should shift over time in therapy, from the beginning stages where dialectics feel urgent and involve the perception of crisis and immediate threat, to the later stages and where dialectics feel difficult, even irreconcilable, but unavoidable and manageable.

ESSENTIAL COMPONENTS OF DBT THERAPY

Regardless of the stage of therapy, DBT involves the following essential components:

- Dialectic analysis (identification of paradox, conflict, and emotional strain) and coaching patients to think dialectically about their own situation

- Validation of the patient's feelings, thoughts, and experiences

- Balance of acceptance strategies with change strategies

- Emotional exposure strategies to reduce emotional escape and avoidance

- Balance of emotion-focused and solution-focused coping

- Prompting improved shifting of attention from internal cues to external cues

- Prompting improved shifting of attention from short-term objectives to long-term objectives

- Balance of emotion-focused and behavior-focused skills and strategies

- Nonpejorative interpretation of the patient's behavior and affect

- Teaching new psychological coping skills for "old" situations

- Balance of attention to both threat and safety cues

TRANFERENCE: PSYCHOANALYTIC AND BEHAVIORAL

The psychoanalytic concept of transference is that the patient projects feelings and dynamics onto the therapist, the object of such projections frequently having to do with the (inadequate) mother or (overcontrolling or unavailable) father. In dynamic psychotherapy the transference relationship is seen as one of the most powerful elements of the therapy because the transference is used both as a diagnostic tool (to identify the underlying thoughts, motivations, needs, and fears of the patient) and as a method of treatment (to rework the infantile and primitive psychological defenses the patient continues to use from childhood in the here-and-now projected interpersonal relationship of the patient and psychoanalyist). In DBT, transference is regarded differently.

Transference may be projection, but the transference is viewed in terms of rigidity of strategy. The patient uses schemas they have developed over time and fails to access information about the particular situation they confront. The patient treats everyone the same. How is this different from the psychoanalytic notion? Is this semantic shift important?

In psychoanalytic theory, the goal is to change psychological defense mechanisms—to decrease primitive defenses and to engage more mature defenses. The goal is not different with DBT. However, in psychoanalytic approaches, transference is seen as useful. The transference (projection) is worked with as a primary therapeutic target to change psychological coping mechanisms through the development of insight. In psychoanalytic approaches, transference is seen as helpful, while in DBT it's seen as harmful. DBT redefines transference. Using schemas that ignore current realities—failing to shift attention from cognitions developed in the past that may not apply to the current moment—is seen as pathological. Rather than use these projections to promote health, as in psychoanalytic approaches, DBT uses them as evidence that different strategies are needed. Psychoanalytic approaches welcome transference, and DBT approaches attempt to extinguish it.

Psychoanalytic theory promotes transference through ambiguity in the therapeutic relationship, and DBT decreases transference through transparency in this relationship. The DBT therapist will use judicious self-disclosure, clearly articulate the procedures and interventions being used (the patient is not left guessing), provide direct feedback (both emotional and cognitive) to the patient, and use interpretation to clarify situations rather than to prompt the patient to engage in their own insight generation. In spite of such clarity in the therapeutic relationship, some patients, particularly those with personality disorders, will continue to project their core psychological issues onto the therapist. Transference sometimes occurs in spite of the DBT therapist's transparency.

How does the DBT therapist handle such transference issues? Surprisingly, they will engage in some of the same strategies that a psychoanalytically oriented therapist will use. The behavior may be similar, but the outcome expected is different. The DBT therapist will verbalize that the feelings the patient is attributing to them are the same ones they experienced with important others, frequently their early childhood caregivers. However, the DBT therapist does not stop there and have the patient ponder what this means and what they should do about it. The DBT therapist coaches the patient to examine how these assumptions, anticipations, and emotional reactions are sustained over time. The patient's schemas are explicitly analyzed, explored, and verbalized.

The Role of Schemas

The notion of schemas in psychology is not new (Kelly, 1955). Schemas can be preverbal (Markus, 1990), manifesting themselves as motoric, affective, or physiological representations, what Kelly (1955) referred to as "speechless impulses." Schemas can also be quite specific, offering both a view of the world and a method of dealing with it. In a very interesting article on schema vacillation, oscillation, and nonlinearity (Elliott and Lassen, 1997), the authors propose that all people, not just those with personality disorders, have schemas that guide their behavior. They suggest that the difference between pathological and healthy use of schemas has to do with flexibility and the ability to see beyond dichotomous thinking. The healthy individual jumps from one schema to another, depending on situational variables, while the maladaptive individual sticks with fewer schemas and applies them rigorously to all situations. Nonlinearity proposes that dramatic shifts in behavior and strategy can occur for most people, depending on the meaning attributed to a situation or purpose.

Unlike schema-focused cognitive therapy for personality disorders (Young, 1990), DBT does not place emphasis upon object relations theory, psychoanalytically informed developmental models, or rational disputation of early maladaptive schemas to produce clinical change. Instead, DBT views schemas as well-rehearsed belief systems that control attention (thus predicting what kinds of information will be attended to), predict emotional avoidance and escape strategies, and result in self-fulfilling prophecies that are subsequently reinforced by selective attention. While there is thus considerable overlap between schema-focused therapy and DBT, DBT attends to dialectic conflict rather than developmental conflicts from earlier stages of development and relies more upon exposure and validation compared to confrontation and logic used by schema-focused therapy.

Schemas, rather than libidinal cathexis and countercathexis, can thus explain transference phenomena in psychotherapy.

The patient's perspective is validated in DBT. "Yes, there are similarities between how you viewed your mother and how you view me. Your conclusions are reasonable." The psychotherapy relationship does predispose dependency issues, authority conflicts, trust issues, and feelings of inadequacy. There is no way to effectively and totally avoid such conflicts. The patient is right that there are similarities between the psychotherapy relationship and how they felt as a dependent child who looked for the authority figure to provide safety and meet their needs.

The DBT therapist also points out the differences. "When you were a child you *were* totally dependent—you were supposed to be. Now you are not totally dependent; you have your own resources that together we can help you more effectively deploy. I can see why you see me as the authority, but I'm really your coach and mentor, not your guardian. Your mother may have been absent when you really wanted her present, and the same will be true for me because I won't always be there when you need me the most. But my prayers will always be with you, and we'll work on strategies you can use even when you're all alone."

Table 23: Transference Examples

Historical Dynamics	Therapy Dynamics Projected
My mother held all of the power in the family. She did not give me what I wanted.	You hold all of the power in this relationship. You are not giving me what I want.
My mother was always setting limits, telling me what I should and should not do.	You are always setting limits, telling me what I should and should not do.
My father was not there when I really needed him.	You are not there when I really need you.
My mother could have made me happy if she really wanted to.	You can make me happy if you really want to.
My father really didn't care about me, or he would have protected me better.	You really don't care about me, or you would protect me better.

Transference issues are thus articulated and fully spelled out: What are the assumptions being made? What are the patient's interpretations of those assumptions (their impact and significance)? What are the feelings these assumptions bring, and how do they influence the patient's behavior? The DBT therapist does not deny the similarities, the feelings such similarities invoke, or the way those feelings will influence how the patient treats the therapist. Instead, the DBT therapist articulates all of these issues and examines how those processes will help or hurt therapy and how they may reflect rigidity of information processing (focusing too much on the past, assuming contingencies now are the same as in the past, failing to attend to the current environment, basing thoughts on feelings from the past, etc.). It has been asserted that all information processing is emotional "in that emotion is the energy level that drives, organizes, amplifies, and attenuates cognitive activity and in turn is the experience and expression of that activity" (Dodge, 1991, p. 159). It should thus not be surprising that the intimate relationship between therapist and patient should be influenced by important emotional processes in the patient's life.

The DBT therapist is careful not to be invalidating when pointing out the rigidity of information processing. The safe tack to take is that these tendencies are natural, occur in most of us, but hurt us, so we work to intentionally give them up. It is not a signal of inferiority that we develop rigid strategies. In fact, typically it is adaptive that strong threat brings automatic responses. It is an evolutionary safety valve for such automatic behaviors to be instinctual rather than volitional. Our biological tendencies toward survival, however, are not as relevant in modern society, where threats are mostly psychological rather than physical. Transference issues are normal but not helpful. They, like many other dynamics in the DBT psychotherapy process, such as emotional avoidance and escape, are evaluated in terms of their effectiveness in both short-term and long-term ways.

INTERPRETATION IN DBT

Good psychotherapy involves interpretation. Interpretation articulates what motivates behavior, how behavior may be a symbolic expression of larger needs and wants, and that tend to be recurrent issues with a particular patient. Interpretation should be intended to illustrate meaningful aspects of the patient's situation, rather than simply point out defenses and resistances. Interpretation within the DBT framework is thus about meaning, want, desire, conflict, frustration, and fear. The DBT therapist verbalizes such meanings, wants, and fears in order to bring into focus dialectic conflict. Interpretations are thus not so much about insight per se, as about re-focusing attention on values and aspirations. Interpretations in DBT should point to a solution to a problem or create a better definition of a problem to be solved, rather than simply amplify psychopathological processes. In interactions with patients, the DBT therapist is not simply attempting to increase the patient's psychological insight into their own dynamics. The DBT therapist does not train the patient in becoming a junior psychologist.

Interpretations in DBT psychotherapy should focus insights on target behaviors and their precursors; explore current, observable, public behavior and events; focus on eliciting and maintaining variables; and describe implications of the interpretation on the patient's behavior (Linehan, 1993b). In short, DBT psychotherapy has as its goal decreasing maladaptive emotionality and increasing psychological coping strategies to current psychosocial stressors. Interpretation has a role in accomplishing these objectives, but DBT is not about increasing intellectual insight into problems for the sake of insight.

DISRUPTIVE BEHAVIORS AND THEIR SOLUTIONS

Compliance issues may be seen as particularly important in DBT. DBT is not necessarily short-term symptom-focused treatment, since it is designed to treat acute mental disorders that have underlying emotional dysregulation. Simply reducing arousal through teaching relaxation skills alone is most often ineffective since the patient responds to so many threat cues in the environment. DBT thus targets emotional arousal patterns, shifting and multiple dialectic conflicts that result in maladaptive responses to variegated situational prompts, learning to tolerate rather than automatically escape and avoid emotional arousal, and increasing the skillful means a patient uses in problem solving situations that prompt aversive affect. Treatment targets are diverse, covering attentional strategies, behavioral strategies, cognitive processing, affective strategies, and interactions between these dimensions. In order for the complex array of DBT technologies to work, the patient must comply with fundamental requirements of treatment. It is the therapist's skill in nurturing compliance with treatment procedures that will define success, rather than their referring to nebulous concepts of "patient resistance." The therapist taxes their own skills rather than those of the patient in order to decrease disruptive behaviors.

Table 24: Disruptive Therapy Problems and Solutions

Disruptive Therapy Behaviors	Therapist Solutions
The patient does not show up for treatment sessions.	■ Initiate contracting (the patient pays cash for missed appointments). ■ Assess (along with the patient) if therapy is too emotionally challenging or not sufficiently emotionally challenging. ■ Work on commitment to psychotherapy.
The patient shows up late for treatment sessions.	■ Work on commitment to psychotherapy. ■ Explore with the patient if this is another form of emotional avoidance. ■ Maintain time limitations: end on time no matter when the patient arrives. ■ Practice strategic behavior skills.
The patient does not complete homework assignments.	■ Explore fears (interpretations, expectations) about change. ■ Explore procrastination as a form of emotional avoidance. ■ Reduce complexity of homework assignments to more manageable levels. ■ Begin homework assignments with behavior that already occurs (begin with existing habits; begin with noticing and describing behaviors).
The patient consistently redirects therapy time to immediate situational crises and resists focus on long-term objectives.	■ Point this out to the patient each time it occurs. ■ Ask the patient what they think the behavior means. ■ Explore fears of change, feelings of hopelessness. ■ Validate importance of current needs. ■ Validate importance of sacrificed long-term needs.

Disruptive Therapy Behaviors	Therapist Solutions
The patient uses distractibility to refocus attention away from affect.	▪ Increase use of relaxation skills (deep breathing, visualization, direct therapist suggestions for soothing) prior to engaging in verbal psychotherapy. ▪ Express confidence in the patient's commitment to change, and acknowledge that this is scary. ▪ Reduce the pace of change expected; increase acceptance and validation.
The patient engages in high-risk behaviors between or within sessions to elicit emergency (caretaking) behavior from the therapist.	▪ Validate emotional vulnerability. ▪ Increase self-soothing responses. ▪ Perform dialectic analysis of the needs the patient is satisfying in the moment, and point out alternatives while validating those needs. ▪ Confront self-loathing and the sense of inadequacy. ▪ Focus on capabilities and how to use them in the moment. Reinforce healthy behaviors, not dependency behaviors. ▪ Establish behavioral contracts for no self-harm. ▪ Practice emotion regulation skills. ▪ Practice distress tolerance skills.
The patient blocks or dissociates so they don't have to engage in acceptance strategies.	▪ Increase therapist verbal guidance during mindfulness training. ▪ Shift to external focus of attention (soothing elements in the environment). ▪ Practice distress tolerance skills. ▪ Shift to systematic desensitization; build a hierarchy with smaller steps. ▪ Teach structured relaxation skills, such as progressive muscle relaxation. Encourage use of both emotion regulation skills and distress tolerance skills. ▪ Break goals into smaller, more manageable steps.

The patient is passive and waits for the therapist to provide all structure, defeating an interactive and collaborative stance in treatment.	<ul><li>Validate the patient's desire to change.</li><li>Validate the patient's fear of change.</li><li>Validate how the patient's current condition may at least be partially acceptable to them (it's known and predictable).</li><li>Ask the patient if they are afraid of the therapy interaction itself (identify the fear).</li><li>Increase therapist disclosure or transparency.</li><li>Increase the conversational tone of therapy.</li><li>Predict silence as anxiety and avoidance (acceptingly).</li></ul>
The patient is verbally combative or competitive and rejects most interventions the therapist offers.	<ul><li>Redirect focus to patient affect in the moment.</li><li>Explore patient doubts about the effectiveness of psychotherapy in general.</li><li>Explore patient doubts about the effectiveness of this psychotherapy.</li><li>Explore the trust versus suspiciousness dialectic.</li><li>Identify patient short-term goals within this session (validate).</li></ul>
The patient is cooperative but does not comply with practice of new strategies between sessions.	<ul><li>Identify fears of change.</li><li>Explore the power of habit and routine.</li><li>Identify long-term objectives and what needs are being sacrificed by current behavior.</li><li>Practice and rehearse behavior expected between sessions during the session; increase both competence and confidence in new skills.</li><li>Establish behavioral contracting.</li><li>Express faith and confidence in the patient.</li></ul>
The therapist becomes angry, afraid, frustrated, annoyed, or hostile toward the patient.	<ul><li>Consult with colleagues.</li><li>Perform dialectic analysis on self: What needs, wants, or urges is the patient triggering in the therapist?</li><li>Consider referral of the patient to another professional and accept responsibility for the failure.</li></ul>

Dialectical behavior therapy is a robust and powerful treatment technology for use with acute mental disorders. One of the distinguishing factors of DBT is that the therapist assumes that the patient wants to change but is fearful of these changes. The therapist uses skillful means in order to support the desire for change, while recognizing the terror some patients experience when such change is imminent.

Book Summary

DBT is not a simple set of treatment strategies to apply to a patient. Instead, it offers a comprehensive theory of pathogenesis, pathotopology, and treatment. DBT is thus a new school of psychology that shares many elements of previous theories, but has substantial differences. DBT returns to Freud's original ideas of compromise formation, gestalt's ideas of conflict and avoidance, behavior theories of learning and motivation, and humanistic theories of safety and acceptance. The critical and most influential factor in the development of psychopathology, according to DBT theory, is emotion regulation. Feelings, rather than thoughts, are at the core of dysfunction. While psychological traumas have powerful and enduring effects upon the person throughout the life course, they are enduring and damaging mostly through neurobiological and neuroanatomical changes that occur with intense or prolonged stress (rather than through issues of psychosocial stages of development or psychodynamic fixations). Kindling effects (the lowering of emotional reactivity thresholds) and the development of neural net pathway potentials (increasing the probability that emotional arousal produces static rather than flexible responding) specify the emotional pain and turmoil that most patients with acute mental disorders experience.

Experience itself is an essential element of DBT theory. Our patients do not incorrectly feel their experience. Rather, they understand the implications of their experience only too well. They feel their pain, and develop compensatory mechanisms to reduce such pain. The pleasure and pain principles are clearly at work. The emotional arousal is too great to tolerate, so anticipatory avoidance and simple escape become automatic and routine. The overarching goal of DBT is to help the patient ignore their emotional pain, for just a few moments at a time, in order to remember their values and desires. DBT also helps the patient to accept their emotional pain, for just a few moments at a time, in order to remember that their feelings are right and normal given their experiences. Reducing secondary emotional reactions, frequently guilt and shame that they feel what they feel, helps to reduce their anguish to painful but more tolerable levels.

No one wants to feel emotional pain. It hurts. We want to be normal. We want to enjoy life. The exquisite sense of urgency to reduce suffering is understandable. The DBT therapist validates the patient's experience, finds the conscious or unconscious strategies the patient uses to reduce their suffering, and helps the patient to feel understood that their strategies work for them in some ways, and cause important losses as well.

Acceptance strategies, perhaps, separate DBT most from traditional cognitive and cognitive behavioral therapies. Welcoming experience, as well as efforts to change it, and balancing acceptance and change, is the most elemental dialectical conflict both the patient and therapist together experience.

It is difficult for a person who has never experienced an urge to use drugs (bringing immediate and dependable relief from want) to understand, on an experiential basis, the internal chaos and conflict such urges bring. It is difficult for a person who has never had a panic attack to understand the impending sense of death and doom, coming from the inside of one's own body, that such episodes cause. It is difficult for a person who has never had overwhelming depression, the sense that life is futile, with prolonged and unending pain, to understand the desire of the person to commit suicide. The world is a dangerous and manipulative place for a person who has character disorder, and keeping composure and sense of peace when one lives in the experience of torture and war is more than taxing (it's unlivable). Chronic emotional pain changes the brain, neurochemistry, sense of identity, relationships, behavior strategies, and the essential self.

Prolonged emotional pain changes people. They don't believe what they have, they can't use what they have, and they misuse what they have. Pain causes frantic attempts to escape pain. What a normal response!

APPENDIX

How to Use the Weblinks

DBT is bifurcated into two separate but equally important components: dialectically informed individual psychotherapy and training in psychological coping skills. This appendix focuses on the skills teaching, while most of the book refers to the theory and practice of DBT individual psychotherapy. This appendix should be reviewed in conjunction with chapter 7 of the text and the weblink contents (go to nhpubs.com/29064). The general content and theory are reviewed in chapter 7, while this appendix reviews the specific PowerPoint slides that can used as the curricula (teaching points) for the psychosocial education component of DBT. This appendix thus explains how to specifically use the downloadable materials in the DBT treatment process.

WHAT'S ON THE WEBLINK

The weblink included with this text contains two classes of information: slides (visual aids for teaching) and worksheets.

PowerPoint Presentations

The zip file on the included weblink labeled "Presentations" has five separate files, each one a complete DBT psychological coping skills module: mindfulness skills (Mindful.ppt), containing 66 slides with a suggested three hours of patient contact meetings; meaning-making skills (Meaning.ppt), containing 52 teaching slides presented over three hours of patient contact; emotion regulation skills (Emotion.ppt), containing 124 slides with a suggested six hours of patient education; distress tolerance skills (Distress.ppt), containing 62 sides for three hours of patient education; strategic behavior skills (Strategic.ppt), containing 127 slides for six hours of suggested patient education; and dialectical thinking (Dialectic.ppt), which has 8 slides. Dialectical thinking is not intended as a separate skill module, but can be used by the psychoeducational instructor whenever it appears that the patient is not attending to the critical component of compromise formation: that we are constantly gaining something but sacrificing something else in service of this gain. Both mindfulness skills (allowing exposure to and identification of emotions) and dialectical thinking (gaining something and sacrificing something else) should permeate the teaching of all modules.

Table 25: Dialectical Behavior Therapy Psychological Coping Skills Program		
Program	Suggested Number of Sessions	Number of Slides
Mindfulness skills	3	66
Meaning-making skills	3	52
Emotion regulation skills	6	124
Distress tolerance skills	3	62
Strategic behavior skills	6	127
Dialectical thinking	-	8
Total program	21	439

Worksheets and Handouts

The second zip file on the weblink is labeled "Forms." The Forms folder contains worksheets, handouts, and practice logs that your patients can use to record their application of the concepts, steps, and processes that DBT demands. The table below shows the forms, worksheets, and handouts, including their labeling inside the zip files, organized by psychological coping skills program.

Table 26: Worksheets for DBT Psychological Coping Skills Program

Program	Name of File	Worksheet Name
Mindfulness Skills	MindfulWkst1.pdf	Mindfulness Practice Record Sheet
Emotion Regulation Skills	ERWkst1.pdf	Emotion Regulation vs. Emotion Tolerance
	ERWkst2.pdf	Blame and Guilt
	ERWkst3.pdf	There Is Something Wrong with Me
	ERWkst4.pdf	Emotion Regulation: Mindfulness to Current Emotions
	ERWkst5.pdf	Discomfort with Your Primary Emotions
	ERWkst6.pdf	Discomfort with Secondary Emotions
	ERWkst7.pdf	Dealing with Feelings from Assumptions
	ERWkst8.pdf	Dealing with Feelings about Your Identity
	ERWkst9.pdf	Emotion Regulation: EMOTIONS
	ERWkst10.pdf	Emotion Regulation: Discriminate Primary from Secondary Emotions
	ERWkst11.pdf	Emotion Regulation: Challenge Your Assumptions
	ERWkst12.pdf	Emotion Regulation: Increase Positive Experiences Mindfully
	ERH1.pdf	Biopsychosocial Model of Emotions
	ERH2.pdf	Emotion Regulation Skills Assumptions
Distress Tolerance Skills	DTWkst1.pdf	Distress Tolerance: Acceptance
	DTWkst2.pdf	Distress Tolerance: ACCEPT
	DTWksht3.pdf	Distress Tolerance: DISTRACT
		Distress Tolerance: VISION
Meaning-Making Skills	MeaningWkst1.pdf	SPECIFIC PATHS (6 pages)
	MeaningWkst2.pdf	Meaning Making: Short-Term vs. Long-Term Planning
	MeaningWkst3.pdf	Meaning Making: SPECIFIC PATHS
	MeaningH1.pdf	Supreme Concerns: Questions to Ask (page 2) Possible Supreme Concerns
Strategic Behavior Skills	StrategicWkst1.pdf	OBJECTIVES
	StrategicWkst2.pdf	TRUST
	StrategicWkst3.pdf	BEHAVIOR
	StrategicWkst4.pdf	CARES
	StrategicWkst5.pdf	Strategic Behavior: CARES
	StrategicH1.pdf	Emotional Expressiveness and TRUST
	StrategicH2.pdf	BEHAVIOR Explained and Examples

Practice Logs	DBTLog1.pdf	DBT Log
	DBTLog2.pdf	DBT Practice Sheet
	MnemonicsH1.pdf	Mnemonic Review
Dialectics	DialecticWkst1.pdf	Forming Compromises
	DialecticWkst2.pdf	Dialectics

Most of these worksheets are taken from *Depressed & Anxious: A Dialectical Behavior Therapy Workbook for Overcoming Depression and Anxiety*, published by New Harbinger Publications (2004). With higher-functioning patients, you may suggest that they purchase this workbook so that they have access to all the rationales for the exercises. Even with lower-functioning patients, I have found that many feel more comfortable having information at their fingertips even if the therapist needs to walk them through each of the exercises.

USING POWERPOINT IN TEACHING

Chapter 8 of this text reviews the critical importance of shifting from psychotherapy mode to teaching mode in DBT. This is, in part, embracing the change versus acceptance dialectic inherent and critical in the DBT treatment approach. The easiest way to shift from therapy to teaching is to have two treatment formats set up specifically for this purpose: traditional (and dialectical) psychotherapy and group psychoeducation. This appendix describes the group psychoeducational component. However, as mentioned in the text, this bifurcation of the treatment process may not be practical in a private practice setting. Although the group format for training offers advantages (cost, efficiency, normalization of experience, and ease of delivery of service), psychoeducation can also occur in an individual format.

If the DBT therapist delivers the psychoeducation in group or individual format, there are a number of advantages to delivering the content via the PowerPoint slide presentations. First, it reinforces the notion that the skills portion of therapy is about learning (change) rather than disclosure of emotions and information (acceptance). Second, it provides a teaching outline (curriculum) for the therapist that prompts delivery of the necessary information. Third, it helps to bring both the therapist and the patients back to the teaching function when the inevitable drift into personal experiences and emotions occurs. Lastly, it prompts the therapist/psychoeducational instructor in sequential presentation of complex material.

The drawbacks of using a PowerPoint method of psychoeducational intervention is that the patients may perceive it as too academic or school-like. However, this gets at the core of the DBT theory of psychopathology: high emotional arousal causes patients to use mood-dependent and emotion-focused coping responses. Even when patients have sophisticated existing psychological insight, they fail to use such insight and introspection when emotional arousal is high. The mnemonics and skills modules are designed to increase the probability that patients use their coping skills, including extant skills, when they are required.

Therapists may dislike using the PowerPoint method to teach skills for the same reason—it feels like school rather than therapy. If the therapist is so uncomfortable teaching new psychological coping skills to their patients, then perhaps they should conclude that the DBT approach is not for them and they should pursue other theoretical methods and assumptions. Teaching is a necessary condition for effective delivery of the DBT approach to psychopathology. If you don't use the PowerPoint slides (in either group or individual modalities), then you'll need to develop an alternative method to deliver the content of skills training.

ALTERNATIVES TO THE USE OF POWERPOINT

If your computer skills are nonexistent, you don't have a computer in your office, you are just too uncomfortable turning your computer screen toward the patient and lecturing from the slides included in the downloadable materials, or your office setup just won't allow presentation of the slides to patients, an alternative is to print out the slides onto paper and use the printed version of the slides as visual aids. You can also review the slides and become sufficiently comfortable with the content that you can deliver a lecture presentation with the course outline provided below. The manner in which you decide to deliver the content is less important than that the full content be delivered; the graphics and visual aids are just prompts for the curricula. The specificity, length, and form of delivery are less important than assessment of the needs of the patients that you are treating. Clinical judgment about needs of the patient supersede the suggested curricula.

PSYCHOSOCIAL TEACHING CURRICULA

This section deals with how to use the PowerPoint slides directly in the psychosocial teaching process. If you are using an alternative teaching approach, this section may still be helpful to you since it describes the content of the education. The "slides" are teaching points, which you can use even with a verbal (without visual aid) or printed method of presentation.

Clicking the Mouse

If you are using PowerPoint for presentation, some of the slides deliver the content sequentially; it may take more than one click of the mouse to go from slide to slide. Don't panic. When you click the mouse once, a graphic or written presentation will appear. You describe the content as the graphic or words appear. For some slides, several clicks of the mouse or keyboard are required before the next slide appears. People have become increasingly visually oriented learners, and the slower presentation of graphics on some slides is used to accommodate this learning style. If you have PowerPoint rather than PowerPoint Viewer installed on your computer, you will have to go to the "Slide Show" menu and select (highlight) "View Show" for the visual presentation to appear.

Computer Screen vs. Projector

If you are presenting to a group of patients rather than an individual, it is recommended that you project the slides onto a projection screen. LCD projectors have decreased in price and increased in performance over the last decade. Many agencies and groups own such LCD projectors that easily connect to a laptop computer. Check with your group or agency to see if one is available for your use. Follow the directions from your projector manual about connecting the projector to the computer. If you are presenting to three or fewer patients, you can simply turn your computer monitor to face them and have them view the slides from the same monitor you routinely use in your office.

Suggested Session Information

The number of sessions to devote to each set of slides are estimates only and will entirely depend on the format (group or individual training), diagnostic acuity of patients (suicidality, degree of mood-dependent behavior, urgency, and acting-out behaviors), and length of each session provided. Certainly, patients who are more introspective, psychologically minded, and higher functioning will need less time with each skill module than patients who are less so. Use your clinical skill in determining the needs of the patients you are serving to determine the length and division of teaching sessions.

On the following five tables you will find a general index of each of the psychosocial skills to teach in DBT. The first column in each table gives the suggested session number and slide numbers; the second column lists the general session content; the third column lists the teaching point for those slides (including which patient worksheet to print out and distribute and when); and the last column provides the chapter number and page number from this text where the content is explained. If the therapist uses this table (going back and forth between the text and the slides) and reviews the content prior to presentation, they should be able to deliver training in the psychosocial skills effectively without further reference to the text.

Table 27: Mindfulness Skills Training

Slide Numbers	Content	Teaching Point	Page #
Session 1 1-7	States of mind	Doing Mind	102-103
		Being Mind	186-187
8	Wisdom	Wisdom	207
9	Mindfulness is Looking	Not about thinking	21-31
10	ONE MIND	ONE MIND	188
11-13	How Skills	Awareness Watchful	
14-21	Function of language	Describing Maps Perspectives Prescriptive and proscriptive	191-192
22-23	Mindful breathing	Mindful breathing Distribute MindfulWKST1.pdf	
Session 2 25-26	Review homework	Mindful breathing	
28-52	Mindfulness as meditation	Mindful theory Mindfulness as observation Nonevaluative	30, 23
53-55	Body scan	Body scan	
Session 3 56-66	Review homework Review concepts	Body scan ONE MIND Wisdom Observing When Being Mindful Be engaged Nonjudgmental Practice Distribute new copy of MindfulWKST1.pdf	192-193

Table 28: Meaning-Making Skills Training			
Slide Numbers	**Content**	**Teaching Point**	**Page #**
1-3	Purpose of skill set	Purpose	103-108
4-13	What is meaningful	We create it As perspectives As faith Like love Obstacles: fear Distribute MeaningH1.pdf	193-194
14	Assumptions	Assumptions	
15-22	SPECIFIC PATHS	SPECIFIC PATHS Distribute MeaningWKST1.pdf	194-195
23-24	Identify meaning	Supreme concern	
Session 2 25-28	Review	Meaning theory SPECIFIC PATHS	
29-45	Practice SPECIFIC PATHS	SPECIFIC PATHS	
46	Homework	Distribute MeaningWKST2.pdf	
Session 3 47-52	Review	Distribute MeaningWKST3.pdf	

Table 29: Emotion Regulation Skills Training

Slide Numbers	Content	Teaching Point	Page #
Session 1 1-4	Goals of emotion regulation	Goals Distribute ERH2.pdf	196-197
5-7	High arousal	Avoidance	68-75
8-16	Primary and secondary emotions	Secondary emotions overshadowing Distribute ERWKST10.pdf	198-200
17-18	Goals	Goals	
19-22	Be honest about how you feel	Break your feelings down Primary and secondary Distribute ERWKST4.pdf	
23-24	Discomfort with primary emotion	Discomfort with primary emotion Distribute ERWKST5.pdf	
25	Homework	Distribute ERWKST1.pdf Distribute ERWKST2.pdf Distribute MindfulWKST1.pdf	
Session 2 26-28	Review	Review homework	
29	Misconceptions	Obstacles	
30-31	Increase your resilience	Emotionalism Distribute ERWKST3.pdf Distribute ERWKST6.pdf CARES	200 211
32-35	Increase pleasure	Distribute ERWKST12.pdf	200-201
36-38	Don't practice your emotions	Take opposite action	201-202
39-44	Urgency is an enemy	Distribute ERWKST7.pdf Being Mind	
45	Homework	Guide completion of worksheets	
Session 3 46-58	Review Biopsychosocial model	Biopsychosocial model Distribute ERH1.pdf	197-198
59-62	Rule-governed behavior	Rule-governed behavior	202

63	Body components of emotions	Body components of emotions	
64-67	Emotional sensitivity	Expressiveness	209-210
68-72	Identity	Distribute ERWKST8.pdf	
72	Identity	Prompt completion of ERWKST8.pdf	
Session 4 75-102	Biopsychosocial model	Biopsychosocial model Kindling effects Being Mind Distribute ERWKST11.pdf	197-198 59-62
97	Avoidance	Acceptance	
102	Homework	Prompt use of worksheets	
Session 5 105-119	Review homework EMOTIONS	EMOTIONS Distribute ERWKST9.pdf	203
1200	Homework	Prompt use of worksheet	
Session 6 121-124	Review	Distribute ERWKST9.pdf Practice mindfulness	

Table 30: Distress Tolerance Skills Training			
Slide Numbers	**Content**	**Teaching Point**	**Page #**
Session 1 1-5	Goals	Goals	203-204
6-8	Pain is a part of life	Acceptance Experience Dialectics	
9-27	Acceptance	Avoidance ONE MIND Acceptance ACCEPT DISTRACT Distribute DTWKST1.pdf Distribute DTWKST2.pdf Distribute DTWKST3.pdf	204
28	Homework	Prompt completion of worksheet and mindfulness	
Session 2 31-49	Use your senses Distraction	Review homework Self-soothing Distribute DTWKST4.pdf	204-205
50	Radical acceptance		
51-60	Homework and review	Mindfulness VISION Radical acceptance	205
Session 3 53-62	Review	Review homework ACCEPT VISION DISTRACT Practice mindfulness	204 205 205-206

Table 31: Strategic Behavior Skills			
Slide Numbers	**Content**	**Teaching Point**	**Page #**
Session 1 1-8	Goals	Goals Wisdom Intelligence Dialectics	109-112 207 208
9-17	Strategic behavior	Urgency Short- vs. long-term objectives	
18-24	Emotions vs. behavior	Mood-dependent	74
Session 2 25-40	Review OBJECTIVES	Review OBJECTIVES Distribute StrategicWKST1.pdf	 209
41	Homework	Homework	
Session 3 42-57	Review Sensitivity	Review Sensitivity Distribute StrategicWKST2.pdf Distribute StrategicH1.pdf	 209-210 210-211 237-238
58	Homework	Homework	
Session 4 59-82	Review Behavior focus	Review Distribute StrategicWKST3.pdf Distribute StrategicH2.pdf	 212-213
83	Homework	Prompt homework	
Session 5 84-127	Review CARES	Mindfulness Emotion regulation Distress tolerance Meaning making Strategic behavior Emotionalism CARES Distribute StrategicWKST4.pdf Distribute StrategicWKST5.pdf	239 241 211-212

Dialectical Thinking

Dialectical thinking is not a separate psychosocial skill set to be presented to patients during psychosocial skills intervention. Instead, eight slides are included on the weblink (Dialectics.ppt) for the psychosocial skills teacher to switch to during any of the previous modules when it is clear that patients are not thinking dialectically. These slides should help remind patients that wisdom and adequate psychological coping come only through understanding that compromises must be made between competing needs and demands.

\multicolumn{2}{c}{Table 32: Dialectic Teaching Points}	
Slide	**Teaching Point**
1	Dialectics are about conflict and opposition.
	The point is not to be on one side of the teeter-totter or the other but to shift back and forth as your objectives (not moods) demand.
2	Dialectics are broad dimensions that encompass feelings, behavioral strategies, needs, wants, and environmental demands.
3	Feelings can be contradictory. This is normal but can confuse your strategies to solve problems.
4	Thoughts can be contradictory. This is normal but can confuse your strategies to solve problems.
5	Values can be contradictory. This is normal but can confuse your strategies to solve problems.
6	Strategies to solve your problems can be contradictory. This is normal but can confuse both you and those in your environment, and thus may not be strategic and in line with your true objectives.
7	Conflict is normal and unavoidable. The goal is to move from self-blame to problem solving.
8	Explain the reasons (from the slide) to think dialectically.
	Distribute DialecticWKST1.pdf and DialecticWKST2.pdf as appropriate to your group needs.

References

Abramowitz, J. S., and Foa, E. B. (2000). Does major depressive disorder influence outcome of exposure and response prevention for OCD? *Behavior Therapy, 31*(4), 795-800.

Abramowitz, J. S., Franklin, M. E., and Cahill, S. P. (2003). Approaches to common obstacles in the exposure-based treatment of obsessive-compulsive disorder. *Cognitive and Behavioral Practice, 10*(1), 14-22.

Abramowitz, J. S., Franklin, M. E., Street, G. P., Kozak, M. J., and Foa, E. B. (2000). Effects of comorbid depression on response to treatment for obsessive-compulsive disorder. *Behavior Therapy, 31*(3), 517-528.

Adamec, R. E., and Stark-Adamec, C. (1983). Limbic kindling and animal behavior—implications for human psychopathology associated with complex partial seizures. *Biological Psychiatry, 18*(2), 269-293.

Addis, M. E. (1997). Evaluating the treatment manual as a means of disseminating empiriclly validated psychotherapies. *Clinical Psychology: Science and Practice, 4*(1), 1-11.

Addis, M. E., and Hatgis, C. (2000). Values, practices, and the utilization of empirical critiques in the clinical trial. *Clinical Psychology: Science and Practice, 7*(1), 120-124.

Agnosti, V. (1999). Predictors of persistent social impairment among recovered depressed outpatients. *Journal of Affective Disorders, 55*(2-3), 215-219.

Alexander, C. N., Langer, E. J., Newman, R. I., Chandler, H. M., and Davis, J. L. (1989). Transcendental Meditation, mindfulness, and longevity: An experimental study with the elderly. *Journal of Personality and Social Psychology, 57*(6), 950-964.

American Psychiatric Association. (1994). *Diagnostic and statistical manual of mental disorders* (Fourth ed.). Washington, DC.

Arnow, B., Kennedy, J., and Agras, W. S. (1992). Binge eating among the obese: A descriptive study. *Journal of Behavioral Medicine, 15*, 155-170.

Astin, J. A. (1997). Stress reduction through mindfulness meditation: Effects on psychological symptomatology, sense of control, and spiritual experiences. *Psychotherapy and Psychosomatics, 66*(2), 97-106.

Baer, R. A. (2003). Mindfulness training as a clinical intervention: A conceptual and empirical review. *Clinical Psychology: Science and Practice, 10*(2), 125-143.

Baltes, P. B., and Staudinger, U. M. (2000). Wisdom: A metaheuristic (pragmatic) to orchestrate mind and virtue toward excellence. *American Psychologist, 55*(1), 122-136.

Bandura, A., Blanchard, E. B., and Ritter, B. (1969). Relative efficacy of desensitization and modeling approaches for inducing behavioral, affective, and attitudinal changes. *Journal of Personality and Social Psychology, 13*(3), 173-199.

Barbieri, P. (1996). Confronting stress: Integrating control theory and mindfulness to cultivate our inner resources through mind/body health methods. *Journal of Reality Therapy, 15*(2), 3-13.

Barley, W. D., Buie, S. E., Peterson, E. W., Holligsworth, A. S., Griva, M., Hickerson, S. C., et al. (1993). The development of an inpatient cognitive-behavioral treatment program for borderline personality disorder. *Journal of Personality Disorders, 7*(3), 232-240.

Barnes, S. J., and Pinel, J. P. (2001). Conditioned effects of kindling. *Neuroscience Biobehavioral Review, 25*(7-8), 745-751.

Baum, M. (1970). Extinction of avoidance responding through response prevention (flooding). *Psychological Bulletin, 74*(4), 276-284.

Beck, A. T., Emery, G., and Greenberg, R. L. (1985). *Anxiety disorders and phobias: A cognitive perspective.* New York: Basic Books.

Beck, A. T., Freeman, A., and Davis, D. D. (2004). *Cognitive therapy of personality disorders* (Second ed.). New York: Guilford Press.

Beck, A. T., Rush, A. J., Shaw, F. F., and Emery, G. (1979). *Cognitive therapy of depression.* New York: Guilford Press.

Berman, J. S., and Katzev, R. D. (1972). Factors involved in the rapid elimination of avoidance behavior. *Behaviour Research and Therapy, 10*(3), 247-256.

Berman, S. L., Weems, C. F., Silverman, W. K., and Kurtines, W. M. (2000). Predictors of outcome in exposure-based cognitive and behavioral treatments for phobic and anxiety disorders in children. *Behavior Therapy, 31*(4), 713-731.

Beutler, L. E., and Howard, M. (2003). Training in psychotherapy: Why supervision does not work. *National Register, 56*(4), 12-16.

Beutler, L. E., Machado, P. P., and Neufeldt, S. (1994). Therapist variables. In S. L. Garfield and A. E. Bergin (Eds.), *Handbook of psychotherapy and behavior change* (pp. 259-269). New York: Wiley.

Bishop, S. R. (2002). What do we really know about mindfulness-based stress reduction? *Psychosomatic Medicine, 64*(1), 71-83.

Blowers, G. H., and O'Connor, K. P. (1995). Construing contexts: Problems and prospects of George Kelly's personal construct psychology. *British Journal of Clinical Psychology, 34 (Pt. 1)*, 1-16.

Bohus, M., Haaf, B., Stiglmayr, C., Pohl, U., Bohme, R., and Linehan, M. (2000). Evaluation of inpatient dialectical-behavioral therapy for borderline personality disorder—a prospective study. *Behaviour Research and Therapy, 38*(9), 875-887.

Borkovec, T. D., and Craighead, W. E. (1971). The comparison of two methods of assessing fear and avoidance behavior. *Behaviour Research and Therapy, 9*(3), 285-291.

Bowlby, J. (1969). *Attachment and loss: Vol. 1. Attachment.* New York: Basic Books.

Boyd, J. H., Burke, J. D., Gruenberg, E., Holtzer, C. E., Rae, D. S., George, L. K., et al. (1984). Exclusion criteria of *DSM-III:* A study of co-occurrence of hierarchy-free syndromes. *Archives of General Psychiatry, 41,* 983-959.

Bradley, R. G., and Follingstad, D. R. (2003). Group therapy for incarcerated women who experienced interpersonal violence: A pilot study. *Journal of Traumatic Stress, 16*(4), 337-340.

Bradley, S. J. (2000). *Affect regulation and the development of psychopathology.* New York: Guilford Press.

Breslin, F. C., Zack, M., and McMain, S. (2002). An information-processing analysis of mindfulness: Implications for relapse prevention in the treatment of substance abuse. *Clinical Psychology: Science and Practice, 9*(3), 275-299.

Brown, D., Forte, M., and Dysart, M. (1984a). Differences in visual sensitivity among mindfulness meditators and non-meditators. *Perceptual and Motor Skills, 58*(3), 727-733.

Brown, D., Forte, M., and Dysart, M. (1984b). Visual sensitivity and mindfulness meditation. *Perceptual and Motor Skills, 58*(3), 775-784.

Brown, G. W., and Harris, T. O. (1993). Aetiology of anxiety and depressive disorders in an iner-city population: 1. Early adversity. *Psychological Medicine, 23,* 143-154.

Carek, D. J. (1990). Affect in psychodynamic psychotherapy. *American Journal of Psychotherapy, 44,* 274-282.

Carlson, L. E., Speca, M., Patel, K. D., and Goodey, E. (2003). Mindfulness-based stress reduction in relation to quality of life, mood, symptoms of stress, and immune parameters in breast and prostate cancer outpatients. *Psychosomatic Medicine, 65*(4), 571-581.

Carter, C. S., Perlstein, W., Ganguli, R., Brar, J., Mintun, M., and Cohen, J. D. (1998). Functional hyperfrontality and working memory dysfunction in schizophrenia. *American Journal of Psychiatry, 145*, 578-583.

Carter, F. A., McIntosh, V. V. W., Joyce, P. R., Sullivan, P. F., and Bulik, C. M. (2003). Role of exposure with response prevention in cognitive-behavioral therapy for bulimia nervosa: Three-year follow-up results. *International Journal of Eating Disorders, 33*(2), 127-135.

Cassidy, J., and Kobak, R. R. (1988). Avoidance and its relation to other defensive processes. In J. Belsky and N. T. (Eds.), *Clinical impications of attachment* (pp. 200-232). Hillsdale, NJ: Erlbaum.

Castonguay, L. G., Goldfried, M. R., Wiser, S., Rause, P. J., and Hayes, A. M. (1996). Predicting the effect of cognitive therapy for depression: A study of unique and common factors. *Journal of Consulting and Clinical Psychology, 64*, 497-504.

Chambless, D. L., and Ollendick, T. H. (2001). Empirically supported psychological interventions: Controversies and evidence. *Annual Review of Psychology, 52*, 685-716.

Chambless, D. L., Sanderson, W. C., Shoham, V., Johnson, S. B., Pope, K. S., Crits-Christoph, P., et al. (1996). An update on empircally validated therapies. *The Clinical Psychologist, 49*(2), 5-14.

Charney, D. S., Deutch, A. Y., Krystal, J. H., Southwick, S. M., and Davis, M. (1993). Psychobiologic mechanisms of posttraumatic stress disorder. *Archives of General Psychiatry, 50*, 294-305.

Clark, L. A., and Watson, D. (1991). Theoretical and empirical issues in differentiating depression from anxiety. In J. Becker and A. Kleinman (Eds.), *Psychosocial aspects of depression* (pp. 39-65). Hillsdale, NJ: Erlbaum.

Cloninger, C. R. (1987). A systematic method for clinical description and classification of personality variants: A proposal. *Archives of General Psychiatry, 44*, 573-588.

Coles, M. E., and Heimberg, R. G. (2000). Patterns of anxious arousal during exposure to feared situations in individuals with social phobia. *Behaviour Research and Therapy, 38*(4), 405-424.

Craske, M. G., DeCola, J. P., Sachs, A. D., and Pontillo, D. C. (2003). Panic control treatment for agoraphobia. *Journal of Anxiety Disorders, 17*(3), 321-333.

Crits-Christoph, P., Baranackie, K., Kurcias, J. S., Beck, A. T., Carroll, K., Perry, K., et al. (1991). Meta-analysis of therapist effects in psychotherapy outcome studies. *Psychotherapy Research, 2*, 81-91.

Cunningham, K., Wolbert, R., and Lillie, B. (2004). It's about me solving my problems: Clients' assessments of dialectical behavior therapy. *Cognitive and Behavioral Practice, 11*(2), 248-256.

Dallman, M. F., Pecoraro, N., Akana, S. F., La Fleur, S. E., Gomez, F., Houshyar, H., et al. (2003). Chronic stress and obesity: A new view of "comfort food." *Proceedings of the National Academy of Sciences USA, 100*(20), 11,696-11,701.

Davidson, R. J., and Goleman, D. J. (1977). The role of attention in meditation and hypnosis: A psychobiological perspective on transformations of consciousness. *International Journal of Clinical and Experimental Hypnosis, 25*(4), 291-308.

Davidson, R. J., and Irwin, W. (1999). The functional neuroanatomy of emotion and affective style. *Trends in Cognitive Science, 3*, 11-21.

Davidson, R. J., Kabat-Zinn, J., Schumacher, J., Rosenkranz, M., Muller, D., Santorelli, S. F., et al. (2003). Alternations in brain and immune function produced by mindfulness meditation. *Psychosomatic Medicine, 65*(4), 564-570.

Davidson, S. E. (2002). Principles of managing patients with personality disorder. *Advances in Psychiatric Treatment, 8*, 1-9.

de Girolamo, G., and Reich, J. H. (1993). *Epidemiology of mental disorders and psychosocial problems: Personality disorders.* Geneva, Switzerland: World Health Organization.

Derryberry, D., and Reed, M. (1996). Regulatory processes and the development of cognitive representations. *Development and Psychopathology, 9*, 633-652.

Dimeff, L. A., Koerner, K., and Linehan, M. M. (2001). *Research on dialectical behavior therapy: Summary of the data to date.* Seattle, WA: The Behavioral Technology Transfer Group.

Dimidjian, S., and Linehan, M. M. (2003). Defining an agenda for future research on the clinical application of mindfulness practice. *Clinical Psychology: Science and Practice, 10*(2), 166-171.

Dodge, K. A. (1991). Emotion and social information processing. In J. G. Garber and K. A. Dodge (Eds.), *The development of emotion regulation and dysregulation* (pp. 159-181). Cambridge, England: Cambridge University Press.

Dowson, J. H., and Grounds, A. T. (1995). *Personality disorders, recognition and clinical management.* Cambridge, England: Cambridge University Press.

Dreikurs, R. (1957). Psychotherapy as correction of faulty social values. *Journal of Individual Psychology, 13*, 150-158.

Dugas, M. J., Ladouceur, R., Leger, E., Freeston, M. H., Langolis, F., Provencher, M. D., et al. (2003). Group cognitive-behavioral therapy for generalized anxiety disorder: Treatment outcome and long-term follow-up. *Journal of Consulting and Clinical Psychology, 71*(4), 821-825.

Dunn, B. R., Hartigan, J. A., and Mikulas, W. L. (1999). Concentration and mindfulness meditations: Unique forms of consciousness? *Applied Psychophysiology and Biofeedback, 24*(3), 147-165.

Eisenberg, N., Fables, R. A., Guthrie, I. K., Murphy, B. C., Maszk, P., Holmgren, R., et al. (1996). The relations of regulation and emotionality to problem behavior in elementary school children. *Development and Psychopathology, 8,* 141-162.

Eisenberger, N. I., Lieberman, M. D., and Williams, K. D. (2003). Does rejection hurt? An fMRI study of social exclusion. *Science, 10*(302), 290-292.

Elkin, I., Shea, T., Watkins, J. T., Imber, S. D., Sotsky, S. M., and Collins, J. F. (1989). National Institute of Mental Health Treatment of Depression Collaborative Research Program: General effectiveness of treatments. *Archives of General Psychiatry, 46,* 971-982.

Elliott, C. H., and Lassen, M. K. (1997). A schema polarity model for case conceptualization, intervention, and research. *Clinical Psychology: Science and Practice, 4*(1), 12-28.

Evans, K., Tyrer, P., Catalan, J., Schmidt, U., Davidson, K., Dent, J., et al. (1999). Manual-assisted cognitive-behaviour therapy (MACT): A randomized controlled trial of a brief intervention with bibliotherapy in the treatment of recurrent deliberate self-harm. *Psychological Medicine, 29*(1), 19-25.

Fava, G. A., Grandi, S., Rafanelli, C., Ruini, C., Conti, S., and Belluardo, P. (2001). Long-term outcome of social phobia treated by exposure. *Psychological Medicine, 31*(5), 899-905.

Fava, G. A., Rafanelli, C., Grandi, S., Conti, S., Ruini, C., Magelli, L., et al. (2001). Long-term outcome of panic disorder with agoraphobia treated by exposure. *Psychological Medicine, 31*(5), 891-898.

Fernandes, P. P. (2003). Rapid desensitization for needle phobia. *Psychosomatics: Journal of Consultation Liason Psychiatry, 44*(3), 253-254.

Ferster, C. B. (1973). A functional analysis of depression. *American Psychologist, 28*(10), 857-870.

Field, T. (1994). The effects of mother's physical and emotional unavailability on emotion regulation. *Monographs of the Society for Research in Child Development 59*(2-3, Serial No. 240) 208-227.

Foa, E. B., Rothbaum, B. O., and Furr, J. M. (2003). Augmenting exposure therapy with other CBT procedures. *Psychiatric Annals, 33*(1), 47-53.

Forsyth, J. P., and McNeil, D. W. (2002). Mastery of Your Anxiety and Worry: A multimodal case study of effectiveness of a manualized treatment for generalized anxiety disorder. *Cognitive and Behavioral Practice, 9*(3), 200-212.

Franklin, M. E., Abramowitz, J. S., Kozak, M. J., Levitt, J. T., and Foa, E. B. (2000). Effectiveness of exposure and ritual prevention for obsessive-compulsive disorder: Randomized compared with nonrandomized samples. *Journal of Consulting and Clinical Psychology, 68*(4), 594-602.

Freeston, M. H., Leger, E., and Ladouceur, R. (2001). Cognitive therapy of obsessive thoughts. *Cognitive and Behavioral Practice, 8*(1), 61-78.

Fresco, D. M., Wolfson, S. L., Crowther, J. H., and Docherty, N. M. (2002). *Distinct and overlapping patterns of emotion regulation in the comorbidity of generalized anxiety disorder and the eating disorders.* Paper presented at the annual meeting of the Society for Research in Psychopathology, San Francisco.

Freud, S. (1914). On the history of the psychoanalytic movement. *The standard edition of the complete psychological works of Sigmund Freud* (pp. ??-??). London: Hogarth Press, 1953-1964.

Garvey, M., Noyes, R., Jr., Anderson, D., and Cook, B. (1991). Examination of comorbid anxiety in psychiatric inpatients. *Comprehensive Psychiatry, 32*, 277-282.

Gilbert, M. E. (1994). The phenomenology of limbic kindling. *Toxicology in Industrial Health, 10*(4-5), 343-358.

Goldapple, K., Segal, Z., Garson, C., Lay, M., Bieling, P., Kennedy, S., et al. (2004). Modulation of cortical-limbic pathways in major depression: Treatment-specific effects of cognitive behavior therapy. *Archieves of General Psychiatry, 61*, 34-41.

Goldberg, S., MacKay-Soroka, S., and Rochester, M. (1994). Affect, attachment and maternal responsiveness. *Infant Behavior and Development, 167*, 335-339.

Goldstein, A. (1973). Behavior therapy. In R. Corsini (Ed.), *Current Psychotherapies* (pp. 207-249). Itasca, IL: F. E. Peacock Publishers.

Goleman, D. (1978). A taxonomy of meditation-specific altered states. *Journal of Altered States of Consciousness, 4*(2), 203-213.

Goleman, D. (2003). *Destructive emotions: How can we overcome them? A scientific dialogue with the Dalai Lama.* New York: Bantam Books.

Gray, J. A. (1991). Neural systems, emotion and personality. In J. Madden IV (Ed.), *Neurobiology of learning and affect* (pp. 273-306). New York: Raven Press.

Greenberg, M. T., Kusche, C. A., and Speltz, M. (1992). Emotional regulation, self-control, and psychopathology: The role of relations in early childhood. In D. Cicchetti and S. L. Toth (Eds.), *Rochester Symposium on Developmental Psychopathology: Vol. 2. Internalizing and externalizing expressions of dysfunction* (pp. 21-55). Hillsdale, NJ: Erlbaum.

Gregory, R. J., Canning, S. S., Lee, T. W., and Wise, J. C. (2004). Cognitive bibliotherapy for depression: A meta-analysis. *Professional Psychology: Research and Practice, 35*(3), 275-280.

Grilo, C. M., McGlashan, T. H., Morey, L. C., Gunderson, J. G., Skodol, A. E., Shea, M. T., et al. (2001). Internal consistency, intercriterion overlap and diagnostic efficiency of criteria sets for DSM-IV schizotypa, borderline, avoidant and obsessive-compulsive personality disorders. *Acta Psychiatrica Scandinavica Supplementum, 104*(4), 264-272.

Grilo, C. M., McGlashan, T. H., and Skodol, A. E. (2000). Stability and course of personality disorders: The need to consider comorbidities and continuities between axis I psychiatric disorders and axis II personality disorders. *Psychiatric Quarterly, 71*(4), 291-307.

Gross, J. J. (1995). The emerging field of emotion regulation: An integrative review. *Clinical Psychology: Science and Practice, 2,* 151-164.

Gross, J. J., and Munoz, R. F. (1995). Emotion regulation and mental health. *Clinical Psychology: Science and Practice, 2,* 151-164.

Gunderson, J. G., Shea, M. T., Skodol, A. E., McGlashan, T. H., Morey, L. C., Stout, R. L., et al. (2000). The Collaborative Longitudinal Personality Disorders Study: Development, aims, design, and sample characteristics. *Journal of Personality Disorders.*

Gunnar, M. R., and Barr, R. G. (1998). Stress, early brain development, and behavior. *Infants and Young Children, 11,* 1-14.

Hahlweg, K., Fiegenbaum, W., Frank, M., Schroeder, B., and von Witzleben, I. (2001). Short- and long-term effectiveness of an empirically supported treatment for agoraphobia. *Journal of Consulting and Clinical Psychology, 69*(3), 375-382.

Hall, C. S. (1954). *A Primer of Freudian Psychology.* New York: New American Library.

Hanh, T. N. (1976). *The miracle of mindfulness.* Boston: Beacon Press.

Hawkins, K. A., and Sinha, R. (1998). Can line clinicians master the conceptual complexities of dialectical behavior therapy? An evaluation of a State Department of Mental Health training program. *Journal of Psychiatric Research, 32*(6), 379-384.

Hawton, K., Townsend, E., Arensman, E., Gunnell, D., Hazell, P., House, A., et al. (2000). Psychosocial versus pharmacological treatments for deliberate self harm. *Cochrane Database Syst Rev*(2), CD001764.

Hayes, S. C., Follette, V. M. and Linehan, M. M. (2004). *Mindfulness and acceptance: Expanding the cognitive-behavioral tradition.* New York: Guilford Press.

Hayes, S. C., Strosahl, K. D., and Wilson, K. G. (1999). *Acceptance and commitment therapy: An experienial approach to behavior change.* New York: Guilford Press.

Hayes, S. C., and Wilson, K. G. (2003). Mindfulness: Method and process. *Clinical Psychology: Science and Practice, 10*(2), 161-165.

Hayes, S. C., Wilson, K. W., Gifford, E. V., Follette, V. M., and Strosahl, K. D. (1996). Emotional avoidance and behavioral disorders: A functional dimensional approach to diagnosis and treatment. *Journal of Consulting and Clinical Psychology, 64,* 1152-1168.

Hayes, S. C., Zettle, R. D., and Rosenfarb, I. (1989). Rule following. In S. C. Hayes (Ed.), *Rule-governed behavior: Cognition, contingencies, and instructional control.* (pp. 191-220). New York: Plenum Press.

Hazlett-Stevens, H., and Borkovec, T. D. (2001). Effects of worry and progressive relaxation on the reduction of fear in speech phobia: An investigation of situational exposure. *Behavior Therapy, 32*(3), 503-517.

Heatherton, T. F., and Baumeister, R. F. (1991). Binge eating as escape from self-awareness. *Psychological Bulletin, 110,* 86-108.

Henke, P. G., and Sullivan, R. M. (1985). Kindling in the amygdala and susceptibility to stress ulcers. *Brain Research Bulletin, 14*(1), 5-8.

Henry, W. P. (1998). Science, politics, and the politics of science: The use and misuse of empirically validated treatment research. *Psychotherapy Research, 8,* 126-140.

Hibbs, E. D., Hamburger, S. D., Leanane, M., Rapoport, J. L., Kruesi, M. J. P., Keysor, C. S., et al. (1991). Determinants of expressed emotion in families of disturbed and normal children. *Journal of Child Psychology and Psychiatry, 32,* 757-770.

Higgit, A., and Fonagy, P. (1992). Psychotherapy in borderline and narcissistic personality disorder. *British Journal of Psychiatry, 161,* 23-43.

Hlastala, S. A., Frank, E., Kowalski, J., Sherrill, J. T., Tu, X. M., Anderson, B., et al. (2000). Stressful life events, bipolar disorder, and the "kindling model." *Journal of Abnormal Psychology, 109*(4), 777-786.

Hofer, M. A. (1995). Hidden regulators: Implications for a new understanding of attachment, separation, and loss. In R. Goldberg, R. Muir, and J. Kerr (Eds.), *Attachment theory: Social, developmental, and clinical perspectives* (pp. 203-231). Hillsdale, NJ: Analytic Press.

Hofmann, S. G. (2000). Self-focused attention before and after treatment of social phobia. *Behaviour Research and Therapy, 38*(7), 717-725.

Horowitz, M., Marmar, C., Krupnick, J., Wilner, N., Kaltreider, N., and Wallerstein, R. (1984). *Personality styles and brief psychotherapy.* New York: Basic Books.

Horvath, A. T. (1998). *Sex, drugs, gambling, and chocolate: A workbook for overcoming addictions.* San Luis Obispo, CA: Impact Publishers.

Hudson, J. I., and Pope, H. G. (1990). Affective spectrum disorder: Does antidepressant response identify a family of disorders with a common pathophysiology? *American Journal of Psychiatry, 147,* 552-564.

Huppert, J. D., and Baker-Morrisette, S. L. (2003). Beyond the manual: The insider's guide to panic control treatment. *Cognitive and Behavioral Practice, 10*(1), 2-13.

Jacobson, N. S., Dobson, K. S., Truax, P. A., Addis, M. E., Koerner, K., Gollan, J. K., et al. (1996). A component analysis of cognitive-behavioral treatment for depression. *Journal of Consulting and Clinical Psychology, 64,* 295-304.

Johnson, E. O., Kamilaris, T. C., Chrousos, G. P., and Gold, P. W. (1992). Mechanisms of stress: A dynamic overview of hormonal and behavioral homeostasis. *Neuroscience and Biobehavioral Reviews, 16,* 115-130.

Johnson, J. G., Cohen, P., Brow, J., Elizabeth, M., Smailes, M. A., and Bernstein, D. A. (1999). Childhood maltreatment increases risk for personality disorders during early adulthood. *Archieves of General Psychiatry, 56*, 600-606.

Johnson, J. G., Cohen, P., Skodol, A. E., Oldham, J. M., Kasen, S., and Brook, J. S. (1999). Personality disorders in adolescence and risk of major mental disorders and suicidality during adulthood. *Archieves of General Psychiatry, 56*(9), 805-811.

Johnson, J. G., Cohen, P., Smailes, E. M., Skodol, A. E., Brown, J., and Oldham, J. M. (2001). Childhood verbal abuse and risk for personality disorders during adolescence and early adulthood. *Comprehensive Psychiatry, 42*(1), 16-23.

Kabat-Zinn, J. (1984). An outpatient program in behavioral medicine for chronic pain patients based on the practice of mindfulness meditation: Theoretical considerations and preliminary results. *ReVISION, 7*(1), 71-72.

Kabat-Zinn, J. (1994). *Wherever you go, there you are: Mindfulness meditation in everyday life.* New York: Hyperion.

Kabat-Zinn, J. (2003). Mindfulness-based interventions in context: Past, present, and future. *Clinical Psychology: Science and Practice, 10*(2), 144-156.

Kabat-Zinn, J., Lipworth, L., and Burney, R. (1985). The clinical use of mindfulness meditation for the self-regulation of chronic pain. *Journal of Behavioral Medicine, 8*(2), 163-190.

Kabat-Zinn, J., Lipworth, L., Burney, R., and Sellers, W. (1986). Four-year follow-up of a meditation-based program for self-regulation of chronic pain: Treatment outcomes and compliance. *Clinical Journal of Pain, 2*, 159-173.

Kabat-Zinn, J., Massion, A. O., Kristeller, J., Peterson, L. G., Fletcher, K. E., Lenderking, W. R., et al. (1992). Effectiveness of a meditation-based stress reduction program in the treatment of anxiety disorders. *American Journal of Psychiatry, 149*, 936-943.

Kabat-Zinn, J., Wheeler, E., Light, T., Skillings, A., Scharf, M. J., Cropley, T. G., et al. (1998). Influence of a mindfulness meditation-based stress reduction intervention on rates of skin clearing in patients with moderate to severe psoriasis undergoing phototherapy (UVB) and photochemotherapy (PUVA). *Psychosomatic Medicine, 60*(5), 625-632.

Kagan, J. (1989). The concept of behavioral inhibition to the unfamiliar. In J. S. Reznick (Ed.), *Perspectives on behavioral inhibition* (pp. 1-23). Chicago: University of Chicago Press.

Kagan, J. (1994). On the nature of emotion. In The development of emotion regulation: Biological and behavioral considerations. *Monographs of the Society for Research in Child Development 59*(2-3, Serial No. 240), 7-24.

Kagan, J., Reznick, J. S., and Snidman, N. (1987). The physiology and psychology of behavioral inhibition in children. *Child Development, 58*, 1459-1473.

Kalynchuk, L. E., Davis, A. C., Gregus, A., Taggart, J., Chris Dodd, C., Wintink, A. J., et al. (2001). Hippocampal involvement in the expression of kindling-induced fear in rats. *Neuroscience and Biobehavioral Reviews, 25*(7-8), 687-696.

Kalynchuk, L. E., Pinel, J. P., Treit, D., and Kippin, T. E. (1997). Changes in emotional behavior produced by long-term amygdala kindling in rats. *Biological Psychiatry, 41*(4), 438-451.

Kandel, E. (1998). A new intellectual framework for psychiatry. *American Journal of Psychiatry, 155*, 457-469.

Kaplan, K. H., Goldenberg, D. L., and Galvin-Nadeau, M. (1993). The impact of a meditation-based stress reduction program on fibromyalgia. *General Hospital Psychiatry, 15*(5), 284-289.

Kazdin, A. E. (1973). Covert modeling and the reduction of avoidance behavior. *Journal of Abnormal Psychology, 81*(1), 87-95.

Kelly, A. E. (1999). Revealing personal secrets. *Current Directions in Psychological Science, 8*(4), 105-109.

Kelly, G. A. (1955). *The psychology of personal constructs: The theory of personality.* (Vol. 1). New York: Norton.

Kempler, W. (1973). Gestalt therapy. In R. Corsini (Ed.), *Current Psychotherapies* (pp. 251-286). Itasca, IL: F. E. Peacock Publishers.

Kendler, K. S., Thornton, L. M., and Gardner, C. O. (2000). Stressful life events and previous episodes in the etiology of major depression in women: An evaluation of the "kindling" hypothesis. *American Journal of Psychiatry, 157*(8), 1243-1251.

Kendler, K. S., Thornton, L. M., and Gardner, C. O. (2001). Genetic risk, number of previous depressive episodes, and stressful life events in predicting onset of major depression. *American Journal of Psychiatry, 158*(4), 582-586.

Kessler, R. C., Davis, C. G., and Kendler, K. S. (1997). Childhood adversity and adult psychiatric disorder in the U.S. National Comorbidity Survey. *Psychological Medicine, 27*, 1101-1119.

Ketter, T. A., George, M. S., Kimbrell, T. A., Benson, E., and Post, R. M. (1996). Functional brain imaging, limbic function, and affective disorders. *The Neuroscientist, 2*, 55-65.

Kiraly, S. J., Ancill, R. J., and Dimitrova, G. (1997). The relationship of endogenous cortisol to psychiatric disorder: A review. *Canadian Journal of Psychiatry, 42*, 415-420.

Koerner, K., and Linehan, M. M. (2000). Research on dialectical behavior therapy for patients with borderline personality disorder. *Psychiatric Clinic of North America, 23*(1), 151-167.

Koons, C. R., Robins, C. J., Tweed, J. L., Lynch, T. R., Gonzalez, A. M., Morse, J. Q., et al. (2001). Efficacy of dialectical behavior therapy in women veterans with borderline personality disorder. *Behavior Therapy, 32*, 371-390.

Kraemer, G. W. (1992). A psychobiological theory of attachment. *Behavioral and Brain Sciences, 15,* 493-541.

Kraemer, G. W., Ebert, M. H., Schmidt, D. E., and McKinney, W. T. (1989). A longitudinal study of the effect of different social rearing conditions on cerebrospinal fluid norepinephrine and biogenic amine metabolites in rehesus monkeys. *Neuropsychophamocology, 2,* 175-189.

Kristeller, J. L., and Hallett, C. B. (1999). An exploratory study of a meditation-based intervention for binge eating disorder. *Journal of Health Psychology, 4*(3), 357-363.

Kutz, I., Borysenko, J. Z., and Benson, H. (1985). Meditation and psychotherapy: A rationale for the integration of dynamic psychotherapy, the relaxation response, and mindfulness meditation. *American Journal of Psychiatry, 142*(1), 1-8.

Lambert, M. J. (1992). Psychotherapy outcome research: Implications for integrative and eclectic therapists. In J. C. Norcorss and M. R. Goldfried (Eds.), *Handbook of psychotherapy integration* (pp. 94-129). New York: Basic Books.

Lazarus, R. S., and Folkman, S. (1984). *Stress, appraisal and coping.* New York: Springer.

Le Gal La Salle, G. (1982). Amygdaloid organization related to the kindling effect. *Electroencephalography and Clinical Neurophysiology Supplement, 36,* 239-248.

LeDoux, J. E. (1993). Emotional networks in the brain. In M. Lewis and J. M. Haviland (Eds.), *Handbook of emotions.* New York: Guilford Press.

LeDoux, J. E. (1996). *The emotional brain.* New York: Simon and Schuster.

Leichsenring, F., and Leibing, E. (2003). The effectiveness of psychodynamic therapy and cognitive behavior therapy in the treatment of personality disorders: A meta-analysis. *American Journal of Psychiatry, 160*(7), 1223-1232.

Levenson, M. R., Aldwin, C. M., Bosse, R., and Spiro, A., III. (1988). Emotionality and mental health: Longitudinal findings from the normative aging study. *Journal of Abnormal Psychology, 97,* 94-96.

Levy, L. H., and Derby, J. F. (1992). Bereavement support groups: Who joins; who does not; and why. *American Journal of Community Psychology, 20*(5), 649-662.

Linehan, M. M. (1987). Dialectical behavior therapy for borderline personality disorder: Theory and method. *Bulletin of the Menninger Clinic, 51*(3), 261-276.

Linehan, M. M. (1993a). Dialectical behavior therapy for treatment of borderline personality disorder: Implications for the treatment of substance abuse [Monograph]. *National Institute for Drug Abuse Research Monographs, 137,* 201-216.

Linehan, M. M. (1993b). *Cognitive-behavioral therapy for borderline personality disorder.* New York: Guilford Press.

Linehan, M. M. (1993c). *Skills training manual for treating borderline personality disorder.* New York: Guilford Press.

Linehan, M. M., Armstrong, H. E., Suarez, A., Allmon, D., and Heard, H. L. (1991). Cognitive-behavioral treatment of chronically parasuicidal borderline patients. *Archives of General Psychiatry, 48*(12), 1060-1064.

Linehan, M. M., Dimeff, L. A., Reynolds, S. K., Comtois, K. A., Welch, S. S., Heagerty, P., et al. (2002). Dialectical behavior therapy versus comprehensive validation therapy plus 12-step for the treatment of opioid dependent women meeting criteria for borderline personality disorder. *Drug and Alcohol Dependence, 67*(1), 13-26.

Linehan, M. M., Heard, H. L., and Armstrong, H. E. (1993). Naturalistic follow-up of a behavioral treatment for chronically parasuicidal borderline patients. *Archives of General Psychiatry, 50*(12), 971-974.

Linehan, M. M., Schmidt, H., III, Dimeff, L. A., Craft, J. C., Kanter, J., and Comtois, K. A. (1999). Dialectical behavior therapy for patients with borderline personality disorder and drug-dependence. *American Journal of Addictions, 8*(4), 279-292.

Linehan, M. M., Tutek, D. A., Heard, H. L., and Armstrong, H. E. (1994). Interpersonal outcome of cognitive behavioral treatment for chronically suicidal borderline patients. *American Journal of Psychiatry, 151*(12), 1771-1776.

Loftus, E. F. (1993). The reality of repressed memories. *American Psychologist, 48*(5), 518-537.

Loftus, E. F. (1994). The repressed memory controversy. *American Psychologist, 49*(5), 443-445.

Loftus, E. F. (2003). Make-believe memories. *American Psychologist, 58*(11), 867-873.

Logsdon-Conradsen, S. (2002). Using mindfulness meditation to promote holistic health in individuals with HIV/AIDS. *Cognitive and Behavioral Practice, 9*(1), 67-71.

London Department of Health. (2000). *NHS hospital in-patient data for the period of 1 April 1998 to 31 March 1999.*

Luborsky, L., Crits-Christoph, P., McLellan, T., Woody, G., Piper, W., Lieberman, B., et al. (1986). Do therapists vary much in their success? Findings from four outcome studies. *American Journal of Orthopsychiatry, 51,* 501-512.

Luborsky, L., Diguer, L., Seligman, D. A., Rosenthal, R., Krause, E. D., Johnson, S., et al. (1999). The researcher's own therapy allegiances: A "wild card" in comparisons of treatment efficacy. *Clinical Psychology: Science and Practice, 6,* 95-106.

Lynch, T. R., Morse, J. Q., Mendelson, T., and Robins, C. J. (2003). Dialectical behavior therapy for depressed older adults: A randomized pilot study. *American Journal of Geriatric Psychiatry, 11*(1), 33-45.

Main, M. (1995). Recent studies in attachment: Overview, with selected implications for clinical work. In S. Goldberg, R. Muir, and J. Kerr (Eds.), *Attachment theory: Social, developmental, and clinical perspectives* (pp. 407-474). Hillsdale, NJ: Analytic Press.

Marks, I., and Dar, R. (2000). Fear reduction by psychotherapies: Recent findings, future directions. *British Journal of Psychiatry, 176,* 507-511.

Markus, H. (1990). Unresolved issues of self-representation. *Cognitive Therapy and Research, 14,* 241-253.

Marlatt, G. A. (2002). Buddhist philosophy and the treatment of addictive behavior. *Cognitive and Behavioral Practice, 9*(1), 44-49.

Marra, T. (2004). *Depressed and anxious: A dialectical behavior therapy workbook for overcoming depression and anxiety.* Oakland, CA: New Harbinger Press.

Mavissakalian, M., and Hamman, M. S. (1987). DSM-III personality disorder in agoraphobia: II. Changes with treatment. *Comprehensive Psychiatry, 28,* 356-361.

McCann, R. A., Ball, E. M., and Ivanoff, A. (2000). DBT with an inpatient forensic population: The CMHIP forensic model. *Cognitive and Behavioral Practice, 7*(4), 447-456.

McGlashan, T. H., Grilo, C. M., Skodol, A. E., Gunderson, J. G., Shea, M. T., Morey, L. C., et al. (2000). The Collaborative Longitudinal Personality Disorders Study: Baseline axis I/II and II/II diagnostic co-occurrence. *Acta Psychiatrica Scandinavica Supplementum, 102*(4), 256-264.

McKendree-Smith, N. L., Floyd, M., and Scogin, F. R. (2003). Self-administered treatments for depression: A review. *Journal of Clinical Psychology, 59*(3), 275-288.

McMillan, T. M., Robertson, I. H., Brock, D., and Chorlton, L. (2002). Brief mindfulness training for attentional problems after traumatic brain injury: A randomised control treatment trial. *Neuropsychological Rehabilitation, 12*(2), 117-125.

McWilliams, N. (1994). *Psychoanalytic diagnosis: Understanding personality structure in the clinical process.* New York: Guilford Press.

Meador, B. D., and Rogers, C. R. (1973). Client-centered therapy. In R. Corsini (Ed.), *Current Psychotherapies* (pp. 119-165). Itasca, IL: F. E. Peacock Publishers.

Mehta, M. R., Dasgupta, C., and Ullal, G. R. (1993). A neural network model for kindling of focal epilepsy: Basic mechanism. *Biological Cybernetics, 68*(4), 335-340.

Meichenbaum, D. (2003). *Treating individuals with angry and aggressive behaviors: A life-span cultural perspective.* Atlanta, GA: Annual Meeting of the Georgia Psychological Association.

Mennin, D. S., Heimberg, R. G., Turk, C. L., and Fresco, D. M. (2002). Applying an emotion regulation framework to integrative approaches to generalized anxiety disorder. *Clinical Psychology: Science and Practice, 9*(1), 85-90.

Messer, S. B., and Warren, C. S. (1995). *Models of brief psychodynamic therapy: A comparative approach.* New York: Guilford Press.

Mesulam, M. M. (1985). *Principles of behavioral neurology.* Philadelphia: Davis.

Miller, A. L., Rathus, J. H., Leigh, E., and Landsman, M. (1996). *A pilot study: Dialectical behavior therapy adapted for suicidal adolescents.* New York: International Society for the Improvement and Teaching of Dialectical Behavior Therapy.

Miller, J., Fletcher, K., and Kabat-Zinn, J. (1995). Three-year follow-up and clinical implications of a mindfulness-based stress reduction intervention in the treatment of anxiety disorders. *General Hospital Psychiatry, 17,* 192-200.

Mody, I. (1993). The molecular basis of kindling. *Brain Pathology, 3*(4), 395-403.

Mohlman, J., and Zinbarg, R. E. (2000). What kind of attention is necessary for fear reduction? An empirical test of the emotional processing model. *Behavior Therapy, 31*(1), 113-133.

Moran, P. (1999). *Antisocial personality disorder: An epidemiological perspective.* London: Gaskell.

Mosak, H. H., and Dreikurs, R. (1973). Adlerian psychotherapy. In R. Corsini (Ed.), *Current psychotherapies* (pp. 35-83). Itasca, IL: F. E. Peacock Publishers.

Nishizuka, M., Okada, R., Seki, K., Arai, Y., and Iizuka, R. (1991). Loss of dendritic synapses in the medial amygdala associated with kindling. *Brain Research, 552*(2), 351-355.

Norcross, J. C., and Hill, C. E. (2003). Empirically supported (therapy) relationships: ESRs. *National Register, 56,* 22-27.

O'Brien, J. T. (1997). The 'glucocorticoid cascade' hypothesis: Prolonged stress may cause permanent brain damage. *British Journal of Psychiatry, 170,* 199-201.

Panksepp, J. (1993). Neurochemical control of moods and emotions: Amino acids to neuropeptides. In M. Lewis and J. M. Haviland (Eds.), *Handbook of emotions* (pp. 87-107). New York: Guilford Press.

Park, J.-M., Mataix-Cols, D., Marks, I. M., Ngamthipwatthana, T., Marks, M., Araya, R., et al. (2001). Two-year follow-up after a randomised controlled trial of self- and clinician-accompanied exposure for phobia/panic disorders. *British Journal of Psychiatry, 178,* 543-548.

Pennebaker, J. W. (1990). *Opening up: The healing power of confiding in others.* New York: Morrow.

Pennebaker, J. W., and Kiecolt-Glaser, J. K. (1988). Disclosure of traumas and immine function: Health implications for psychotherapy. *Journal of Consulting and Clinical Psychology, 56,* 239-245.

Perkins, D. D. (1995). Speaking truth to power: Empowerment ideology as social intervention and policy. *American Journal of Community Psychology, 23*(5), 765-794.

Persons, J. B., Bostrom, A., and Bertagnolli, A. (1995, June). *Clinically significant change in patients treated with cognitive-behavior therapy for depression in a private practice setting.* Paper presented at the Society for Psychotherapy Research, Vancouver, British Columbia, Canada.

Persons, J. B., Burns, B. D., and Perloff, J. M. (1988). Predictors of drop-out and outcome in cognitive therapy for depression in a private practice setting. *Cognitive Therapy and Research, 12,* 557-575.

Pina, A. A., Silverman, W. K., Weems, C. F., Kurtines, W. M., and Goldman, M. L. (2003). A comparison of completers and noncompleters of exposure-based cognitive and behavioral treatment for phobic and anxiety disorders in youth. *Journal of Consulting and Clinical Psychology, 71*(4), 701-705.

Pontius, A. A. (1993). Overwhelming remembrance of things past: Proust portrays limbic kindling by external stimulus—Literary genius can presage neurobiological patterns of puzzling behavior. *Psychological Reports, 73*(2), 615-621.

Post, R. M. (1992). Transduction of psychosocial stress into the neurobiology of recurrent affective disorder. *American Journal of Psychiatry, 149*, 999-1010.

Post, R. M., Denicoff, K. D., Frye, M. A., Dunn, R. T., Leverich, G. S., Osuch, E., et al. (1998). A history of the use of anticonvulsants as mood stabilizers in the last two decades of the 20th century. *Neuropsychobiology, 38*(3), 152-166.

Post, R. M., and Kopanda, R. T. (1976). Cocaine, kindling, and psychosis. *American Journal of Psychiatry, 133*(6), 627-634.

Post, R. M., and Weiss, S. R. (1998). Sensitization and kindling phenomena in mood, anxiety, and obsessive-compulsive disorders: The role of serotonergic mechanisms in illness progression. *Biological Psychiatry, 44*(3), 193-206.

Raine, A. (1997). Autonomic nervous system factors underlying disinhibited, antisocial, and violent behavior. *Annals of the New York Academy of Sciences, 794*, 46-59.

Rappaport, H. (1972). Modification of avoidance behavior: Expectancy, autonomic reactivity, and verbal report. *Journal of Consulting and Clinical Psychology, 39*(3), 404-414.

Ray, O. (2004). How the mind hurts and heals the body. *American Psychologist, 59*(1), 29-40.

Reibel, D. K., Greeson, J. M., Brainard, G. C., and Rosenzweig, S. (2001). Mindfulness-based stress reduction and health-related quality of life in a heterogeneous patient population. *General Hospital Psychiatry, 23*(4), 183-192.

Riccio, D. C., and Silvestri, R. (1973). Extinction of avoidance behavior and the problem of residual fear. *Behaviour Research and Therapy, 11*(1), 1-9.

Rimm, D. C., and Masters, J. C. (1979). *Behavior therapy: Techniques and empirical findings* (Second ed.). New York: Academic Press.

Rizvi, S. L., and Linehan, M. M. (2001). Dialectical behavior therapy for personality disorders. *Current Psychiatry Reports, 3*(1), 64-69.

Robertson, H. A., and Cottrell, G. A. (1985). Some observations on the kindling process. *Progress in Neuropsychopharmacological and Biological Psychiatry, 9*(5-6), 539-544.

Rogers, C. R. (1957). The necessary and sufficient conditions of therapeutic personality change. *Jounal of Consulting Psychology, 21*, 95-103.

Rosenbaum, J. F., Biederman, J., Gersten, M., Hirshfield, D. R., Meminger, S. R., Herman, J. B., et al. (1988). Behavioral inhibition in children of parents with panic disorder and agoraphobia: A controlled study. *Archives of General Psychiatry, 45*, 463-470.

Roth, A., and Fonagy, P. (1996). *What works for whom? A critical review of psychotherapy research.* New York: Guilford Press.

Russell, P. S., and John, J. K. (1999). Self-injurious behaviour: A kindling phenomenon? *Pediatric Rehabilitation, 3*(1), 1-4.

Safer, D. L., Telch, C. F., and Agras, W. S. (2001). Dialectical behavior therapy for bulimia nervosa. *American Journal of Psychiatry, 158*(4), 632-634.

Samoilov, A., and Goldfried, M. R. (2000). Role of emotion in cognitive-behavior therapy. *Clinical Psychology: Science and Practice, 7*, 373-385.

Sanislow, C. A., Morey, L. C., Grilo, C. M., Gunderson, J. G., Shea, M. T., Skodol, A. E., et al. (2002). Confirmatory factor analysis of DSM-IV borderline, schizotypal, avoidant and obsessive-compulsive personality disorders: Findings from the Collaborative Longitudinal Personality Disorders Study. *Acta Psychiatrica Scandinavica Supplementum, 105*(1), 28-36.

Sapolsky, R. M. (1994). *Why zebras don't get ulcers: A guide to stress, stress-related diseases, and coping.* New York: Freeman.

Sapolsky, R. M. (2000). Glucocorticoids and hippocampal atrophy in neuropsychiatric disorders. *Archieves of General Psychiatry, 57*, 925-935.

Schulkin, J., McEwen, S. S., and Gold, P. W. (1994). Allostasis, amygdala, and anticipatory angst. *Neuroscience and Biobehavioral Reviews, 18*, 385-396.

Schwalberg, M. D., Barlow, D. H., Alger, S. A., and Howard, L. J. (1992). Comparison of bulimics, obese binge eaters, social phobics, and individuals with panic disorder on comorbidity across DSM-III-R anxiety disorders. *Journal of Abnormal Psychology, 101*, 675-681.

Segal, Z. V., Williams, J. M., and Teasdale, J. D. (2002). *Mindfulness-based cognitive therapy for depression: A new approach to preventing relapse.* New York: Guilford Press.

Segal, Z. V., Williams, J. M., Teasdale, J. D., and Gemar, M. (1996). A cognitive science perspective on kindling and episode sensitization in recurrent affective disorder. *Psychological Medicine, 26*, 371-380.

Shapiro, D. (1965). *Neurotic Styles.* New York: Basic Books.

Shapiro, S. L., Bootzin, R. R., Figueredo, A. J., Lopez, A. M., and Schwartz, G. E. (2003). The efficacy of mindfulness-based stress reduction in the treatment of sleep disturbance in women with breast cancer: An exploratory study. *Journal of Psychosomatic Research, 54*(1), 85-91.

Shapiro, S. L., Schwartz, G. E., and Bonner, G. (1998). Effects of mindfulness-based stress reduction on medical and premedical students. *Journal of Behavioral Medicine, 21*(6), 581-599.

Shea, M. T., and Yen, S. (2003). Stability as a distinction between Axis I and Axis II disorders. *Journal of Personality Disorders, 17*(5), 373-386.

Shearin, E. N., and Linehan, M. M. (1992). Patient-therapist ratings and relationship to progress in dialectical behavior therapy for borderline personality disorder. *Behavior Therapy, 23*(4), 730-741.

Shearin, E. N., and Linehan, M. M. (1994). Dialectical behavior therapy for borderline personality disorder: Theoretical and empirical foundations. *Acta Psychiatrica Scandinavica Supplementum, 379*, 61-68.

Shore, A. N. (1994). *Affect regulation and the orgins of the self.* Hillsdale, NJ: Erlbaum.

Siegeltuch, M. B., and Baum, M. (1971). Extinction of well-established avoidance responses through response prevention (flooding). *Behaviour Research and Therapy, 9*(2), 103-108.

Simpson, E. B., Pistorello, J., Begin, A., Costello, E., Levinson, J., Mulberry, S., et al. (1998). Use of dialectical behavior therapy in a partial hospital program for women with borderline personality disorder. *Psychiatric Services, 49*(5), 669-673.

Singer, T., Seymour, B., O'Doherty, J., Kaube, H., Dolan, R. J., and Frith, C. D. (2004). Empathy for pain involves the affective but not the sensory components of pain. *Science, 20*(303), 1157-1162.

Skodol, A. E., Gunderson, J. G., McGlashan, T. H., Dyck, I. R., Stout, R. L., Bender, D. S., et al. (2002). Functional impairment in patients with schizotypal, borderline, avoidant, or obsessive-compulsive personality disorder. *American Journal of Psychiatry, 159*(2), 276-283.

Skodol, A. E., Stout, R. L., McGlashan, T. H., Grilo, C. M., Gunderson, J. G., Shea, M. T., et al. (1999). Co-occurrence of mood and personality disorders: A report from the Collaborative Longitudinal Personality Disorders Study (CLPS). *Depression and Anxiety, 10*(4), 175-182.

Spangler, G., and Grossmann, K. E. (1993). Biobehavioral organization in securely and insecurely attached infants. *Child Development, 64*, 1439-1450.

Speca, M., Carlson, L. E., Goodey, E., and Angen, M. (2000). A randomized, wait-list controlled clinical trial: The effect of a mindfulness meditation-based stress reduction program on mood and symptoms of stress in cancer outpatients. *Psychosomatic Medicine, 62*(5), 613-622.

Sperry, L. (1999). *Cognitive behavior therapy of DSM-IV personality disorders: Highly effective interventions for the most common personality disorders.* Philadelphia: Brunner/Mazel.

Spoont, M. R. (1992). Modulatory role of serotonin in neural information processing: Implications for human psychopathology. *Psychological Bulletin, 112*, 330-350.

Spradlin, S. E. (2003). *Don't let your emotions run your life: How dialectical behavior therapy can put you in control.* Oakland, CA: New Harbinger Press.

Springer, T., Lohr, N. E., Buchtel, H. A., and Silk, K. R. (1996). A preliminary report of short-term cognitive-behavioral group therapy for inpatients with personality disorders. *Journal of Psychotherapy Practice and Research, 5,* 57-71.

Stanley, B., Ivanoff, A., Brodsky, B., and Oppenheim, S. (1998). *Comparison of DBT and "treatment as usual" in suicidal and self-mutilating behavior.* Paper presented at the proceedings of the 32nd Association for the Advancement of Behavior Therapy Convention, Washington, DC.

Steketee, G., Chambless, D. L., and Tran, G. Q. (2001). Effects of axis I and II comorbidity on behavior therapy outcome for obsessive-compulsive disorder and agoraphobia. *Comprehensive Psychiatry, 42*(1), 76-86.

Strelau, J. (1994). The concepts of arousal and arousability as used in temperment studies. In J. E. Bates and T. D. Wachs (Eds.), *Temperament: Individual differences at the interface of biology and behavior* (pp. 117-141). Washington, DC: American Psychological Association Press.

Swenson, C. R., Sanderson, C., Dulit, R. A., and Linehan, M. M. (2001). The application of dialectical behavior therapy for patients with borderline personality disorder on inpatient units. *Psychiatric Quarterly, 72*(4), 307-324.

Teasdale, J. D., Segal, Z. V., and Williams, J. M. G. (2003). Mindfulness training and problem formulation. *Clinical Psychology: Science and Practice, 10*(2), 157-160.

Teasdale, J. D., Segal, Z., and Williams, J. M. G. (1995). How does cognitive therapy prevent depressive relapse and why should attentional control (mindfulness) training help? *Behaviour Research and Therapy, 33*(1), 25-39.

Teasdale, J. D., Segal, Z. V., Williams, J. M., Ridgeway, V., Soulsby, J., and Lau, M. (2000). Prevention of relapse/recurrence in major depression by mindfulness-based cognitive therapy. *Journal of Consulting and Clinical Psychology, 68,* 615-623.

Telch, C. F., Agras, W. S., and Linehan, M. M. (2001). Dialectical behavior therapy for binge eating disorder. *Journal of Consulting and Clinical Psychology, 69*(6), 1061-1065.

Thayer, J. F., Friedman, B. H., Borkovec, T. D., Johnsen, B. H., and Molina, S. (2000). Phasic heart period reactions to cued threat and nonthreat stimuli in generalized anxiety disorder. *Psychophysiology, 37,* 361-368.

Thomas, A. K., Bulevich, J. B., and Loftus, E. F. (2003). Exploring the role of repetition and sensory elaboration in the imagination inflation effect. *Memory and Cognition, 31*(4), 630-640.

Thompson, R. A. (1994). Emotion regulation: A theme in search of definition. The development of emotion regulation: Biological and behavioral considerations. *Monographs of the Society for Research in Child Development, 59*(2-3, Serial No. 240), 53-72.

Toro, J., Cervera, M., Feliu, M. H., Garriga, N., Jou, M., Martinez, E., et al. (2003). Cue exposure in the treatment of resistant bulimia nervosa. *International Journal of Eating Disorders, 34*(2), 227-234.

Trupin, E. W., Stewart, D. G., Beach, B., and Boesky, L. (2002). Effectiveness of a dialectical behaviour therapy program for incarcerated female juvenile offenders. *Journal of Child and Adolescent Mental Health, 7*(3), 121-127.

Tsao, J. C. I., and Craske, M. G. (2000). Timing of treatment and return of fear: Effects of massed, uniform-, and expanding-spaced exposure schedules. *Behavior Therapy, 31*(3), 479-497.

Turner, R. M. (1987). The effects of personality disorder diagnosis on the outcome of social anxiety symptom reduction. *Journal of Personality Disorders, 1*, 136-143.

Turner, R. M. (2000). Naturalistic evaluation of dialectical behavior therapy-oriented treatment for borderline personality disorder. *Cognitive and Behavioral Practice, 7*(4), 413-419.

Tuschen-Caffier, B., Voegele, C., Bracht, S., and Hilbert, A. (2003). Psychological responses to body shape exposure in patients with bulimia nervosa. *Behaviour Research and Therapy, 41*(5), 573-586.

Tyrer, P., Seivewright, N., Ferguson, B., Murphy, S., Darling, C., Brothwell, J., et al. (1990). The Nottingham study of neurotic disorder: Relatioship between personality status and symptoms. *Psychological Medicine, 20*(2), 423-431.

Valentine, E. R., and Sweet, P. L. G. (1999). Meditation and attention: A comparison of the effects of concentrative and mindfulness meditation on sustained attention. *Mental Health, Religion and Culture, 2*(1), 59-70.

van der Kolk, B. A. (1996). The body keeps the score: Approaches to the psychobiology of posttramatic stress disorder. In B. A. van der Kolk, A. C. McFarlane, and L. Weisaeth (Eds.), *Traumatic stress: The effects of overwhelming experience on mind, body, and society* (pp. 3-23). New York: Guilford Press.

Vaughan, C. E., and Leff, J. (1976). The influence of family and social factors on the course of psychiatric illness. *British Journal of Psychiatry, 129*, 125-137.

Verheul, R., Van Den Bosch, L. M., Koeter, M. W., De Ridder, M. A., Stijnen, T., and Van Den Brink, W. (2003). Dialectical behaviour therapy for women with borderline personality disorder: 12-month, randomised clinical trial in the Netherlands. *British Journal of Psychiatry, 182*, 135-140.

Vieth, A. Z., Strauman, T. J., Kolden, G. G., Woods, T. E., Michels, J. L., and Klein, M. H. (2003). Self-system therapy (SST): A theory-based psychotherpy for depression. *Clinical Psychology: Science and Practice, 10*(3), 245-268.

Visser, S., and Bouman, T. K. (2001). The treatment of hypochondriasis: Exposure plus response prevention vs cognitive therapy. *Behaviour Research and Therapy, 39*(4), 423-442.

Vodde, T. W., and Gilner, F. H. (1971). The effects of exposure to fear stimuli on fear reduction. *Behaviour Research and Therapy, 9*(3), 169-175.

Wachtel, P. L. (1977). *Psychoanalysis and behavior therapy: Toward an integration.* New York: Basic Books.

Wagner, A. W., and Linehan, M. M. (1999). Facial expression recognition ability among women with borderline personality disorder: Implications for emotion regulation? *Journal of Personality Disorders, 13*(4), 329-344.

Wagner, E. E., Miller, A. L., Greene, L. I., and Winiarski, M. G. (2004). Dialectical behavior therapy for substance abusers adapted for persons living with HIV/AIDS with substance use diagnoses and borderline personality disorder. *Cognitive and Behavioral Practice, 11*(2), 202-212.

Waidhofer, K. (2004). *My baby can talk.* Scotts Valley, CA: Baby Hands Productions/Allison and Partners.

Wampold, B. W. (2001). *The great psychotherapy debate: Models, methods, and findings.* Mahwah, NJ: Erlbaum.

Watson, J. B., and Rayner, R. (1920). Conditional emotional reaction. *Journal of Experimental Psychology, 3*(1), 1-14.

Wegner, D. (1994). Ironic processes of mental control. *Psychological Review, 101,* 34-52.

Wells, A. (2002). GAD, metacognition, and mindfulness: An information processing analysis. *Clinical Psychology: Science and Practice, 9*(1), 95-100.

Westen, D. (2000). The efficacy of dialectical behavior therapy for borderline personality disorder. *Clinical Psychology: Science and Practice, 7*(1), 92-94.

Westen, D., and Morrison, K. (2001). A multidimensional meta-analysis of treatments for depression, panic, and generalized anxiety disorder: An empirical examination of the status of empirically supported therapies. *Journal of Consulting and Clinical Psychology, 60,* 875-899.

Whitmont, E. C., and Kaufmann, Y. (1973). Analytical psychotherapy. In R. Corsini (Ed.), *Current psychotherapies* (pp. 85-117). Itasca, IL: F. E. Peacock Publishers.

Williams, K. A., Kolar, M. M., Reger, B. E., and Pearson, J. C. (2001). Evaluation of a wellness-based mindfulness stress reduction intervention: A controlled trial. *American Journal of Health Promotion, 15*(6), 422-432.

Wilson, K. G., and Roberts, M. (2002). Core principles in acceptance and commitment therapy: An application to anorexia. *Cognitive and Behavioral Practice, 9*(3), 237-243.

Wiser, S., and Telch, C. F. (1999). Dialectical behavior therapy for binge-eating disorder. *Journal of Clinical Psychology, 55*(6), 755-768.

Wolpe, J. (1958). *Psychotherapy by reciprocal inhibition.* Stanford, CA: Stanford University Press.

Yen, S., Shea, M. T., Battle, C. L., Johnson, D. M., Zlotnick, C., Dolan-Sewell, R., et al. (2002). Traumatic exposure and posttraumatic stress disorder in borderline, schizotypal, avoidant, and obsessive-compulsive personality disorders: Findings from the Collaborative Longitudinal Personality Disorders Study. *Journal of Nervous and Mental Disease, 190*(8), 510-518.

Young, J. E. (1990). *Cognitive therapy for personality disorders: A schema-focused approach.* Sarasota, FL: Professional Resource Press.

Zanarini, M. C., Skodol, A. E., Bender, D. S., Dolan, R. J., Sanislow, C. A., Schaefer, et al. (2000). The Collaborative Longitudinal Personality Disorders Study: Reliability of axis I and II diagnoses. *Journal of Personality Disorders, 14*(4), 291-299.

Zimmerman, M., Pfohl, B., Stangl, D., and Corenthal, C. (1986). Assessment of DSM-II personality disorders: The importance of interviewing an informant. *American Journal of Psychiatry, 142*(12), 1437-1441.

Zimmerman, M., Posternack, M. A., and Chelminski, I. (2002). Symptom severity and exclusion from antidepressant efficacy trials. *Journal of Clinical Psychopharmacology, 22*(6), 610-614.

Zoellner, L. A., Echiverri, A., and Craske, M. G. (2000). Processing of phobic stimuli and its relationship to outcome. *Behaviour Research and Therapy, 38*(9), 921-931.

Index